MW01700326

101

Helpful Hints for

IELTS

General Training Module

By Garry Adams & Terry Peck

Adams & Austen Press - Sydney, Australia
mk book distributors - Ahmedabad - 380 015, India

Publisher's Acknowledgements

The publishers are grateful for permission to use copyright material. We would like to acknowledge the original sources of text material listed below. Permission has been sought to reproduce all material whose source could be identified. Information that will enable the publishers to rectify any error or omission in subsequent editions will be welcome.

The nine Band Score descriptions on page 12 are reproduced from *The IELTS Handbook*, a joint publication of the University of Cambridge Local Examinations Syndicate, The British Council, and IDP Education Australia: IELTS Australia. The reading passage *"Studying in Sydney, Australia–An Overview for International Students"* on page 94, is adapted from The 1995 International Undergraduate Prospectus of the University of New South Wales, Sydney, Australia, with permission of Mr. Harry Lo, Senior Education Consultant, University of New South Wales International Office. The reading passage *"The Recreation and Sports Association"* on page 114, is adapted from The Recreation and Aquatic Centre 1994 information booklet of the University of Wollongong, with permission of Ms. Mary Sparks, Wollongong Recreation and Sports Association. The reading passage *"International Students 'Down Under' "* on page 134, is adapted from The ELICOS Student Contextualised – Facts & Figures by Ms. C.M. Bundesen.

Authors' Acknowledgements

We would like to acknowledge the assistance and support of the following people:

Leo Liang, David Kimsey, Andrew Thomas (Sydney English Language Centre, Bondi Junction, Australia) and Soon-Young Youn.

Also Available:

Interactive Online IELTS Course

'101 Helpful Hints Interactive Online Course for IELTS'

http://aapress.com.au/ielts101

Revised Indian Edition – 2016/2017
ISBN 978-81-901159-1-9

First published in Sydney, Australia

Adams & Austen Press Pty. Ltd.

PO Box 509, Marrickville, NSW 1475,

Australia

Phone: 612-9590-4469 Fax: 612-9590-4471

E-mail: aap@aapress.com.au ***www.aapress.com.au***

About the Authors

Terry Peck and Garry Adams have extensive IELTS coaching experience, both having been involved in implementing and designing IELTS coaching programmes. Terry Peck was an IELTS examiner for a number of years in Sydney, Australia.

By the Authors

'101 Helpful Hints for IELTS – Academic Module' International Edition (Indian):

Book & Audio CD: 978-81-901159-0-2

'202 Useful Exercises for IELTS – Academic/General' International Edition (Indian):

Book & Audio CDs(2): 978-81-901159-2-6

Published by Adams & Austen Press

'404 Essential Tests for IELTS – Academic Module' International Edition (Indian):

Book & Audio CDs(2): ISBN 81-901159-3-6 Study Guide CD-ROM: ISBN 81-901159-7-9***

'404 Essential Tests for IELTS – General Training Module' International Edition (Indian):

Book & Audio CDs(2) & Study Guide CD-ROM: ISBN 81-901159-4-4***

* *the listening test is the same for both Modules of the test*
** *Multimedia CD-ROM – video, audio and practice tests*

English Test Vocabulary Kit

'Activating 1001 Academic Words for IELTS'
– a unique method for all English test candidates

Book and Multimedia CD: ISBN 81-901159-8-7

This book published in India by

mk book distributors

1, Tulsi, 2 Azad Society, Ambawadi, Ahmedabad 380 015, India

Phone: 079-2676 3012 / 3022

E-mail: mkbooksd@gmail.com

www.mkbooksd.com

This edition is authorized for sale in India, Bangladesh, Bhutan, Burma, Mauritius, Maldives, Nepal, Pakistan, Sri Lanka and U.A.E.

Printed and bound by **ANAND PRESS**, *Anand - 388 001, India. Tel: 9428076569 / 02692-253933, 255507*

CONTENTS

INTRODUCTION

101 HELPFUL HINTS

THE PRACTICE TESTS

APPENDICES

INDEX

INTRODUCTION

HOW TO USE THIS BOOK

STEP 1

Read the Introduction "What is IELTS?" on page 5, so that you have a better understanding of what the examination is about and what is expected of you.

STEP 2

Complete Practice Test One under test conditions. Follow the instructions on page 85. Check your answers with the Answer Key on page 152. Check your ability using the Score Interpreter on page 154.

STEP 3

Use the Hints Section starting on page 11 to review with care any mistakes you might have made in Practice Test One.

STEP 4

Complete Practice Test Two under test conditions. Check your answers with the Answer Key on pages 152 and 153. Check your ability using the Score Interpreter on page 154.

STEP 5

Refer to the Hints Section again to review with care any mistakes you might have made in Practice Test Two.

STEP 6

Complete the more difficult Practice Tests Three and Four under test conditions. Check your answers with the Answer Key on page 153. Check your ability using the Score Interpreter on page 154.

STEP 7

Contact your nearest IELTS Administration Centre and fill in an application form to take the test. Apply only when you feel you have adequately prepared and are ready for the examination.

WHAT IS IELTS?

AN OVERVIEW

- The International English Language Testing System (IELTS) examination can be taken in over 100 different countries in the world. It is primarily designed to assess whether candidates are ready to study or train in further or higher education courses held in English at college or university.
- The examination takes 2 hours and 45 minutes to complete, and consists of four Sub-tests in the skills of listening, reading, writing and speaking.
- There are two IELTS test modules available: the Academic Module and the General Training Module. The results of the Academic Module may be used to determine a candidate's suitability for study at undergraduate or postgraduate level. The General Training Module is suitable for candidates wishing to continue their studies at diploma level only. The General Training Module is also used for immigration purposes to many English-speaking countries (e.g. Australia, Canada and New Zealand), and for students who wish to complete their secondary education in an English-speaking country. The General Training Reading and Writing Sub-tests are less demanding than the corresponding Academic Module Sub-tests, but the Listening and Speaking Sub-tests are the same for both modules.
- It does not matter what subject you are going to study in the future – or have studied in the past – all students taking the desired module do the same test. You will not be tested on your specific knowledge of a subject; only your English language skills are assessed.
- You may write on the question papers, but you may not take the question papers from the examination room. All your answers must be written on the Answer Sheet provided.
- You can apply to take the IELTS examination at any IELTS Administration Centre. For further details of your nearest centre, consult the *IDP British Council UCLES IELTS Handbook* or refer to the official IELTS website on the Internet: ***http://www.ielts.org/***
- At certain IELTS Administration Centres it is possible to choose between a computerised version of the Listening, Reading and Writing Sub-tests (CB IELTS) and the usual paper-based version. This option is available to Academic Module candidates only at the present time.
- You cannot pass or fail the IELTS examination. The college or institution in which you wish to enrol (or government department in the case of immigration) will inform you of the overall IELTS Band Score they require. Note that you may also need to achieve a minimum score in a particular Sub-test (often the Writing or Speaking Sub-test).
- You will be given a Band Score between 0 and a maximum of 9 for each of the 4 Sub-tests. Half mark scores may be given in all the Sub-tests: 4.5, 5.5, 6.5 etc. Your Overall Band Score is an average of the 4 Sub-test Band Scores, with fractional scores rounding up or down to the nearest *x*.0 or *x*.5 score (with *x*.25 and *x*.75 always rounding up.)

Therefore, if you score	6.5	in the Listening Sub-test
	5	in the Reading Sub-test
	7	in the Writing Sub-test
and	6	in the Speaking Sub-test
Your total score is	24.5	

By averaging the scores (dividing the total score 24.5 by 4) in the example above, you would achieve an Overall Band Score of 6.0 (which is 6.125 rounded down).

- You will usually receive your results within two weeks of the date of your test.
- If you want to take the examination again, you no longer have to wait a minimum of three months as you did in the past; you can take the test as often as you wish and there is no limit to the number of times you can sit for IELTS.

THE LISTENING SUB-TEST

- The Listening Sub-test takes 30 minutes: approximately 20 minutes to listen to the tape and answer the questions, and 10 minutes to transfer your answers to an Answer Sheet provided with the test booklet.
- The test consists of 4 sections, and you will hear the tape only once. There are 40 questions in total.
- The listening passages become more difficult as you progress through the test.
- Section 1 is based on social or life situations: for example, travel arrangements, visiting a new city, or making arrangements to go out. This is usually a conversation between at least two speakers.
- Section 2 is also based on social or life situations: for example, a news broadcast, or a description of college facilities. This is usually a passage with only one person speaking.
- Section 3 is usually based on education and training situations: for example, a group of students planning a project, or a tutor and a student discussing career options. This is often a conversation with up to four speakers.
- Section 4 is also based on education and training: for example, a lecture or a talk of general academic interest.
- Both grammar and spelling are important in the Listening Sub-test (only certain spellings are now acceptable). You must spell words 100% correctly when they are spelt out for you in the recording.
- Your answers need to be legible, that is, they must be able to be read. This applies to all the types of answers you give: letters, numbers and phrases.
- You write your answers on the question paper as you do the Listening Sub-test, and when it is completed, you have 10 minutes to transfer them carefully onto the Answer Sheet. Make sure that each answer is transferred accurately and is legible.

THE READING SUB-TEST

- The General Training Module Reading Sub-test takes 60 minutes and is in 3 parts or sections. Parts 1 and 2 usually contain 2 short passages each, and Part 3 a longer single passage. The combined length of the texts is 2000–2750 words with a total of 40 questions.
- The reading passages become more difficult as you progress through the test.
- Part One, social survival, consists of one or more texts with tasks involving the extraction of factual information at a basic level of English.
- Part Two, workplace survival, usually consists of two short texts, both being relevant to the work environment; for example, applying for a job, or pay and conditions. They contain more complex language.
- Part Three, general reading, contains a text that is of general interest, and is instructive or descriptive in content. The language is at a more complex level than the other two sections.
- The questions may come before or after the reading passages in the examination booklet, and instructions and examples are given at the beginning of a new group of questions.
- When giving your answers in the Reading Sub-test, both grammar and spelling are important (only certain spellings are now acceptable).
- You must write your answers during the Reading Sub-test on the Answer Sheet provided.

THE WRITING SUB-TEST

- The General Training Module Writing Sub-test takes 60 minutes.
- There are two writing tasks.
- The first task will take approximately 20 minutes, and you are required to write a minimum of 150 words. The second task will take approximately 40 minutes with a minimum of 250 words.
- For Task 1 you must write a letter in response to a given problem. The letter will require an explanation of the situation, and may involve a request for necessary information. You should write in the style appropriate for the type of letter required - either personal, or in a semi-formal correspondence style.
- For Task 2 you are asked to write a short essay or a general report in which you might have to provide general information concerning a given topic, offer a solution to a particular problem, present and justify an opinion, or evaluate and challenge a given argument.
- In both tasks you must write in the style appropriate to the question task. The Task 2 essay should be written in a formal (or semi-formal) style. You will also be marked on your ability to organise your writing, and on your choice of content within your answers.
- The question tasks do not require any specialised knowledge of a particular subject.

THE SPEAKING SUB-TEST

- The Speaking Sub-test takes between 11 and 14 minutes.
- The Sub-test consists of an interview with a trained examiner, and is recorded on a tape recorder. This recording is made to ensure the interview is conducted properly and for use if the test is to be reassessed at a later date.
- There are 3 parts to the Speaking Sub-test.
- Part 1: you answer questions about your home life or family life, work or study, your interests and other familiar topics of a general nature to reveal your background.
  (4–5 minutes)
- Part 2: you are given exactly 1 minute to prepare yourself to talk about a particular topic. The instructions to guide your talk are written on a card given to you by the examiner. Your talk should last for 1–2 minutes. The examiner will ask one or two questions at the end.
  (3–4 minutes – including preparation time of 1 minute)
- Part 3: you have a discussion with the examiner based on themes connected to the topic given in Part 2. This part of the test requires discussion of more abstract ideas.
  (4–5 minutes)

  The interview is then closed and the Speaking Sub-test is completed.
- Most of the questions asked in the Sub-test are scripted; they come from a bank of questions prepared by the test authorities. These questions are being continually added to and updated.
- The Speaking Sub-test Band Score is calculated from a comprehensive checklist of speaking skills in four distinct areas of ability:

Fluency and Coherence	Lexical Resource
Grammatical Range and Accuracy	Pronunciation

(See Hint 85 on page 74 for an explanation of these skills.)

Ten Myths about the IELTS Test*

* Commonly held beliefs which are untrue!

1. The IELTS test is more difficult than other English tests.	Well, no. The IELTS test is not necessarily any more difficult than other tests, but not all tests assess the same skills. The IELTS test will certainly challenge you because the training course you are considering will be tough, too.
2. I can choose which module of the IELTS test I wish to take.	Not quite. If you want to do a degree course, you MUST take the Academic Module. The General Training Module is for diploma level courses and immigration purposes. But it is true that the IELTS test module you take is determined by the choices you make about your future.
3. The IELTS tests are different in various parts of the world.	No. There are many *versions* of the test, and at any given examination there may be a different version being given at a centre. However, IELTS is a standardised, global test.
4. I can get a better score at some IELTS testing centres than at others.	Absolutely not. IELTS officials use many means to ensure standardisation of Band Scores throughout the world. Of course, it could be true that taking IELTS in an English-speaking country is beneficial, but only because you are being exposed to English every day.
5. I can only take the IELTS test a total of 3 times.	Not true. You can now take the IELTS test as many times and as often as you wish. But it is sensible to wait at least two and preferably three months – continuing to practise – before you get tested again. This should increase your score.
6. I can successfully study for the test by myself.	We do not think so. The authors realise that every student has his or her own particular study method, but to prepare effectively for the IELTS test you should get professional advice from a tutor, either in a class or privately. You should also realise that General English Course practice is useful in addition to a specialised IELTS Course.
7. To get a good result in the IELTS test I should do as many practice tests as possible.	Really? Achieving a satisfactory Overall Band Score is the result of a number of strategies, not of just taking practice tests. And, definitely, if you do a practice test, you must work out why you made each and every mistake; otherwise you are missing out on valuable "learning" time.
8. The Listening Test is the most difficult of the IELTS Sub-tests.	Many students believe that one particular Sub-test is more difficult than all the others. Of course, all they are really saying is that they need extra practice in that skill area. Sorry, it is a myth.
9. If I don't think my score is accurate, there is nothing I can do about it.	If you receive a Band Score that you believe is not an accurate assessment, you can have all or any of your test papers and speaking assessment re-evaluated. This costs extra, unless your score increases. The second assessment becomes official, but IELTS will not lower your original score.
10. If I get a good score, I can use it as proof of my ability at any time in the future.	Not at any time in the future, no. There is a time limit on the usefulness of the Test Report Form which you receive after having taken the IELTS test. This period is about two years, provided you can prove that you have maintained your English.

Ten Truths about the IELTS Test

Facts you should know about the test, but probably do not!

✓

1. The IELTS test is unlike any other English test in the world.	It's true! The IELTS test is the only English test of its kind. It is primarily a test of English for academic study, but also includes a General Training examination option for candidates whose English requirements are at diploma level. This includes English for immigration purposes.
2. The IELTS test is extremely accurate.	Each new version of the IELTS test is put through an exhaustive and carefully analysed trialling process. In fact, you may be asked to help with the trial of a new test 30 minutes before your actual test begins.
3. If I wish, I can choose to take a computerised version of the IELTS test.	Versions of the IELTS Listening, Reading and Writing Sub-tests are available in computerised format (CB IELTS) at certain centres. Candidates choosing CB IELTS still have the option of performing the Writing Sub-test on paper if they wish, instead of using the keyboard and screen.
4. I can write on all the Question Papers.	Yes, you can. However, you cannot take the Question Papers from the Testing Room, and the examiners will only look at your Answer Sheets.
5. Unlike some English language tests, the IELTS test is made up of a number of different question types.	Yes, the question types are varied, and this means you should have adequate practice in all the types of question before you take the test. We also recommend advance planning, with two attempts at the actual test if possible – the first time as a "trial", and the second time for "real".
6. The IELTS Listening Test is designed to increase in difficulty as it continues, and each section is heard once only.	It is true that both the Listening and Reading Sub-tests become more difficult as they progress, and, yes, the Listening Test recording is heard only once. The test is given in stages, and you have time to read the next set of questions before you the tape continues. One minute is given at the end of a section to recall what you have heard.
7. There are two writing tasks, and I must complete both to score well in the Writing Sub-test.	Yes, you must complete both writing tasks to get a good writing Band Score. Since running out of time is usually a problem for candidates, it is vital that, when practising, you gradually decrease the extra amount of time you allow yourself to finish, until eventually you can complete both tasks in the given time of one hour.
8. The questions asked in the IELTS Speaking Test are determined in advance by the test authorities.	The majority of questions you will be asked come from a large bank of questions prepared beforehand by the IELTS test authorities. This standardisation of spoken questions means all candidates receive a fair speaking assessment.
9. The results of the IELTS test are made available soon after the test is taken.	True. Unlike some other tests, the official results are issued to all candidates two weeks from the test date. Unfortunately, the results cannot yet be made available sooner.
10. Even if I get a satisfactory Overall Band Score, I may not be accepted into the course I wish to take.	The IELTS test results can be used for a number of purposes, but the examination itself does not determine your successful acceptance into a particular course. Your intended course may require a minimum Band Score in a particular Sub-test in addition to a satisfactory Overall Band Score.

Some interesting World Wide Websites for students and teachers...

http://hotpot.uvic.ca/ [3]
http://international.ouc.bc.ca/pronunciation/ [19]
www.unifon.org/spelling-tests.html [17]
www.lextutor.ca/levels/ [10 16]
www.talkenglish.com [13]
www.rong-chang.com [12-14]
www.elllo.org/ [13]
www.eslcafe.com/discussion [12]
www.eslcafe.com [5]
http://eslcafe.com/help [15]
www.english-forum.com [10]
www.englishpage.com [12]
www.linguistic-funland.com/esloop/esloop.html [5]
www.englishlistening.com [13]
www.english-zone.com [10 11]
http://webster.commnet.edu/grammar/quiz_list.htm [11 15]
http://ksuweb.kennesaw.edu/~shagin/punct.htm [15 18]
www.wordsmyth.net [14-16 18]
www.englishtown.com.br [13]
www.eslpartyland.com [11]

www.spelling.hemscott.net/ [17]
www.bbc.co.uk/worldservice/learningenglish [14]
www.breakingnewsenglish.com/podcast.html [14]
www.churchillhouse.com [7] www.uefap.co.uk [14]
www.edufind.com/english/practice/test-ces.html [10]
http://languagetesting.info [6] www.soon.org.uk/page17.htm [5]
www.bebc.co.uk [3] www.englishjet.com [8 10]
www.ielts.org [1 2]
http://perso.wanadoo.es/autoenglish [11]
www.junketstudies.com/rulesofw [14]
www.englishlearner.com/tests/index.shtml [10]
www.englishlearner.com/teachers/ [6]

www.educationuk.org/ [8]
www.studygroup.com/embassyces/english/ [11]
www.lydbury.co.uk/grammar [15]
www.europa-pages.com/uk/ [7 8]
www.edufind.com/english/grammar/ [15]
www.langsci.ucl.ac.uk/ipa/ [19] www.englishuk.com/ [8]
www.blcu.edu.cn/exam-center/ielts.htm [1]
www.englishdaily626.com/ [13]
http://iteslj.org/ESL.html [5]
http://iteslj.org/links/Various/Web_Links/ [5]
http://a4esl.org/ [11]
www.manythings.org [11]
www.studyesl.com [7 8 9]
www.towerofenglish.com/ [5]
www.studyinternational.com.ph [3]
www.mkbooksd.com [3]
www.aapress.com.au [1 3 5]
www.aapress.com.au/ielts/english/message.html [20]
www.wfi.fr/volterre/teacher.html [6]
www.britishcouncil.org/au.htm [2]
http://ielts.webtrain.com.au [4]
www.idp.com/students/ [1 2]
www.fonetiks.org [19]
www.britishcouncil.org/nz.htm [2]

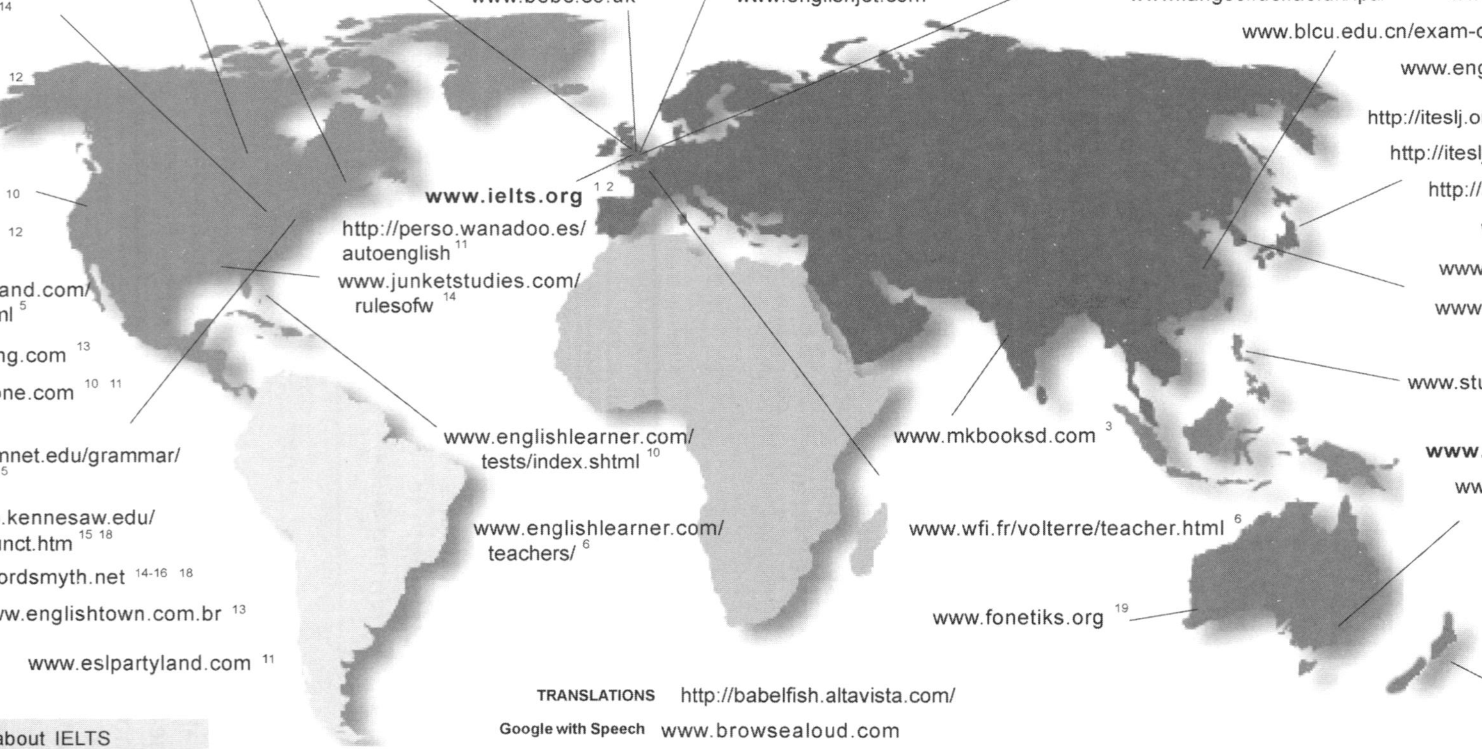

TRANSLATIONS http://babelfish.altavista.com/
Google with Speech www.browsealoud.com

KEY

1 general information about IELTS
2 IELTS testing centres
3 publishers/distributors of IELTS practice books/software or ESL books/software
4 101 Online IELTS course
5 ESL and/or EFL links to other sites
6 ESL & IELTS information for teachers
7 English language schools/colleges – directories
8 study English UK
9 study English Australia & NewZealand
10 test your English
11 English quizzes
12 English language or IELTS help online
13 listening and/or speaking help links
14 writing and/or reading help links
15 grammar help links
16 vocabulary help links
17 spelling help links
18 punctuation help links
19 pronunciation help links
20 IELTS forum

IELTS centres now exist in most countries of the world

NB: All links on this page are available to copy from *www.aapress.com.au/ielts/english/links2.html*

101 HELPFUL HINTS

HOW TO SUCCEED AT IELTS

There is now a great deal of IELTS practice material available in bookshops and online.

For any skill to develop, practice is essential. Students can now study from:

- books designed to give them a taste of the actual test – **Sample Tests, Practice Tests**
- books designed to give them **exercises** to build skills for the test
- books designed to help with **formulating strategies** for how to deal with the test
- **multimedia CD-ROMS** designed to bring a visual aspect to skill acquisition
- **online courses** designed to allow for practice at the keyboard
- **free materials** online
- **private tutors** online and face to face
- **IELTS classes** in schools or institutions.

All have their place. However, we do not recommend the extensive use of what is usually disorganised study from free IELTS online information sources. This is because our investigations show that students who use these services seldom get what they set out to achieve, i.e. a good score. The amount of information online is now so vast – anyone can write a few pages about IELTS – that it has become very difficult to know who is well qualified to turn to for advice. Even some popular free IELTS downloads are of questionable value and, in our opinion, may do more harm than good.

On page 10 we recommend some useful websites to visit. The web is always changing, but at the time of publication, these sites can be trusted. However, if you want to learn how to play the guitar, you shouldn't spend much time reading about how to do it from some unknown person online. You should practise at home from a good book and hire a professional tutor for face to face assistance. Naturally, you would be wary of people who guarantee you'll be playing guitar like a pro in a few hours – thanks to their "unique" advice. All skill development takes time and some hard work. That is no less true of learning a language. Successful students know this.

Absolutely, we consider a professional tutor or recognised IELTS class the ideal way to study for the test. Of course, not all tutors have sufficent expertise in IELTS. Before you spend money on a course, you should investigate how well that course prepares its students. Ask to attend a class first before you sign up. Fortunately, the majority of IELTS tutors we have worked with are dedicated and hard-working professionals who are glad to do all they can to help you succeed – if you will take their advice.

USING THE HINTS

The 101 Helpful Hints for IELTS book is not a book of "secrets". The strategies discussed in the Hints are ways to make you hear, see, write and speak the way successful candidates do. Exercising your brain in this way will expand your language "muscles" – even if you do not need to use every strategy in the actual IELTS test.

Follow the advice on how to use the book and how to take the tests on page 4, and use the Hints to study how an answer can be found. Sometimes a Hint will *directly* reference a test question, and sometimes a Practice Test question will require a strategy from a particular Hint.

After you have taken Practice Listening Test One and Practice Reading Test One, refer to the notes for those tests on pages 91–92 and 104 respectively. More notes for the other Practice Tests are available online at:

http://www.aapress.com.au/101hints/

- Four icons are used throughout the Hints Section and in the Practice Tests:

  The icons indicate sections of practice for the Listening,

  Reading, Writing, and Speaking Sub-tests.

IELTS TEST – BASIC HINTS

BEFORE THE TEST

1 CHOOSE A REALISTIC AND ACHIEVABLE GOAL

To obtain a satisfactory IELTS Band Score, it is necessary to be realistic. If the goal is to reach a certain level of English proficiency, success can only be achieved with much practice. It is important to know what an IELTS score in any of the Sub-tests means before you set yourself a goal. An outline of the Overall Band Scale levels is given below:

9	**Expert User**	Has fully operational command of the language: appropriate, accurate and fluent with complete understanding.
8	**Very Good User**	Has fully operational command of the language with only occasional unsystematic inaccuracies and inappropriacies. Misunderstandings may occur in unfamiliar situations. Handles complex detailed argumentation well.
7	**Good User**	Has operational command of the language, though with occasional inaccuracies, inappropriacies and misunderstandings in some situations. Generally handles complex language well and understands detailed reasoning.
6	**Competent User**	Has generally effective command of the language despite some inaccuracies, inappropriacies and misunderstandings. Can use and understand fairly complex language, particularly in familiar situations.
5	**Modest User**	Has partial command of the language, coping with overall meaning in most situations, though is likely to make many mistakes. Should be able to handle basic communication in own field.
4	**Limited User**	Basic competence is limited to familiar situations. Has frequent problems in in understanding and expression. Is not able to use complex language.
3	**Extremely Limited User**	Conveys and understands only general meaning in very familiar situations. Frequent breakdowns in communication occur.
2	**Intermittent User**	No real communication is possible except for the most basic information using isolated words or short formulae in familiar situations and to meet immediate needs. Has great difficulty understanding spoken and written English.
1	**Non User**	Essentially has no ability to use the language beyond possibly a few isolated words.
0	**Did Not Attempt The Test**	No assessable information provided.

(Source: http://www.ielts.org/)

It takes three months of regular intensive practice to improve by one overall Band

2 FOLLOW A REGULAR STUDY PLAN

Set aside the maximum number of hours you can spare each day to practise English for all four Sub-tests. Do not concentrate only on your weakest areas. Be regular in your practice, and give yourself a rest between tasks. Take at least one day out of your week to rest and forget the test completely. The secret of success is to work towards your goal slowly, steadily and regularly.

Take every opportunity to listen to English whenever and wherever you can. Watch TV programmes and films, listen to radio programmes and English language CDs – even songs in English on the Internet. Have as many conversations with native English speakers as you can, and practise in English as often as possible with your non-native English-speaking friends.

Try to read texts in English at least once every day. You should always be in the process of reading a book in English – a page or two each night before bedtime is an excellent plan. Read newspapers, magazines, and novels written for your English level (available from good language bookshops). General Training Module candidates should read widely and often. Always carry English texts with you, so you can read when you have spare time that would otherwise be wasted.

Do not worry about understanding every word. Read some articles in detail and some for speed.

3 INCREASE YOUR PERSONAL SPEED

In the IELTS test, time is your enemy. Candidates who have taken the test and did not perform as well as they had hoped often complain that they were unable to give all the answers in the Listening Test because the recording was too fast, and that they ran out of time in the Reading Test.

To begin with, do not worry if you do not finish the tests. Remember, the test is designed to measure candidates over a range of scores from 0 to 9 (0 indicates the test was not attempted). Candidates whose English is near perfect can expect to score 9, but even native English-speaking people would be unlikely to complete every Listening Test answer perfectly or finish the Reading Test a long time before the examination ends. Remember, the test is meant to be challenging.

The IELTS test measures many aspects of your English ability including the speed at which you listen, read, write, speak, and think in English. Your personal speed is not something which changes a great deal from day to day, but does change considerably over a longer period of time, as a direct result of practice in working with the English language.

Your personal speed and ability in the 5 areas previously mentioned is pretty well fixed at any given time. The official IELTS Band Scores you receive are extremely accurate, since each test is trialled extensively to achieve standardised results for candidates at all English levels. Nonetheless, there are certainly many things you can do, before and on the day of the test, to help maximise the use of your time and give yourself the best chance of success.

Consider the following situation: although a racing car cannot go faster than its maximum speed, the race can still be won, and its maximum speed maintained for longer, if an expert driver is at the wheel. An expert racing car driver will:

(before the race)

...spend a great deal of time practising at the wheel before race day,
...visit the track so that he or she knows where to go and what to expect,
...get enough sleep before the day of the big race,
...eat a good breakfast on race day morning;

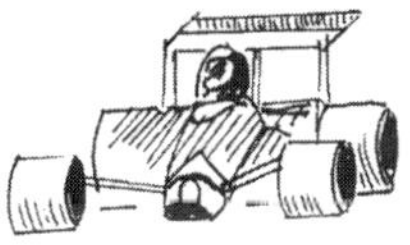

(during the race)

...check his or her watch constantly to monitor the car's progress,
...keep moving along the track and not get stuck on a bad corner,
...breathe long and deeply to relax and keep the oxygen going to the brain,
...drink water (but not too much!) when the car is at the pit-stop.

The Listening, Reading, and Writing Tests are given in that order, and are usually held on a single morning. The combined length of those three tests is 2 hours and 30 minutes. (The Speaking Test is usually conducted at an appointed time in the afternoon or the morning of the next day.) Only one short break is given between the Reading and Writing Tests, so you need to be at your best for a long period of time, which is why you must sleep and eat well before the test. The hints and guidelines in this book should help you achieve your "maximum speed". The more effort you put in, the faster your personal speed will be on the day. (See also Basic Hints 1 and 2.)

4 INCREASE YOUR SENTENCE READING SPEED

The faster and more accurately you read, the more questions you will be able to answer. In all the tests, the instructions, the example, and the questions themselves need to be read quickly, and must be well understood in order for you to have more time to find the answers. It pays to increase your overall reading speed. (See also Reading Hint 41.)

To increase your reading speed, you must learn to read in groups of words that form logical units of thought within sentences. Look at the following sentence:

Australia has been a popular choice for thousands of international students over many years.

Notice how you can think of the sentence as being made up of 3 main parts:

1	**Australia has been a popular choice**	(What and where?)
2	...**for thousands of international students**	(Who for?)
3	...**over many years.**	(When?)

Note also, that in this case (and many others) all the phrases answer wh/how questions. It may be helpful at first to think of wh/how questions when trying to read in phrases.

If you read each word in a sentence one at a time, you will read very slowly and most likely misunderstand the meaning of much of what you read. So read your sentences in phrases by considering all the words of a phrase as a single unit.

Notice how much quicker it is to read the sentence, and how the meaning of what you say is more clear. Practise reading in phrases everyday. Look ahead on the page as you read, and always aim to find logical places in the sentences where phrases begin and end. Note also that there is often more than one solution as to where the logical breaks between phrases occur within sentences.

Read faster by reading words in groups that form logical units of thought

5 DEVELOP A MEMORY FOR ENGLISH

In the Reading Test, it pays to remember as much as you can of what you have just read, but at least the words can be read again. However, in the Listening Test you cannot go back, and the recording is only played once. If the answer comes before the keyword/phrase, your memory of what you have just heard is even more important. Nevertheless, the answer usually follows the keywords/phrases that you hear, and is close in time to the main keyword/phrase you are listening for. (See also Basic Hint 9.)

To improve your "English memory", try the following exercise: use the pause button on your CD player, and repeat the sentences spoken in the passages on the CD that comes with this book, **gradually increasing the length of what you repeat**. Do not worry about repeating the exact words. Simply aim to remember more of what you have heard.

DURING THE TEST

6 MANAGE YOUR TIME CAREFULLY

The Listening Sub-test

The recording is heard once only, and the questions are answered as you listen. Time is, therefore, managed for you, but you have a short period of time after each passage is heard to check your work.

Do not use this time to transfer your answers to the Answer Sheet because you are given 10 minutes at the end of the test in which to do this.

The Reading Sub-test

An advised period of time is usually given in which to complete each of the three sections of the test. **Keep an eye on the time** as you progress through the Reading Sub-test, and as you complete each question group. Make sure that you stop answering questions when the advised time is up. Move on to the next group of questions even if you have not finished those questions. If you do not, you will probably not complete as many questions as you could. Remember that **you** are in charge of managing your time in the Reading Sub-test.

7 THE GOLDEN RULE OF IELTS

The Golden Rule is **"Always give the monkey exactly what he wants"**.

If a monkey asks for a banana, you must give him a banana and not an apple. In other words, your answer to a question must be exactly what is required. You must be quite sure of the type of information you are asked to give as an answer, and what you must do with that information to give an accurate answer.

You might think that this advice is too simple to be worth remembering. It might seem obvious that you have to do what the test asks you to do and give the answers the test asks you to give.

Yet failure to remember and apply the Golden Rule is one of the main reasons why candidates do not score as well in the test as they believe they should. Read the questions very carefully.

Know the type of information the test asks you to give:

Is the answer a method of transport? ...a person? ...a place? ...a number?
If you know, you have a better chance of giving the correct answer.

Know what you have to do with the information:

Do you have to complete a sentence, or fill in the missing words in a sentence?
If so, your answers must, therefore, be grammatically correct within that sentence.

Do you have to provide an answer with no more than a maximum number of words?
If so, your answer must not contain more than that maximum number of words.

Do you have to name two items that you must hear in the recording, or find in a reading passage?
If so, your answer must contain two items only; three items would be incorrect.

Always know exactly what type of information you need to give and what you have to do with it

8 READ THE INSTRUCTIONS CAREFULLY

Candidates who do not read or listen to the instructions carefully may believe they are saving time, but the instructions contain vital information which must be understood in order to answer correctly.

- The instructions may contain information about the passage topic which helps to predict what you may hear or read. (See Listening Hint 16 & Reading Hint 38.)
- The instructions tell you what to do, what kind of answer to give, and, in the case of the Listening Test instructions, they tell you when to answer.
- It is important to read the instructions quickly and accurately. You might not have time to complete the test if you are too slow at reading the explanatory information.

9 ALWAYS LOOK AT THE EXAMPLE

The example is given to you for a number of very good reasons. It is important to read and/or listen to the example carefully. Some candidates believe they can save time by not looking at the example. This is a mistake. If you do not know how to give the answer, you are very likely to give an incorrect answer or a correct answer in the wrong form.

You will not always be given at example, but if you are, you should read it carefully.

The example tells us 3 very important pieces of information about the task:

1. The example tells you **how** to give the answer to questions.

   You should usually answer questions in the same **form** as the given example.

   ❒ Look at the Example for Questions 1 – 4 in Reading Test One:

   > ***Example:*** ....1788...... – First Fleet arrives from England

Your answers to Questions 1 – 4 can therefore be given in **number form** where applicable. In this case, the answers might also be given as **words** or **phrases**. The instructions will usually tell you in what form the answers are to be given. The example illustrates what the instructions state.

2. The example gives you **information** about the listening or reading passage.

   You will understand more about what you listen to and read if you can predict what is to come. The example gives information that is easily understood and helps you predict information about the ideas behind the main topic of the passage.

   ❒ Look at the Example for Questions 5 – 9 in Reading Test One:

   > ***Example:*** Paragraph (i) ...C.... (Australia – Attractive to International Students)

In this case, the example heading for Paragraph (i) tells you that the introductory paragraph is aboutAustralia and its attractiveness to overseas students. Having read the passage title, you can predict the passage is concerned mainly with the attractiveness of Sydney to overseas students.

3. The example tells you **when** to start listening, or **where** to start reading to find the answers.

   ❒ Look at the Example for Questions 22 – 27 in Reading Test Two:

   > ***Example:*** The Workers' Unions no longer have the power they once had. TRUE

The logical place to commence looking for the answers would not be at the very top of the reading passage, but <u>after</u> the position of the example keyword(s) in the passage. Of course, in the Listening Test, the answers will come <u>after</u> the example that you hear.

10 USE QUESTION KEYWORDS TO FIND THE ANSWERS

The **keywords** or **keyphrases** in the questions help you in your search for the answers. This is true for both the Listening and Reading Sub-tests. First, you must choose which word or phrase to listen for on the tape, or search for in the reading passages. There may be more than one keyword or keyword phrase in a question, and they can be placed before or after the answer. The answer is not always given in sequence.

❒ Look at Question 17 in Listening Test One:

signpost keywords

(fast and easy exit) to (the rooftop) is (a requirement) **(17)** ....

destination keyphrase → ***the answer***

(Tapescript: "The availability of **fast and easy exit** from all lower floors to **the rooftop** was made **a requirement** for every building over two-storeys high **by law**.")

Since topic keywords and keyphrases are heard or read some time before or after the answer is found, they are similar in function to street signposts; they can point forwards to where you are going or back to where you came from. In this book, they are referred to as **signpost keywords/phrases** because they point to where the answer can be found. Other keywords are very close to the answer and often form part of the answer phrase. Here, they are referred to as **destination keywords/phrases**.

Note that signpost keywords are usually heard a short time before the answer is given, and tell you that the answer is coming.

In Question 16 of Listening Test One, the signpost keywords/phrases to listen for are *"fast and easy exit"*, and *"the rooftop"*. The destination keyphrase is *"a requirement"*. You should listen carefully to all the words which follow the destination keyphrase.

Also note that in Question 17 of Listening Test One, two answers are possible: *"by law"* and *"of high buildings"*. These words follow the destination keyphrase – or they may be a choice from those words which fits the requirements of the answer *(i.e.* ***NO MORE THAN THREE WORDS****)*.

You may not hear (or find in a reading passage) all the keywords or keyphrases; you may instead hear (or read) words with the same or similar meaning. You should be aware that flexibility is most important when dealing with keywords. (See also Listening Hint 18 & Reading Hints 49 & 56.)

Circle the important keywords or phrases before you listen or search for the answer

CHECK BEFORE THE END OF THE TEST

11 DO NOT FORGET TO MAKE LOGICAL GUESSES

In the Reading Sub-test, if you are having trouble completing the questions to a particular passage, you should leave a minute or so at the end of each advised time period for that passage (usually 20 minutes) to guess those questions that can be guessed. In the Listening Sub-test, you are given a minute of silence after each section has finished. Candidates who forget to give a logical guess to questions they cannot otherwise answer, do not give themselves any chance at all to get a mark!

❒ Look at Question 11 in Reading Test One: (True/False/Not Given question type)

11 Sydney Harbour is the largest in the world. ....

It is a True/False type question with the added possibility of the statement not being mentioned (**NOT GIVEN**) in the passage.

A guess might be that this statement is likely to be true. The passage states that *"... the 57 square kilometre harbour is one of the largest harbours in the world..."*. Yet, if Sydney Harbour was indeed the largest in the world, the passage would probably have said so.

Remember, though, the instructions tell us to "**Use the information given in the reading passage**." Since the passage does not actually say the harbour is the largest in the world, the answer must be *"NOT GIVEN"*.

❒ Look at Question 13 in Reading Test One:

13 The Entertainment Centre is only for international popular music artists who attract large audiences. ....

A logical guess would be that the statement is likely to be false, which is, in fact, the answer. It is unlikely that an Entertainment Centre in a large city would be *"only for..."* overseas artists.

❒ Look at Question 14 in Reading Test One:

14 There is now a greater variety of restaurants to choose from in Sydney than in the past. ....

It is obviously difficult to guess if a statement is not mentioned in the passage. If in doubt, do not choose a statement that is **likely to be false** as "not given" in the passage. In most cases, only **likely to be true** statements are not mentioned in the text. They are often put there to trap candidates into believing the statement is actually mentioned. The statement in Question 14 is likely to be true, but, in fact, there is no mention of it in the passage.

Also, your own knowledge of the actual truth of a statement might not always be helpful. The answer must be given according to what is said in the passage. Nevertheless, logical thinking is the key to working out (and guessing!) many of the answers in the IELTS test.

12 ARE YOUR ANSWERS GRAMMATICALLY CORRECT?

While it is true that not all words and phrases given as answers to questions in the Listening and Reading Tests need to be grammatically correct, it is often possible to work out the correct answer by using your knowledge of grammar. Always consider whether your choice of answer is grammatically acceptable before making your final decision. This is especially true of the following types of tasks:

- short-answer question tasks
- sentence completion tasks
- all table/chart/diagram/note completion tasks
- gapfill tasks.

❒ Look at Questions 16 and 17 in Listening Test One:

- **Building reconstruction**
  – large buildings near the coast including **(16)** ....
  – fast and easy exit to the rooftop is a requirement **(17)** ....

Question 16 must be **plural**, since *"large buildings"* is plural. The answer is *"hotels and resorts"*, both of which are plural. *"Hotel"* or *"resort"* might not be accepted, (we are not told which grammatical errors are accepted and which are not). The answer to Question 17 is **an adjectival phrase**, *"by law"* or *"of law"*. Although the word *"legal"* might make sense if it was placed before the word *"requirement"*, it does not make English grammatical sense coming after the noun. Take no chances.

Verb forms, plural forms and other grammatical forms can be important when you give Listening and Reading Test answers. A good rule is to always try to give the answer in correct grammatical form. (See Writing Hint 65 for a 10 Point Grammar Checklist, and see Writing Hint 81.)

13 GIVE ONE ANSWER ONLY

Give just one answer to a question, unless you are specifically requested to give more than one answer. Even if one of the multiple answers you give is correct, you might score zero if too many of the other answers are incorrect. Surprisingly, candidates sometimes give more answers than necessary! If you are asked to name just three items that you hear or read about in a passage, it makes no sense to give four items as your answer. You will score zero, even if all four items are correct. Remember the Golden Rule. (See Basic Hint 7.)

Note that with short-answer questions, especially in the Listening Test, there is sometimes a variety of words or phrases that can give the correct answer. However, you waste valuable time if you give more than **one** of the correct answers to short-answer questions. Alternative answers are given to various questions in the Answer Keys for the Listening and Reading Tests contained in this book.

14 CHECK YOUR SPELLING

In the Listening and Reading Tests incorrect spelling may now be penalised. The markers of the test refer to a list of acceptable spellings when assessing your answers. There are no indicators given by the IELTS authorities as to what might constitute an acceptable spelling. However, we must assume that slight variations of the correctly spelt answer will probably be listed.

❐ Look at Question 6 in Listening Test One:

Family Name: 6 ....L A V I L L I E R S ✓

You must spell George's family name exactly as spelt out letter by letter in the recording. In this case, there are no acceptable alternatives to the spelling of the name as given on the CD. Answers to other question types in the Listening and Reading Tests must be sufficiently well spelt to indicate the correct answer. Copy answers from the passages accurately in the Reading Test.

❐ Look at Question 7 in Listening Test One:

Nationality: 7 ....S W E T E R L A N ✗

It would be unlikely for the spelling "Sweterlan" to be accepted as "Switzerland" because it is an inaccurate phonetic approximation of the answer. Besides, you are asked to give the **nationality**, not the country. Remember the Golden Rule. (See Basic Hint 7.)

15 MAKE SURE YOUR ANSWERS ARE EASY TO READ

You cannot expect to do well if your answers cannot be read. Candidates may be unaware that their answers cannot be understood by the examiners who mark the tests. Be careful!

Words: If you have trouble with English letters, you could write your Listening and Reading Test answers in BLOCK LETTERS. Practise, so your letters look like these:

A B C D E F G H I J K L M N O P Q R S T U V W X Y Z

....

a b c d e f g h i j k l m n o p q r s t u v w x y z

....

Your letters must be distinguishable from each other. Pay particular attention to:

E and *F*   *I*, *J* and *L*   *M*, *N* and *W*   *U* and *V*   *I* and *T*

(It is often hard to tell the difference between these letters when candidates write them quickly.)

Numbers: Numbers can be even more difficult to read:

1 2 3 4 5 6 7 8 9 0

....

Many candidates do not realise that their numbers cannot be recognised by the examiners. Practise so that your numbers look similar to those shown above.

LISTENING TEST HINTS

16 BE READY TO LISTEN

Remember that the listening part of the IELTS test is the same for Academic and General Training Module candidates. There are 4 sections, and each is treated separately and **played once only**. The moment you hear the words *"Section 1"*, *"Section 2"* etc. you should:

- be prepared and ready to listen for the instructions that are given
- listen for details about the information contained in the coming passage. (e.g. who? what? where? when? why?)

First, check where the questions are located on the pages in the section to be heard. In the short time given to you before the listening passage begins, which is usually only about ten or twenty seconds at most, you should do your best to predict what you will hear.

When Section 1 begins, the first item to listen for is the **example**. The example is heard first and then again when the passage is played in full; in other IELTS Listening Test Sections no example is given. (See also Basic Hints 8 and 9.)

17 LEARN TO PREDICT

There are many types of IELTS listening question tasks:

- matching tasks
- multiple choice tasks
- short-answer question tasks
- classification tasks
- sentence completion tasks
- chart/ table/notes completion tasks
- gapfill tasks
- diagram labelling tasks

In the Listening Test you use four skills at once. It is not surprising that candidates often find this the most demanding of the four tests. You need to be able to:

- **read** the instructions and questions
- **listen** for general information
- **listen** for specific information
- **write** the answers as you listen for the answers to the questions that follow.

Before each listening passage, in the time given to you to look at each section in the test booklet, you should try to predict information about the listening passage situation. Predict the number of people involved and what they might be doing or planning. Try especially to predict what they might say and the words they might use.

You are given only a short time to look at the questions before the listening passage begins. However, to score well in the Listening Test you need to develop the ability to think ahead. The more effectively you can predict, the quicker your mind will form the correct **word associations** to make with the topic, and the better you will be able to work out the meaning of what you hear.

A useful exercise for helping to develop the ability to predict is to play CDs in English (e.g. the CD that accompanies this book), and pause after every minute or two to ask yourself what will happen and what you will hear next. This can also be done with videos, taped news items on the TV, interviews on the radio etc. It is important to **think about the words that you expect to hear**. Write them down, and then check to see how many you guessed correctly.

The secret to increasing your listening skills is to better predict what you might hear

18 WORK OUT THE WORD VARIABLES

Section 1 of the Listening Test is the easiest of the four sections. Each section becomes progressively more difficult. If you know your English level is average or above average, that is, you have a good understanding of basic survival English, you should have little trouble hearing all the answers in Section 1. Most candidates who are seriously considering tertiary study in an English-speaking country in the near future should be able to score 100% in this section. However, it is so easy to make unnecessary mistakes due to nervousness or lack of preparation. Listen for a general understanding of the situation, and at the same time listen for the specific **keywords or phrases**.

The questions in Section 1 are most likely to be presented to you in the test booklet in the form of notes, tables, simple charts or forms to be completed; but multiple choice or short-answer questions are also common. In many types of questions, multiple choice for example, those variable word/phrase choices are given to you. In other questions, the choice of words you may hear is completely up to you to predict.

❐ Look at Question 2 in Listening Test One:

2 Who do they ask for directions?

A a man on a trolley
B a man sitting down with a hat on
C a man at the check-in desk

It is clear that the words to listen for are given to you. This is not always the case, however. Predicting the words you might hear – in other Sections especially – is easier if you work out the **word variables**. The variables are those words and situations in a possible answer that can vary or change, according to what you hear in the recording.

❐ Look at Question 16 in Listening Test One:

- ***Building reconstruction***
  – large buildings near the coast including **(16)** ....

What kind of large buildings do you find near the coast? Hotels? Mosques? Condominiums? Apartment blocks? These are the word variables.

Now, it is true, you don't have a lot of time to do this in the actual test – almost no time at all in fact – but for practice it is essential that you spend some time **before** you play the CD...brainstorming; that is, guessing possible words that you might hear. Competent teachers will occasionally allow you time to do this as a group exercise before they play the practice listening tests.

By predicting the variable words to listen for, you increase your chances of hearing the answer

19 THE ANSWERS ARE OFTEN STRESSED AND REPEATED

If you listen carefully to the practice CD, you will notice that important information, which includes the answers, is almost always stressed and quite often repeated two or even three times. This surprises many candidates when they know the answer and listen again to the recording.

❐ Look at Question 8 and part of the tapescript for this question in Listening Test One:

Destination: **(8)** ....

George: Well, yes, I live in France now, but I was born in Switzerland.

Clerk: Swiss. Very good. Flight number: FA–492. Destination is...

George: ...**Paris**.

George: Are you connecting with any other flight in **Paris**, or will you be staying there?

Clerk: No, I'm spending my vacation in **Paris**. Well, Sèvres, just outside **Paris**.

The answer "Paris" is mentioned four times (in bold) and is stressed once (bold and underlined).

20 KNOW WHEN TO MOVE ON TO THE NEXT QUESTION

In the IELTS Listening Test each section is considered separately, and you are not told when the next question in a section comes. When the passage is being played, you should:

- be aware of the content of the next question...
- ...as you listen for the answer to the current question.

If you do not think ahead to the next question, and you miss an answer, you might be unable to keep up with the recording. You could still be waiting for an answer that has already been given.

Listen for the question topic keywords/phrases, any marker words/phrases (see below), and the changes in the speaker's inflection or pitch, to help you recognise when the questions change. Once you recognise that the question topic has changed, it is time to move on to the next question, even if you have not completed the previous question.

Only very few Listening Test questions are given out of order. However, you must be flexible enough to look ahead at the test paper in case the answers to questions do not come in the order shown in the test booklet. This is most likely to occur in a gapfill listening task.

Marker words/phrases are those English words/phrases that tell the listener that the topic is changing. Listen for marker words/phrases so that you know to move on to the next question.

e.g.	And now (we will) ...	Now tell me, ...	Next, I'd like to...
	Finally, can you tell us... ?	Right, so the first thing...	To start with...
	Before I move on to...	I'd like now to move on to...	One more thing...
	And what about... ?	Well, that's about it, except for...	

Changes in the speaker's inflection also tell you that the question topic is changing. Usually, when an English speaker changes topic, his or her voice will lift considerably in pitch and in level of excitement. Listen to the CD provided with the book for the above or similar marker words/phrases, and try to hear the changes in pitch and excitement in the voice.

21 LOOK AT OTHER QUESTIONS FOR THE ANSWER

In some cases, the answer to a question could be given in written words later in the test booklet.

❐ Look at Question 1 in Listening Test One.

The answer *"C" (FrancAir Check-In)* is given to you by looking at Question 3. In listening and reading gapfill tasks especially the word or phrase you need is sometimes there in front of your eyes on the page.

❐ Look at Questions 11 – 13 in Listening Test One.

The choice **E measuring of the earthquake** tells you that there is an earthquake (answer **A**) because of the use of the definite article *"the"*.

Clues to the answer, and even the answers themselves, can sometimes be found printed in the test booklet

22 LISTEN FOR THE SPEAKER CHANGING HIS/HER MIND

Often the speaker changes his or her mind and makes a correction before giving the answer that you need. Alternatively, the speaker may correct someone else.

❒ Look at the part of the tapescript which answers Question 7 in Listening Test One:

(Tapescript:) *Clerk:* George...er...L-A-V-I-L-L-I-E-R-S. Good. Now, nationality: French. No, wait a minute. It's a Swiss passport.

The clerk wants to find out George's nationality. He guesses that George is French, but thinks twice when he notices George's passport is Swiss. It would be a mistake to write down the first nationality mentioned, in your hurry to get the right answer.

Listen for the possibility of the speaker making corrections to what is said

23 USE SHORTHAND FOR SPEEDY WRITING

In the Listening Test, you are often required to listen for the next answer while writing down the answer to the previous question. It is one of the measures of effective listening – the examiners want to find out if you can comprehend what is said while attempting another task at the same time. This further tests your listening ability in English.

To write down the answers more quickly, write only **the first two or three letters of the answer** that you hear. This shorthand approach is often effective in a gapfill listening task because some of the answers may come in quick succession, especially at the beginning of the gapfill passage. (See also Listening Hints 24 and 25.) You can complete the words during the short period of time given to you after the passage has finished. You are very likely to remember what the letters mean because they are the first letters of words you have recently heard in context.

❒ Look at Questions 16 – 20 in Listening Test Two:

Estonia is a small, flat country in Europe dotted with numerous islands and lakes. The manufacture of agricultural machinery and **(16)** ..e......m................ are the major industries, with **(17)** ..gr.............. and vegetables the main **(18)** ..cr.........s.... .

Once a part of Greater Russia, the nation is now an independent **(19)** ..dem...........rep

Although many people speak Russian, the official language is Estonian. The weather in Estonia in summer is **(20)** ..mi.............. .

This method can enable you to return quickly to giving your whole attention to listening for the next answer. However, it does require some practice. Note that you would not try to use this method to remember numbers, but with word answers you can almost always remember the words again. Then, all you need to do is give the **correct grammatical form** of the answers. (See also Basic Hint 12.)

24 PRACTICE FOR LISTENING GAPFILLS

Gapfill tasks are usually considered by candidates to be the most difficult of the IELTS listening tasks. Your grammatical knowledge is as important as your listening ability, for answers should be grammatically correct within the given sentences.

The most common type of IELTS listening gapfill task requires you to listen to a passage of spoken English containing information concerning a particular topic or event. In the tests in this book the gapfill listening tasks are based on news items or TV reports. It is good practice to listen to the news either on the TV or radio, and try to complete a chart such as the one on the next page:

Item	What?	Where?	When?	Who?	How?	Why?
News Item 1						
News Item 2						

Not only news items, but all kinds of informative talks can provide practice of this kind. First, what you should do here is listen for **general information**. This is essential because unless you can understand the general idea of what is being said, you will be unable to understand the specific information in the talk. Most listening gapfill questions require you to listen for specific information.

Make a video or audio clip of your news items or talks from the TV or radio. Now go back over the excerpt you have made and listen for **specific information**. It is useful to make an audio clip of a video item because it is easier to play back the information and to focus on what you are hearing, rather than seeing. Do not try to understand every word. You should train your ear to listen for the words you are already familiar with, but did not catch on the first listening for general information.

You can also use the passages on the CD that accompanies this book for the same purpose. Check the words that you miss by referring to the Practice Listening Test Tapescripts in Appendix 6 starting on page 162. More exercises are available from the companion practice book *"202 Useful Exercises for IELTS"*. (See also Reading Hint 55.)

25 LISTENING GAPFILLS – STEP BY STEP

❒ **Before you listen:**

Read the instructions carefully.

(See Basic Hints 7 and 8.)

Always look at and listen for the example.

(See Basic Hint 9.)

❒ **As you listen:**

Choose the keywords/phrases to listen for, and be aware of the question changing.

(See Basic Hint 10 and Listening Hint 20.)

Be aware that some of the answers may come quickly one after the other.

(See Listening Hint 23.)

Be aware that one or two of the answers may not be given in question order.

(See Listening Hint 20.)

Be aware that the word or phrase you need may already be on the page.

(See Listening Hint 21.)

Use shorthand to improve the speed at which you write down your answers.

(See Listening Hint 23.)

❒ **In the time given to you at the end of the gapfill:**

Make sure your words and numbers are easy to read.

(See Basic Hints 14 and 15.)

Guess the answers to unanswered questions – do not leave blanks.

(See Basic Hint 11.)

Check that your answers are given in grammatically correct English.

e.g. for answers that should be in plural form.

(See Basic Hint 12.)

26 PRACTICE FOR SHORT-ANSWER QUESTIONS

Some candidates find short-answer question tasks even more challenging than gapfill exercises. Usually, short-answer question tasks come later in the Listening Test, and, therefore, the Listening passages are longer and more difficult to understand.

The IELTS short-answer question tasks require you to listen to a passage of spoken English, often a conversation between two people, and choose words or phrases from the dialogue which best answer the given questions. It is good practice to listen to interviews and conversations with interesting persons on the TV or radio, and make brief notes from short excerpts of what you have chosen to listen to.

Make a video or audio clip of your chosen news item or talk from the TV or radio. Now you can go through the clip and make abbreviated notes of the important points made by the speakers. As previously mentioned, it is useful to make an audio clip of a video item because it is easier to play back the information and to concenetrate on what is being said. Do not worry if you cannot understand every word.

You can also use the passages on the CD that accompanies this book for the same purpose. Check the words that you do not hear clearly by referring to the Practice Listening Test Tapescripts in Appendix 6 starting on page 162.

❒ Look at these notes made from part of the tapescript of Section 3 of Listening Test One:

Sue: Good afternoon and welcome to "Working Lives". My name is Sue Holt. This week we continue our series by looking at a job that is often thought of as adventurous, exotic, and highly desirable. We're going to take a behind-the-scenes look at the airline hospitality industry. What is the reality behind the smart uniform and ever-ready smile of the flight attendant? We're lucky enough to have in the studio Julie Nevard, who works for British AirWorld, and is a senior member of the cabin crew staff.

Sue: Thank you for finding the time to speak to us. I know that you must have a busy schedule.

Julie: My pleasure. Yes, it is a very full-time job, but I think you realise that very early on in your career..

Sue: How long have you been involved in in-flight hospitality?

Julie: Well, I trained for a year at the British AirWorld Training School, and...I'd already taken a Diploma in Hospitality and Tourism after I left school so, all in all, ...about 5 years...no, more like 6 years.

Work^{n} -Lives - Sue H

advent / good job

↓

<u>airline flight attndnt</u>

Julie N (Brit AirWrld)

→ Sen memb cab crew staff

\- (busy sched) f t job

\- traind 1 yr →Brit Air Tr Schl

↓

... Dip (Hosp + Tourism)

@ ? (post sch)

Total = ~~5~~ 6 yrs

The notes above make use of: **abbreviations**

underlining

symbols, (especially dashes, arrows and brackets).

missing vowels etc.

Be aware, however, that your test answers, must not be in note form. This is for practice only.

For practice, you can devise and use your own system of note-taking

27 SHORT-ANSWER QUESTIONS – SPECIFY THE TOPIC

In a question which asks you to provide a short answer to a question, you should first accurately work out the question topic in order to give the correct answer.

❒ Look at Questions 23 and 24 in Listening Test One:

23 What does Julie like most about her job?

....

24 What is Julie's main responsibility when on duty?

....

In Question 23 the topic is not simply what Julie likes about her job, but what Julie likes **most** about her job. Therefore, the answer is *"meeting new people"*, and not *"going to places she has never been before"*, nor any of the other reasons she mentions.

Similarly, in Question 24 the topic is not simply Julie's responsibilities when on duty, but Julie's **main** responsibility when on duty. Therefore, the answer is *"passenger comfort"* and not any one of the other responsibilities she mentions.

Check with the Practice Listening Test One Tapescript in Appendix 6 on page 163 if you are unsure of what Julie says.

If you do not read the question carefully, and do not accurately specify the topic, you might easily give the wrong answer.

Before the passage is played, or as you listen, circle the topic of each question

28 SHORT-ANSWER QUESTIONS – SUMMING UP

The speaker often sums up what he or she says in answer to a specific question. It is natural for a speaker to be sometimes unable to give an instant answer to a question. The speaker will then talk of many connected things before stating directly what he or she wishes to give as the answer at the end of the reply.

❒ Look at part of the tapescript for Section 3 of Listening Test One:

Sue: Then tell me, what is your main responsibility during a flight?

Julie: That's hard to say really. Well, we're responsible for all the needs and demands of each and every passenger, for up to 10 hours on some long haul flights. Not to mention the safety of the plane and all the passengers. I suppose, if I have to come up with a single answer, it'd be passenger comfort.

The above excerpt gives the answer to Question 24 in Listening Test One. Julie cannot instantly give a direct answer to Sue's question, but eventually sums up and states her answer directly: *"passenger comfort"*.

You should wait for the speaker to sum up before giving your short answer to a question. If you do not, you run the risk of writing down an answer which may be incorrect or only partly correct. You might also be too busy writing down what you think is the answer, and not hear the correct answer in the speaker's summing up.

Don't always be satisfied with the first words you hear

29 SHORT-ANSWER QUESTIONS – STEP BY STEP

❒ **Before you listen:**

Read the instructions carefully.

(See Basic Hints 7 and 8.)

Always look at and listen for the example.

(See Basic Hint 9.)

❒ **As you listen:**

Accurately specify the topic before choosing the keywords/phrases to listen for, and be aware of the question changing.

(See Basic Hint 10 and Listening Hints 20 and 27.)

If necessary, wait for the speaker to sum up.

(See Listening Hint 28.)

❒ **In the time given to you at the end of the short-answer questions:**

Make sure your words and numbers are easy to read.

(See Basic Hints 14 and 15.)

Guess the answers to unanswered questions – do not leave blanks.

(See Basic Hint 11.)

Check that your answers are given in grammatically correct English.

e.g. for answers that should be in plural form.

(See Basic Hint 12.)

30 PRACTICE FOR MULTIPLE CHOICE QUESTIONS

Most candidates say that they find the multiple choice question tasks easier than the other listening tasks. This is because in a question with four choices you have a 25% chance of being correct. However, you also have a 75% chance of being wrong, which is why multiple choice questions are harder than they seem. Of course, if you are given 5 choices, your chance is lowered to only 20%!

The IELTS multiple choice question tasks require you to listen to a passage of spoken English, often a **conversation** between two people, or a **lecture or talk**, and make a choice between a number of possible given answer choices. It is good practice to listen to lectures or talks given on interesting topics. CD and tapes can be found on any number of topics at local bookstores and English language bookstores, or you can use the practice material contained on the CD which accompanies this practice book. CDs with exercises for other English language tests conducted mostly in multiple choice format (such as TOEFL or TOEIC) can be bought. Also, more multiple choice exercises are available from the companion practice book *"202 Useful Exercises for IELTS"*.

The choices for answers to a multiple choice question are either **directly or indirectly supported** (correct), **directly or indirectly contradicted** (incorrect), or **not mentioned** at all (incorrect).

When you practise multiple choice question tasks, do not be satisfied with simply finding the correct answer. Decide if the other incorrect choices are either **contradicted** or **not mentioned**. Of course, in the actual test you only have to find the one correct answer, but further practice will help you understand why certain choices cannot be correct. Therefore, carefully examine the 3 (or more) given choices to see how multiple choice questions are constructed. In this way, you get more value out of the practice task.

Note that although there is only one correct solution to a multiple choice question, it is possible that all or even none of the given choices to a multiple choice question may be correct. (See also Listening Hint 31). And if you have to guess, the chance of the first option (A) being correct is less than for the other options.

Multiple choice questions are often harder than they look

First, look at the ways in which answer choices may be incorrect:

1. There is often at least one given answer choice that is **neither sensible nor logical**, and, therefore, cannot be correct.

2. There may be given answer choices that are **contradicted** in the passage.

   A choice may either be

	directly contradicted	– clearly and directly opposite in meaning to what is heard
or	**indirectly contradicted**	– what is heard leads you to conclude that the choice is incorrect
or	**not exactly what is stated**	– almost, but not quite, what the speaker says.

3. There may be given answer choices that are **not mentioned** in the passage. (Note that some answers might not be mentioned in the passage and may also lack logic or sense.)

Next, look at the ways in which answer choices may be correct:

1. A given answer choice may be **directly supported** by what is stated in the passage.
2. A given answer choice may be **indirectly supported** by what is stated in the passage, that is, what is heard leads you to conclude that the choice is the correct answer.

When you practise, ask yourself if the given answer choices in a multiple choice question are:

• directly supported.................... ds	• directly contradicted................ dc
• indirectly supported................ is	• indirectly contradicted............ ic
• not **exactly** what is stated..... ne	• lacking logic or sense............... ls
• not mentioned............................ nm	• all (or none) of the above......... a (or n)

❒ Look at Question 32 in Listening Test One:

32 The reception desk in a hotel is described as:

A impressive at first
B a switchboard operating system
C the nervous centre of the hotel
D the first point of contact with a guest

Choice **A** is not mentioned in the passage. The reception desk is nowhere described as being impressive.

The lecturer simply says there is a
"...need for creating a good first impression..."

Note that choice **A** is not mentioned but is also not a sensible answer. Does the reception desk become less impressive later?

Choice **B** cannot possibly be correct because it lacks logic. A switchboard operating system is mentioned, but it cannot be a description of a reception desk.

Choice **C** is not exactly what is stated in the passage.

The lecturer says
"...the reception desk is both the...er...the face and the nerve centre of a hotel."

Choice **D** is correct because it is directly supported in the passage.

The lecturer says the reception desk is
"...the first point of physical contact with the client, ..."

31 MULTIPLE CHOICE – CONSIDER ALL THE CHOICES

Do not forget to consider all of the possible answer choices. It is possible that the last choice may be one of the following two types:

"**all of the above**" ...answer choices are correct.

or "**none of the above**" ...answer choices is correct.

If you do not read the last choice given, and it asks you to consider all of the other choices as correct or incorrect answers, you might easily make a choice that only partly answers the question.

32 MULTIPLE CHOICE – LENGTH OF THE CHOICES

There is often one possible answer choice that is longer than the others. After you have considered and rejected any illogical choice(s), the next consideration could be whether or not the longest choice given is the correct answer. Yes, correct answers in multiple choice questions are often the choices that are the longest! Of course, this is not always so; however, if you have no alternative but to guess, this hint might help. In addition, statistically, the first answer choice is least likely to be the correct answer.

33 MULTIPLE CHOICE – STEP BY STEP

You do not have much time to read the multiple choice questions in the Listening Test booklet before the passage begins. Therefore, decide which parts of the question task to read first.

❒ **Before you listen:**

You need to understand what the topic of the talk or conversation is about so that you can predict what ideas and words you might hear. Therefore, read the instructions first.

(See also Basic Hints 7 and 8.)

Once you have read the instructions, do not forget to look at the example.

(See Basic Hint 9.)

Next, you should read the first question and all the possible answer choices to that question. By doing this, you will be prepared for the first question when the passage begins. Note that you do not know how much time you have before the passage begins.

(See also Listening Hint 16.)

Underline any keywords/phrases in the question and possible answer choices that you feel might help you in listening for the answer. Make sure that the keywords/phrases refer to the specific topic of the question.

(See also Basic Hint 10.)

Then, you should at least read the other questions for keywords before you read any of the possible answer choices to those questions. This will further assist you with predicting and prepare you to move on to the next question as the questions change.

(See also Listening Hint 20.)

Be ready to give the answer to the first question as soon as the passage begins. Sometimes the answer to the first question is given in the speaker's very first sentence.

(See also Listening Hint 23.)

❒ **As you listen:**

Carefully examine the answer choices for each question as you listen to the passage.

(See Listening Hint 30.)

Do not overlook "all (or none) of the above" answer choices.

(See Listening Hint 31.)

If in doubt, consider the longest answer after rejecting any illogical answers.

(See Listening Hint 32.)

❒ **In the time given to you at the end of the multiple choice questions:**

Check the choices you have made.

(See Listening Hints 31 to 33.)

Guess the answers to unanswered questions – do not leave blanks.

(See Basic Hint 11.)

34 RECOGNISE QUALIFYING WORDS AND PHRASES

You need to recognise any modifying or qualifying words or phrases used in the question statements, and listen for them in the passage.

Below are some words and phrases that help to modify or qualify what is stated:

must	have to	certainly	will	absolutely essential
ought to	should	necessary to	need to	can/may only
don't have to	not required to	unnecessary to	need not (needn't)	it is optional
may	might	can	could	it is possible
must not (mustn't)	should not (shouldn't)	cannot (can't)	won't	strictly prohibited
never	sometimes	often	usually	always
however	but	an exception is	on the other hand	yet

You are sure to find instances of these qualifying words in the IELTS (and other) Listening Tests.

❒ Look at Questions 18 – 19 in Listening Test One:

- ***Contact***
  - telephone lines **(18)** .... (so don't phone direct)
  - only contact **(19)** .... on the hotline

❒ Look at Question 34 in Listening Test One:

34 The lecturer says that a member of a drink and bar service team

A need not have a thorough knowledge of wine.
B must not drink on the job.
C can eventually become a wine maker.
D can eventually manage a cellar dealing only with wines.

Sometimes identifying these words is useful and even essential in order to get the correct answer. In Question 34, for instance, the tapescript says:

"**Two of the main avenues open** are cellar management: dealing **exclusively** with wine and fortified wines...the, er...selection, purchase, storage, and general upkeep of the hotel cellar..."

A member of a drink and bar service team *"can"* choose one of *"two...main avenues open"*, that is, he or she has a choice. Dealing *"exclusively with"* means dealing *"only with"*.

Identify any modifying or qualifying words Listening Test question tasks

35 BEWARE OF "100% WORDS"

Be especially careful of question statements which include words such as *"always"*, *"never"*, *"must"*, *"have to"*, *"only"*, and *"all (the students etc.)"*. This can also apply to other question types such as multiple choice tasks in both the Listening and Reading Tests.

These 100% qualifying words have unconditional or all-inclusive meanings in sentences. However, even though the words you read in the Listening Test booklet may be heard in the passage, they are often qualified later. If you do not listen carefully, you might easily believe these statements are correct when they are not. In fact, statements containing "100% words" are quite often false. They are sometimes purposely included in the test to discover a candidate's true listening ability.

❒ Look at Question 35 in Listening Test Two:

35 The Macintosh computer network

- **A** can only be used by second and third year students.
- **B** can be used by some first year students.
- **C** is reserved for third year student use.

What you hear in the passage is almost the same as what is written in the question statement:

"The Macintosh computer network is reserved for second and third year students only..."

However, the tutor further qualifies what he says in the very same sentence:

"...unless you are a first year student of the Graphic Design course."

Sometimes statements which make 100% claims are not further qualified in the same sentence, but are qualified a little later in the passage. Beware!

36 MULTIPLE CHOICE QUESTIONS WITH MULTIPLE ANSWERS

The IELTS Listening Test no longer contains True/False question types but now has multiple choice questions with a number of answer choices from which you must choose two or maybe three correct answers. The rubric (instruction) tells you how many of the answer choices are correct.

❒ Look at Questions 11 – 13 in Listening Test One:

*Choose **THREE** letters from **A–F**.*

Which **THREE** events have recently taken place?

- **A** an earthquake
- **B** a tsunami
- **C** a giant wave of water
- **D** a chain reaction
- **E** measuring of the earthquake
- **F** airlifting of villagers

In the question set above, this means that three answer choices are **correct** and three are **incorrect**.

As you listen, you must check (✓or circle) answer choices that are correct and dismiss those that are not. This particular question asks if each event has *recently* taken place. That word *"recently"* is important. The events might all have happened, but only three occurred recently. So, reading the rubric accurately is very important.

The words you are listening for will probably be heard in question set order, but this might not be the case. Since three of the answer choices are incorrect – and some might not even be heard in the recording – don't wait for each answer choice to come, but as you listen to the block of spoken text, keep all the choices in mind.

When the time comes at the end of the test to transfer your answers to the Answer Sheet, the **answers to the questions in this question set can be given in any order**.

READING TEST HINTS

37 WRITE YOUR ANSWERS ON THE ANSWER SHEET

It is most important to write your answers on the Answer Sheet as you do the Reading Test. If you do not, you may find yourself in the unfortunate position of having completed the test in the given time of 60 minutes but without having recorded any answers to any questions at all! This would require you to make a special request of the IELTS marking team to refer to your Reading Test booklet for the answers. The problem is that your quickly written answers might be difficult to read. This could easily mean that a correct answer you gave might be marked as incorrect. (See also Basic Hint 15.)

Write your answers on the Answer Sheet provided as you do the Reading Test

38 DO NOT READ THE READING PASSAGE FIRST

It is a mistake to begin reading a passage without first having a reason to read. There are 3 parts to the Reading Test, and many candidates begin each part in the same way – by reading the passage. They might read it in detail, or scan it quickly to find out what the topic of the passage is and to get a general idea of the contents. However, candidates who do this first have forgotten the need to predict information. They do not have a good enough reason to read the passage so soon.

Always have a reason to read a passage before you begin to do so. Have a question in your mind – something you are looking for – otherwise you will not be managing your time well. (See also Basic Hint 6 and Listening Hint 17.)

39 READ THE TEST IN A LOGICAL ORDER

The following sentence gives a suggested order in which to look at the information in any of the 3 parts of the Reading Test:

"**T**o **H**ave **B**right **P**rospects, **I**ntelligently **A**nswer **E**ach **Q**uestion".

Read each part of the test in the order given by the first letter of each word of the sentence:

T – The **TITLE** of the reading passage should give you a rough idea about the main topic of the passage. If you do not understand the meaning of the title or some of the words it contains, it does not matter. Try and work out the meaning of the title while you continue to read.

H – The **HEADINGS** for each section of the passage refer to what is contained in each section, and where information can be located. They also help you to predict what the passage is about.

B – **BOLD PRINTED WORDS** indicate that those words are of some importance. They can also help you to predict information contained in the passage.

P – It is said that a **PICTURE** is worth a thousand words. Always look at illustrations, figures, tables, graphs and diagrams that accompany a reading passage. They often summarise, add important detail, or make information in the passage more clear.

I – The **INSTRUCTIONS** contain important information that you must read. If you do not read the instructions, you will almost certainly answer some of the questions in the wrong manner. The instructions may also contain clues about the information contained in the passage.

A – What kind of **ANSWERS** do you need to give? The instructions will tell you. The kind of answers that are required also tell you more about the information within the passage. Is the answer a name? a date? a number? etc. Remember to apply the Golden Rule. (See Basic Hint 7.)

E – The **EXAMPLE** not only provides you with the correct way to answer the questions, it tells you, in summarised form, more about the passage itself. You are not wasting time by examining the example and the answer it gives.

Q – Finally, the **QUESTIONS** themselves provide valuable hints about the ideas contained in the passage as well as specific information to look for on your first reading.

All of the above should be quickly examined before you read the passage in any detail. It will make scanning the passage much easier, and will help you to predict a large amount of information.

40 CONSIDER THE PASSAGE LAYOUT

In the Reading Test the questions may come before or after the passages. You need to know:

- where each of the 3 parts of the Reading Test begins and ends
- how many questions there are in that part of the test, and where they also begin and end (so that you do not forget to look at questions)
- how long to spend on a group of questions
- which questions to answer first.

There are many types of IELTS reading question tasks:

- matching headings with paragraphs
- short-answer questions
- identifying information – yes/no (true/false) or not given
- notes, summary, table, flowchart or diagram completion
- matching lists/phrases
- identification of a writer's viewpoint – yes, no or not given
- multiple choice
- sentence completion (gapfill)
- classification

Each reading passage requires certain strategies or approaches to take in order to make the best use of your time. The strategies to use depend on the type of question tasks that accompany each passage. You should be flexible enough to use a different approach if it suits the question task. (See also Basic Hint 6.)

With some passages, it is best to spend time reading certain portions of the passage in some detail. This might be the best approach for a particular sentence completion task, for instance. With other passages, it might be better to search the passage for the question topic keywords/phrases (referred to as signpost keywords/phrases in this book), and to look closely around those keywords for further matching keywords/ phrases to obtain the answer you require. This is usually the best way to answer matching task question types. Further reading practice is available in the companion practice book *"202 Useful Exercises for IELTS"*. (See also Basic Hint 10 and Reading Hints 44 and 45.)

Sometimes it is a good idea not to answer certain questions in the order in which they are given. For example, it might be wise to try and complete a gapfill summary of a passage (or part of a passage) first, since a summary gives broad information about that passage quicker than a detailed reading, even with words missing. On the other hand, if you know that a certain type of reading task is more difficult for you, it may be best to attempt another task first. However, it is usually best to answer the questions in the order given in the test.

It is impossible to say which is the best strategy for a group of questions in advance. By studying the reading hints in this book, it should be possible to find the best strategy to use in a given case. Some of the strategies that follow can be applied to more than one question type.

Examine the layout of each part of the test before you read the passage within it

41 SCAN THE READING PASSAGE

Scanning is the method to use when you need to search a page quickly for information that you require. You may be looking for **the general idea of the information** on the page (skim quickly through the information), or you may wish to scan for **specific information**. In either case, the method is to sweep your eyes across the page slowly and smoothly, starting at the top left, and working your way across and down the page in a wavelike motion as in the illustration below.

Practise scanning by applying the scanning technique to this page and other pages of writing of your own choice.

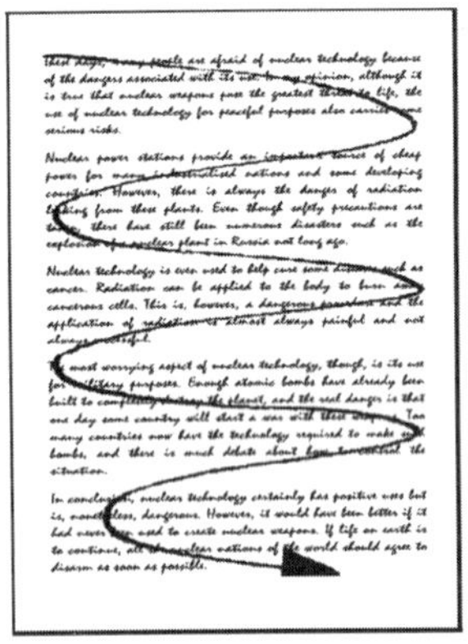

Did you understand the general idea of the topics on the page you just scanned? Did you move smoothly and steadily?

Do not read every word and do not rush. You are simply guiding your eyes with your finger or pen, and picking up information as you go, occasionally stopping for a moment to read something important that you have found, and continuing slowly back and forth, across and down the page.

It takes a little practice at first, but it is the best way to move quickly through a text without getting stuck and wasting time reading a lot of unnecessary information. You are more likely to find what you are looking for because you will have covered all parts of the page.

When scanning, guide your eyes across the page by using your first 3 fingers, or your index finger alone, or even the tip of a pen or pencil. This will prevent your eyes from wandering about on the page. You can increase your general reading speed too, by following your finger with your eyes across the page as you read. Many studies prove how much quicker people read when guiding their eyes across the page. You might be surprised to discover how much faster you will be reading.

42 READ THE TOPIC SENTENCES FIRST

When you are ready to search the reading passage for more information, you have to know which parts of the passage to read first. Remember, you do not usually have time to read every word of the passage, especially if your reading speed is only average.

A reading passage consists of a number of paragraphs, each of which has a **main idea** or **topic** that tells the reader more about the main topic of the passage. You should make certain that you understand the topic of each of the paragraphs in the passage by searching for the topic sentences.

The topic sentence is usually, but not always, **the first sentence of a paragraph**. In fact, the topic sentence might be any one (or two) of the paragraph sentences. In general, when searching for the topic sentence it is wise to follow a particular search order:

check the **first sentence** → then the **second sentence** → and then the **last sentence**

If you still have not discovered the topic of the paragraph, you will have to read the whole paragraph to find out what it is about. (See also Writing Hint 61.)

The **introduction** is a paragraph with a special purpose: it contains the main idea or topic of the entire passage. If the passage is an argument, it should also state the writer's opinion. Note that the first sentence of the introduction is usually the topic sentence. (See also Writing Hint 80.)

In addition, the **conclusion** often summarises the main points of the passage, and is often worth reading directly after looking at the introduction.

43 KNOW WHERE TO START LOOKING FOR AN ANSWER

The quickest way to find the answers to the Reading Test questions is to know where to look for them. If you know what the main idea or topic of each paragraph is, you can first look for the answer to a question in the most likely paragraph in the passage.

❐ Look at Question 10 in Reading Test One: (TRUE/FALSE/NOT GIVEN)

10 Sydney was first established as a settlement for convicted criminals. ....

Having completed Questions 5–9 and matched the headings to the paragraphs in the reading passage, we know that the heading for Paragraph (ii) is answer *"A" (Sydney – Location and History)*. Question 10 refers to a historical feature of Sydney, so it is logical to look in Paragraph (ii) for the answer. A quick scan of Paragraph (ii) reveals that the question statement is *"TRUE"*.

There is usually a logical place to begin looking for the answer to a reading question. This requires an understanding of the **main idea or topic** of each paragraph. You can save yourself a great amount of time if you work out the main idea or topic of each paragraph in the early stages of your assessment of the passage. (See also Reading Hint 42.)

44 READ AROUND THE KEYWORDS/PHRASES

Sometimes the answer to a question can be found without a detailed reading of a paragraph that might contain the answer. First, choose the keyword/phrase from the question, and locate the first instance of it in the reading passage, reading around it to discover the answer. Next, read the sentence that the keyword/phrase is within. Then, if necessary, read the preceding and succeeding sentences. If the answer is not found by reading around the first location of the keyword/phrase, search for the next instance, and repeat the process. Continue until the answer is found.

❐ Look at Question 14 in Reading Test One: (TRUE/FALSE/NOT GIVEN)

14 There is now a greater variety of restaurants to choose from in Sydney than in the past. ....

Paragraph (iv)

Not far from the city centre are the attractive old residential suburbs of Balmain, Glebe, and Paddington, where many people live in smart terraced houses. Art galleries, pubs, and **restaurants** abound in the cosy streets that tend to be quite narrow, whereas the suburbs surrounding the city's colleges and universities consist mainly of family homes and multi-unit blocks - an ideal situation for students looking for a homestay or to rent. Sydney's newer suburbs now have a large multicultural population, and local shopping centres reflect the influences of many cultures.

Dining Out

In Sydney, a vast array of ethnic and local **restaurants** can be found to suit all palates and pockets. In summer, café patrons often sit outside at tables under umbrellas, and enjoy the passing parade of shoppers. Students who prefer to cook at home can choose from several large weekend markets, where fresh fruit, fish, and vegetables may be bought more cheaply than at the local supermarket. Sydney also has its own Chinatown.

Shopper's Delight

In the heart of the city are several big department stores linked by enclosed over-the-street crossings and underground walkways. Most noticeable are the towering Centrepoint complex and the Queen Victoria Building, both containing many shopping arcades, coffee shops and **restaurants**. Out of town, in the suburbs, there are huge regional shopping centres. At the weekend markets, bargains can be had when shopping for clothing as well as for a wide range of assorted goods.

read around the question keyword

A quick **scan** of the paragraphs that contain each instance of the keyword reveals that there is no mention of *"a greater variety of restaurants to choose from in Sydney than in the past"*. It may be true in reality, but the answer must be *"NOT GIVEN"*.

This method of **searching for each instance of the keyword/phrase** should direct you to the answer in the shortest time possible. (See also Basic Hint 10.)

45 MATCHING TASKS

As can be seen from the various reading question types, there is more than one way in which candidates can be asked to match information in the IELTS test, but, basically, there are 2 distinct types:

Type 1 – with a list of items to choose from **equal** in number to the matches to make.

Type 2 – with a **longer** list of items to choose from than the number of matches to make.

Tasks with more items than necessary from which to choose answers (Type 2) are, naturally, more difficult than tasks with an equal number of items to match (Type 1). In both types, there are often 2 or 3 similar items for each question from which you will have to choose the correct answer.

Matching Task Method – for Types 1 and 2

Step 1. Read the instructions carefully. You need to have as much information as possible about the matching task before you begin.

Step 2. Complete the task in the order in which the answers will be given in the passage. It is important to determine the best order in which to do the matching. Random order is not a good idea; a systematic approach is always best. The fastest method is, if possible, to match the items in the order in which the answers to the questions will appear in the passage.

❒ Look at the list of headings for Questions 5 – 9 in Reading Test One:

A Sydney – Location and History
B Residential Inner-City Suburbs
C Australia – Attractive to International Students
D Entertainment for Young and Old
E The Harbour and Surrounding Suburbs
F The Cultural Climate

There are 6 paragraphs, each requiring a heading, and there are 6 headings to choose from. Therefore, this task is a matching task Type 1. The **headings** are to be matched with **paragraphs** in the passage, so the best method in this case is to look at each paragraph to be matched **from top to bottom in the passage**, and seek the correct match from the list of items (not the other way around).

Step 3. Cross off the answers to the example first, but only if an answer cannot be used more than once. Having crossed the example off the list of items, you should then proceed to the first place in the passage where a match is to be made, and seek the match from the list of items.

Step 4. Give yourself a number of choices from the list of possible matches. If you do not, you might easily decide on the first match you think is the answer, but often there are two or three matching items that might match. Of course, only one will be correct.

❒ Look at Question 8 in Reading Test One:

8 Paragraph (v) ....

Paragraph (v)

Sydney is home to the State Art Gallery of New South Wales, the State Conservatorium of Music, the Australian Opera, the Sydney Dance Company, and the Australian Ballet. The world-class Sydney Symphony Orchestra offers superb classical music all year round. Local theatre is innovative and well supported, and large-scale overseas productions tour regularly.

Question 8 asks for the heading of Paragraph (v). The topic of the paragraph deals with forms of entertainment. The likely headings that will match with this paragraph are, therefore, *"D" – (Entertainment for Young and Old)* and *"F" – (The Cultural Climate)*.

If you do not consider both likely choices, you might not choose answer *"F" – (The Cultural Climate)*, which is the correct answer.

Matching Task Method – Type 1 only

Step 5. Leave the most difficult match to last. Sometimes, one of the matching items is more difficult than the others. In a matching task Type 1, you can leave the most difficult match to last because the unmatched item left over at the end will be the answer (provided, of course, your other answers are correct). Do not waste too much time searching for the answer to a difficult matching question in a matching task Type 1 – it is wiser to solve the easiest matches first.

Step 6. Check your answers carefully because if you make an error with one match in a matching task Type 1, you will cause an error to occur with another match.

With both matching task Types 1 and 2, when the task asks you to match a heading with **a single paragraph**, you must be sure of the main topic of the paragraph before you make your match.

Similarly, when you are asked to match a heading with a particular part of the passage (which might contain more than one paragraph), you must be sure that **every paragraph** within that portion of the passage relates in some way to the topic idea of the heading you are considering.

❒ Look at Section (vi) in Part 3 of Reading Test Three:

Section (vi)

While student visa holders took either 10–29 week or 40 week courses, most students on working holiday and tourist visas took courses of less than 10 weeks, or from 10–19 weeks in length.

More than 50% of all students were taking courses of between 10–29 weeks, with the proportion fairly evenly divided between the 10–19 week and 20–29 week ranges. A large proportion of students were taking courses of at least 40 weeks in length, and only a few students indicated enrolment in courses shorter than 10 weeks.

There were noticeable differences between nationalities, with Koreans, Japanese, and Taiwanese taking longer courses than other nationalities, and Swiss and other European students taking much shorter courses.

It is not immediately clear from the first paragraph whether the main topic of Section (vi) is answer *"B" "length of courses"* or *"J" "visas"*. By checking the other paragraphs, however, it can be seen that only the topic *"length of courses"* is **common to all three paragraphs**.

Matched headings need to refer to all parts of the indicated portion of the passage

46 CHECK YOUR ANSWERS ARE CORRECT

Besides matching headings with paragraphs or portions of a passage, you might need to match beginnings with endings of sentences by referring to a reading passage, or match labels with parts of a diagram, table or chart. Your answer must agree with **all** the information in the other half of the match. It is sometimes useful to **match at least 3 areas of information in a possible answer** before choosing that answer.

❒ Look again at the headings for Questions 5 – 9 in Reading Test One:

A Sydney – Location and History
B Residential Inner-City Suburbs
C Australia – Attractive to International Students
D Entertainment for Young and Old
E The Harbour and Surrounding Suburbs
F The Cultural Climate

The first heading can be divided into 3 parts: *"Sydney"*, *"Location"* and *"History"*. Similarly, the second heading can be divided into 3 parts: *"Residential"*, *"Inner-City"* and *"Suburbs"*. The third heading can be divided into 3 parts as well: *"Australia"*, *"Attractive"* and *"to International Students"*. When searching for the answer in a paragraph in a piece of text, make sure that each of the 3 parts of the heading relates to what is stated in the passage.

Not only matching task headings can be divided into 3 parts. Many, but not all, statements and questions in other reading task types contain 3 (or more) areas of information to search for in a passage. The point to remember is that if at least **three matching areas of information** agree with what you read in the passage, you can be fairly certain that the answer you have chosen is correct.

❒ Look at Question 10 in Reading Test One:

10 Sydney was first established as a settlement for convicted criminals. ....

This question is part of a TRUE/FALSE/NOT GIVEN reading task, but the question statement can be divided into (at least) 3 areas of information to check for in the reading passage: *"Sydney"*, *"first established as a settlement"*, and *"for convicted criminals"*.

Each of these 3 areas of information can be matched with what is in the reading passage, and therefore the answer is *"TRUE"*.

Check that all parts of the answer agree with what is stated in the reading passage

47 "PLACE" THE TASK ACROSS THE PASSAGE

If you look at the **example** and the **last question** of a particular set of questions in a reading task, and then locate the topic of the example and the topic of the last question within the passage, the answers to the task questions will generally lie within the area between those two locations. This placing technique shortens the area of the passage in which to search for the answers.

The technique is particularly useful in reading gapfill tasks where you must refer to a reading passage for the missing words. The summary gapfill text can sometimes be divided into sections that correspond to the various paragraphs of the reading passage. It should then be quicker to find the correct paragraph within which to find the answer.

This technique is not limited to gapfill tasks.

❐ Look at the Example and Questions 15 – 17 in Reading Test Two:

start ↑

Example: The economic downturn is the reason that some staff members will be ....seeking employment........... .

15 When an opportunity arises follow it up immediately; in other words, ...

— —

↓ finish

17 When staff lose their jobs due to downsizing, they will receive ....

The topic of the example is given by the keyphrase *"the economic downturn"*. The topic of the last question (Question 17) is given by the keyphrase *"downsizing"*. Therefore, the answers to the set of questions will most likely be found in the area of text **beginning** with the heading *"Economic woes"*, and **ending** with the last word *"downsizing"* of the paragraph headed *"3. The importance of references"*; that is, the answers will probably be in the first column of the passage.

The example above is a simple example of how to apply the placing technique to a question set. In more difficult cases the technique can often prevent much wasted time searching for an answer in the wrong part of the passage.

Know where to look for answers in the reading passage by restricting the search area

48 LOOK FOR CHANGES IN THE SENTENCE ORDER

The information contained in a question sentence (or part sentence) is sometimes written in a different order to that in the equivalent sentence in the passage. This switching of information can be confusing in a difficult question. A simple example is given below.

❐ Look at Question 12 in Reading Test One:

12 The streets of the suburb Paddington are not very wide and contain houses arranged in rows. ....

In the passage it says:

"Not far from the city centre are the attractive old residential suburbs of Balmain, Glebe, and Paddington, where many people live in smart terraced houses. Art galleries, pubs and restaurants abound in the cosy streets that tend to be quite narrow..."

The *"streets"* and *"houses"* of Paddington in the question are referred to in reverse order in the reading passage.

Sometimes not all the keywords/phrases within a particular question can be found close together in the passage, or within a single sentence. In fact, there may be a good deal of interesting but **irrelevant information** between the keywords/phrases in the passage. This may prevent you from finding all you need to know to answer the question. (See also Reading Hint 56.)

Successful IELTS reading test comprehension requires the ability to find question sentences within text

49 LOOK FOR PATTERNS OF WORDS AND PHRASES

Finding the answers to questions in the Reading Test largely depends on your ability to recognise the shapes and patterns in groups of words. There are basically 3 kinds of "patterns" to recognise:

Pattern Type 1:	corresponding words with **exactly the same pattern**
Pattern Type 2:	corresponding words with **a similar pattern**
Pattern Type 3:	corresponding words, but with **a less recognisable pattern**

The best way to explain is by illustration and analysis.

❐ Look at Question 15 in Reading Test One:

15 Some department stores in Sydney are joined by walkways above and below the ground.

	Question Phrase		**Passage Phrase**	
a)	department stores	→	department stores	(Pattern Type 1)
b)	joined by	→	linked by	(Pattern Type 2)
c)	walkways above and below the ground	→	over-the-street crossings and underground walkways	(Pattern Type 3)

The noun phrase *"department stores"* in the question matches **exactly** the noun phrase *"department stores"* in the passage (Pattern Type 1).

The phrase *"linked by"* in the question has a **similar pattern** to the phrase *"joined by"* in the passage (Pattern Type 2). The word *"linked"* in the passage phrase has been substituted with the similar meaning word (synonym) *"joined"* in the question phrase (Pattern Type 2).

The phrase *"walkways above and below the ground"* in the question is similar in meaning to the phrase given in the passage, but the **pattern is less recognisable** (Pattern Type 3).

Note that single words, too, may be substituted in the question for a word (or phrase) in the passage. In Question 15, the word *"some"* is a substitute for *"several"* in the passage.

Now refer to the reading passage starting on page 94, and find the corresponding phrases for those in Question 16 below. To which pattern type does each phrase belong?

❐ Look at Question 16 in Reading Test One:

16 Australians are sports-minded people, but this is not realised by the rest of the world.

	Question Phrase		**Passage Phrase**	
a)	sports-minded people	→	....	(Pattern Type ....)
b)	is not realised	→	....	(Pattern Type ....)
c)	the rest of the world	→	....	(Pattern Type ....)

(Answers are given upside-down at the bottom of page 43).

Note that *"is not realised"* is **opposite** in meaning to the equivalent phrase found in the passage. Therefore, the answer to Question 16 is *"FALSE"*.

Not all questions will contain all three pattern types; nor will all substitutions fall neatly into the three patterns. Nevertheless, being able to recognise and match the patterns when they occur will help greatly with your reading comprehension.

50–54 FIVE QUICK HINTS

50 Read the Glossary

Occasionally a reading text comes with a glossary of words in the passage that may not be easily understood. Do not forget to check a glossary for the meaning of a word.

Also, the IELTS General Training Module, being a test at secondary and post-secondary education (tertiary) level, contains vocabulary often found in such tests. The Glossary on page 169–171 contains a number of such words taken from this book. Check the meanings of the words it contains in a good dictionary and learn them. They are words that you are likely to encounter many times in practice IELTS tests, and probably in the IELTS test itself.

51 Check Difficult Vocabulary

You may not understand every word in the reading passages. Even native English-speaking people might have difficulty fully understanding all the vocabulary presented in an IELTS test. You are **not allowed to use a dictionary** in the examination room, nor is it a good idea to use a dictionary during the first attempt at the tests in this book (or any other practice IELTS test book). Later, of course, it is useful to study the passages carefully and check unknown vocabulary.

The best approach is to guess the meaning of the word from the context, that is, from the words that surround it. However, this is not always an easy task. If you still have no idea what the word means, ask yourself if it contributes a **positive** (+) or **negative** (–) meaning to the sentence. This is usually enough to assist you to work out the meaning or intention of the writer. (See also Reading Hint 55.)

52 Search for Numbers First

Numbers are easier than words to locate within a reading passage. If a number is mentioned in the question, use the keyword approach outlined in Reading Hint 44, and search for the key "number" in the passage. Check around each use of the number to see if the answer you need is located nearby. Remember though, that numbers can also be expressed in word form in a reading passage.

53 Remember Maximum Word Requirements

When the instructions inform you that the maximum number of words to give as an answer is, say, three, you can assume that at least one answer, and possibly more, will contain three words exactly. Therefore, look for phrases that contain the maximum number of words allowed. Remember the Golden Rule, and do not give more words than instructed. (See Basic Hint 7.)

❒ Look at Questions 32 – 35 in Reading Test One and the Answer Key.

In this task, 3 out of 4 of the answers can be exactly **three words long**:

30 – *"for (easy) cleaning"* **32** – *"void (the) warranty"* **33** – *"season the wok"*

54 Check Figures and Diagrams for Answers

Do not forget that the answers you are looking for may be given in a figure, diagram, illustration, graph, table or chart that accompanies the reading passage. Always check footnotes, too.

❒ Look at Question 20 in Reading Test One:

20 When asked, people tend to

A be offended by workers who are unsociable.
B dislike immigrants who make excuses.
C dislike immigrants who repeat mistakes.
D agree that immigrants are unpunctual.

The answer is given **only** in the survey list. It is easy to overlook an illustration, diagram, table or chart etc. when quickly searching for an answer.

55 READING GAPFILLS METHOD

If the first task in a reading passage is to complete the reading passage itself by asking you, for instance, to add headings for various paragraphs or sections, then it is probably best to complete that task first. However, if there is a gapfill task which is a summary of the whole passage, or even part of the passage, consider completing the gapfill first. Summary gapfills help to predict information about the passage, even with some words missing. They may also help to answer questions in other tasks connected to that passage.

There are basically 2 types of gapfill tasks possible in the IELTS Reading Test:

Type 1 – those with **a given list of words or phrases** to choose from to fill in the gaps.

Type 2 – those where you fill the gaps with **words or phrases from the reading passage**.

Gapfill tasks Type 2 are, naturally, more difficult than gapfill tasks Type 1. The text of a gapfill task Type 2 is always a summary of part or the whole of a reading passage. On the other hand, a gapfill task Type 1 may or may not be a summary of part or the whole of a reading passage. Both task types, however, require a good knowledge of grammar.

Reading Gapfill Method – for Type 1

Step 1. First, read the instructions. You need to know if the gapfill is a summary of part or of the whole of the reading passage; if so, you will need to refer to the passage. You also need to know if you can use a word from the list of words **more than once**.

Step 2. Next, read the example and cross the answer to the example off the list, but only if you cannot use a word from the list more than once.

Step 3. Then, scan or skim the gapfill text quickly for a general understanding of the text.

Step 4. Now work out the parts of speech for each of the words in the given list. Place a letter standing for the part of speech next to each word in the list. If the item in the list is a phrase, you should determine the kind of phrase (noun, adjectival, adverbial, prepositional etc.).

If a word can function as two parts of speech, e.g. as a noun and a verb, write down both.

n – noun	**v** – verb	**a** – adjective	**adv** – adverb
p – preposition	**pp** – past participle	**'-ing'** words	**c** – conjunction

By distinguishing the words or phrases according to their function as parts of speech, you need only search through similar functioning words when considering a word or phrase for a gap. In this way, you considerably shorten the time required to find the words or phrases that are possible correct answers.

Remember, if the word either side of the gap:

...is a **noun**, the answer could be an **adjective** (usually before the gap)

...is a **verb**, the answer could be an **adverb**.

...is an **adjective**, the answer could be a **noun** (or an **adverb** if after the gap)

Do not forget this structure: **(pro)noun + (be) + adjective**. e.g. She is happy.

Note that an **adverb** may precede the **adjective** in the above structure.

Step 5. Now turn to the first gap in the task, and try to work out the full meaning of the sentence it is within. You may need to read the sentence before and after, too.

Step 6. Next, work out the part of speech for the gap. Do so, by closely examining the words that come both **before and after** the gap.

Step 7. Then search only through the words in the list that can function as the same part of speech as the missing gap word. Look for **all** the possible answers that you think could fit in the gap. **Make no final choices just yet**. There are usually two or three similar words that could be correct. Write them all above the gap.

Step 8. Refer to the reading passage to help you choose possible answers for the gap if the gapfill text is a summary of part or all of the passage.

Step 9. Complete steps 5 to 8 for each gap in the task.

Step 10. Choose a final answer from the words chosen for each gap. **Cross off the incorrect answers**; do not write them on the Answer Sheet, for you will not be correct if you give more than one answer.

Reading Gapfill Method – for Type 2

Step 1. First, read the instructions. You need to know if the gapfill text is a summary of part or of the whole of the reading passage.

Step 2. Next, read the example for information about the topic of the summary.

Step 3. Then, scan or skim the gapfill text quickly for a general understanding of the text.

Step 4. Now locate the answer to the example in the reading passage.

Step 5. "Place" the summary across the passage to find out where the answers to questions may be found. It is often possible to divide the summary into parts that correspond to various paragraphs or sections of the passage. In this way, it is possible to shorten the area of the passage in which to look for particular answers. (See also Reading Hint 47.)

Step 6. Now turn to the first gap in the task, and try to work out the full meaning of the sentence it is within. You may need to read the sentence before and after, too.

Step 7. Next, work out the part of speech for that gap. Do so, by closely examining the words that come both **before and after** the gap.

Step 8. Then, examine the keywords/phrases to look for in the passage, and locate them in the passage. (See also Basic Hint 10 and Reading Hint 57.)

Step 9. Choose the word that best suits the gap, remembering that the words you find in the passage may not be in the word form you require. You may need a noun, but the word given in the passage might be an adjective. In which case, you must change the form of the word to the word form required in the gapfill text.

Step 10. Complete steps 6 to 9 for each gap in the task.

Gapfill tasks require a good deal of practice to complete successfully

Turn the page upside down to see the **answers to the exercise given on page 40**:

sports-minded people → csports-conscious nation(s) (Pattern 2)

is not realised → tis recognised (**opposite** in meaning) (Pattern 2)

the rest of the worl → (one of the most)... ...in the world (Pattern 3)

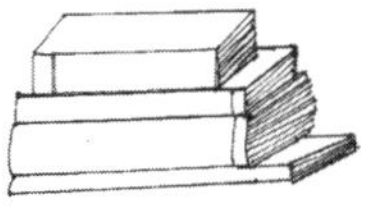

Further Considerations for Type 1 and Type 2 Gapfill Tasks

1. If the missing word is a noun, ask yourself if it is **singular or plural**. If the missing word is a verb, look at the subject of the verb and, if singular, consider if the verb could be third person present singular. If so, the missing word will require an "s" or "es" at the end. (See also Writing Hint 65.)

2. Consider whether the word you need functions **positively** or **negatively** within the sentence. Remember that connectives (linking words) can determine the polarity of the meaning of the words that follow:

"however" / "but" "on the other hand"	**changes** polarity	from + to –	or	from – to +
"also" / "and" / "too"	**maintains** polarity	+ if +	or	– if –
"furthermore" / "moreover"	**maintains** and **strengthens** polarity	from + to + +	or	from – to – –

There are many other connectives you could add to the table above. (See also Writing Hint 66.)

3. Sometimes the word you need is **already part of the gapfill text**. Candidates might be surprised to learn that the word (or even the phrase) that they are seeking may be repeated somewhere in the text. (See Question 22 in point 4 below). Of course, this is not always the case, but is a point worth remembering.

4. Pay special attention to **pronouns** in gapfill tasks and in all reading passages. Each pronoun directs you towards the **noun or noun phrase** it stands for, and usually, but not always, back through the text. Consequently, it is wise to check pronouns that follow gaps, and determine the nouns for which they are substituting.

❒ Look at Questions 22 and 25 in Reading Test One:

> Company policy will change as of ***Example:*** ....*December 1st*......... . Not all of Brandon Webb's employees are currently maintaining their **(22)** .... Employment contracts require that all staff have their health and fitness levels regularly **(23)** .... by the company's own doctors. Under new policy **(24)** .... , it will become **(25)** .... for staff who do not **(26)** .... the Monday gym class to undergo a medical examination. However, this does not apply to staff over 60 years old.

The pronoun *"their"* in the second line above refers back to the noun phrase *"Brandon Webb's employees"*. The pronoun *"their"* is repeated in the third line, which should give you a good clue.

The answer to Question 22 is probably connected with some positive action, since the overall meaning of the sentence is **negative**:

"Not all...employees...are (doing something right)."

Therefore, search the list for something **positive** to maintain. The answer to Question 22 is also part of the gapfill text itself.

The answer to Question 25 is an adjective since the basic structure is

(pro)noun + (auxiliary verb) + linking verb + adjective: *"it will become...(positive or negative?)"*.

The overall meaning of this sentence is **negative**. The polarity of the next sentence shifts because of the connective word *"however"*. The overall meaning of this sentence is, therefore, **positive**: *"this (negative requirement) does not apply to staff over 60 years old"*.

Search the list for a word with a negative association; in this case, it is something the employees have to do...or else! Of course, you should also search the reading text itself for words and ideas.

56 FIND SHORT SENTENCES WITHIN PARAGRAPHS

It is important to develop the ability to "see" a short question sentence within a longer sentence or within a paragraph. The sentences forming the questions usually contain **summarised** information, and are, therefore, almost always shorter than the sentence or sentences in the reading passage which contain the corresponding information.

❐ Look at Question 15 in Reading Test Two:

15 When an opportunity arises follow it up immediately; in other words,

........*do not procrastinate*........

(from the Reading Passage)

Obtain as much information as possible from reliable sources online and off, and be sure to keep a job search diary. Do not procrastinate. Always return calls when they are made to you, and follow up opportunities the moment they present themselves.

It takes practice to "see" the information contained in the sentence of a question within the extra wording in the reading passage, but it is an important skill. Note that sometimes the information in the sentence forming the question is **not given in the same order** as the same information in the passage. Nonetheless, the ability to "see" a shorter sentence within longer sentences is essential when trying to locate the correct answer within a large piece of text. (See also Reading Hint 48.)

57 CONSIDER THE LOCATION OF THE ANSWER

You must be willing to search both before and after the keywords/phrases. The distance of an answer from the keyword/phrase can vary considerably in the Reading Test, but the answer is usually found in the same paragraph as the keyword/phrase with which it is connected.

In this book, certain keywords and phrases in the questions (and passages) are referred to as **signpost keywords/phrases** because they point to paragraphs in the passage where answers are likely to be found. Keywords more closely connected with the answer are referred to as **destination keywords/phrases**. (See also Basic Hint 10.)

❐ Look at Question 16 in Reading Test Two:

16 It is not possible to ...*overemphasise*...... the need for a quality résumé.

2. Work on your résumé.

The importance of a well-presented, accurate and comprehensive résumé cannot be overemphasised. Creating and composing a professional document is essential, but not everyone has specific experience about what and what not to include nor the requisite design skills. To show yourself in your best light, pay someone to perform this task for you. A quality résumé can be worth a hundred times what you spend on it.

signpost keyphrases

destination keyphrase

answer

Notice that sometimes the signpost keyword/phrase can be found long before the answer in a passage. It can also come after the answer.

Note also that when the keywords/phrases in the question are found in the passage they may not be written exactly in the same way. The corresponding keywords/phrases in the passage may contain substituted words, or they may be phrases with a similar meaning. (See also Reading Hint 49.)

Nevertheless, reference to the keywords/phrases in a question can **always** be found somewhere in the reading passage, and most often in the same paragraph. (See also Reading Hints 46 and 56.)

58 CHARTS AND TABLES IN QUESTION TASKS

Keywords, keyphrases, and examples are also features of questions within charts and tables. Do not overlook the words already contained in a chart or table in your hurry to find the answer in the reading passage. These words can also be considered as "examples".

❒ Look at Questions 35 – 40 in Reading Test Three:

Keywords/phrases for Question 35

Table 1. INTERNATIONAL STUDENTS STUDYING IN AUSTRALIA

	Source of Students	Under 20 years old	20–29 years old	Over 30 years old	Interest in Further Studies
75 – 100%	–	–	–	–	Iran / Hong Kong / China / Thailand / Indonesia
50 – 74%	–	**(35)** .... and Hong Kong	**(36)**	**(37)**	**(38)** ....
25 – 49%	*(Ex:) Japan*	–	–	**(39)**	**(40)** .... / European countries (not including Switzerland)
0 – 24%	–	–	–	–	Switzerland

Particular examples for Questions 38 and 40

The keywords/phrases for Question 35 are the headings for the row and column in which the question is found (*"Under 20 years old"* and *"50 – 74%"*). Similarly, the keywords/phrases for Questions 36 – 40 are the appropriate row and column headings.

The particular example for Questions 35 – 38 is *"Hong Kong"* because it is in the same row as the questions. Similarly, the example words for Questions 39 and 40 are the countries found in the same row as the questions. Notice that the answer to Question 40 cannot be a European country.

Remember that in charts and tables, the example words in a row not only help you answer the question, they may also be words or phrases within a particular word set, in this case the word set is "countries".

Be aware that it is possible for the answer to a question in a chart or table to be a word already given somewhere in the same row or column.

Remember to examine all the words and phrases contained in a chart or table

WRITING TEST HINTS

A BASIC UNDERSTANDING

59 PAY ATTENTION TO THE PRESENTATION

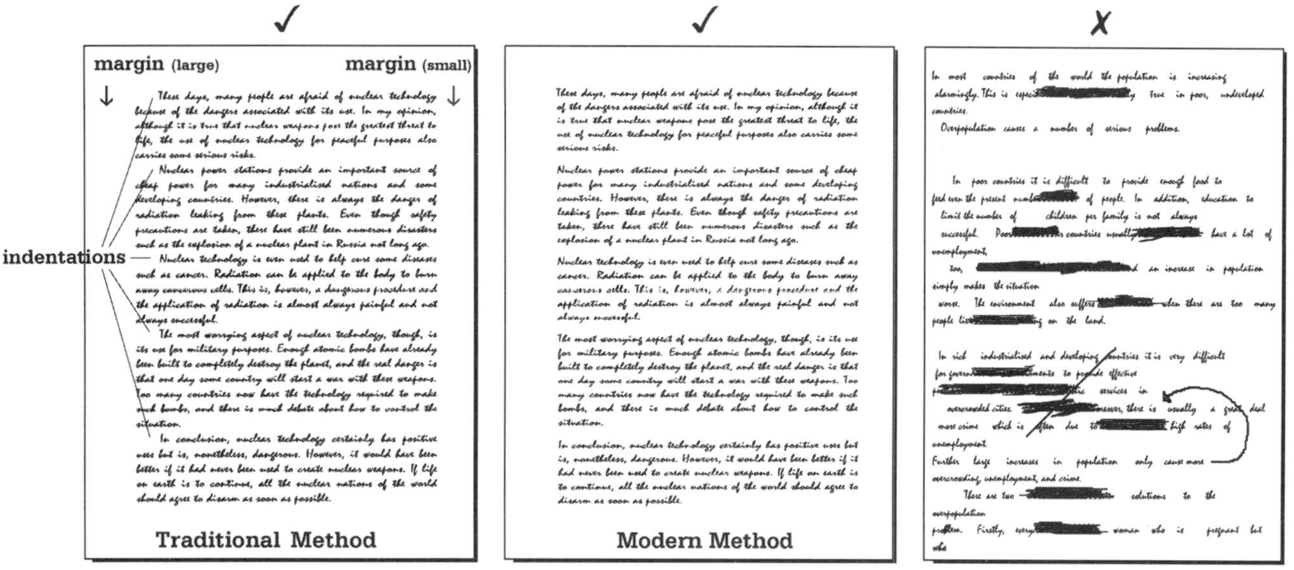

While it is true that the IELTS Writing Test is not marked for neatness, there is the psychological aspect to consider when you are trying to impress an examiner. You are not there in person to present your work, so always aim to make your writing look presentable on the page.

10 Point Guide to Presentation and Layout

1 There is no need for a title in the IELTS test task writings, and do not rewrite the question task.

2 Use left and right margins as in the two good examples above.

3 Use either **indentations** for the first line of each paragraph (traditional method) or **a blank line** between paragraphs (modern method), but do not mix both methods.

4 Do not use double spacing, that is, do not leave a blank line between each line of writing.

5 Use all the line – write from the very edge of the left margin all the way to the very edge of the right margin. This is true for every line, except where the line is short, or where the last word will not fit between the margins. In the latter case, do not continue into the margin area. Start on a new line with the word that is too large.

6 Do not split words. Rather than memorise complex rules for splitting words, do not split them.

7 Write between 10–12 words per line. This will prevent you writing words too large and with gaps larger than a single letter or two between words. It will also make it simpler for you to quickly estimate how many words you have written in the test.

8 *Use cursive writing, that is, with the letters joined together.*

Cursive writing makes your work look more mature; if it can be read easily. The non-cursive writing of some candidates can look immature. Since first impressions are important, impress the examiner by writing the way educated English-speaking adults usually write in English.

9 Write in a thick, not fine, pen, and consider writing in blue ink. Why? From a psychological point of view, a thick pen makes a stronger impression. Similarly, written work in pencil looks weak and impermanent. Pencil users waste time erasing, and sharpening or pumping the lead. Blue ink is more soothing and pleasant to look at than black. Leave behind a positive impression.

10 If you make a mistake, simply cross out the ~~error~~ error with one line. There is no penalty for crossing out. Besides, it shows the examiner that you are capable of error correction.

Quick Punctuation Guide

1.	Use **full-stops** only at the end of a sentence. Begin sentences with a capital letter. Proper nouns also require capital letters.	/ . /	e.g. *the Sydney Opera House* *Newlands High School*
2.	Use **commas** to separate parts of a sentence to avoid any confusion with meaning. Additional information is enclosed within commas.	/ , /	e.g. *To be a good athlete you do not need to use drugs, and long hours of practice will always be more beneficial in the end.* (The comma after "*drugs*" makes it clear that *long hours of practice* ARE necessary. Only drugs are not required.)
	A **comma** is used after most connectives (linking words), and usually before and after a connective in mid-sentence. Commas also separate clauses in most conditional sentences.		e.g. *If all athletes refused to take drugs, sport would be fair and much safer. However, it is unlikely that drugs will ever be excluded from the Olympic Games completely.*
3.	**Semi-colons** are used to separate sub-groups within lists, but more often to join two independent clauses that are grammatically complete but closely related. However, in the latter case, you can always use a full-stop instead.	/ ; /	e.g. *Athletes who are caught taking drugs at the Olympic Games should be banned for life; this is essential to teach others a lesson.*
4.	You may use a **colon** if you need to draw attention to what is to follow.	/ : /	e.g. *Strict punishment is important for the following reasons:*
5.	Use **quotation marks** for quotes and titles. **Apostrophes** show possession or contraction.	/ " " / / ' /	e.g. *He said it was "a great shame"...* *the country's profits* *there's*
6.	Do not use **contractions** in formal writing. Use the full form instead.	/ n't /	e.g. *don't, shouldn't, can't, it's* etc.
7.	Do not use **exclamation marks** in the IELTS Writing Test, and **avoid asking questions**.	/ ! / / ? /	
8.	**Brackets** are useful, especially for quoting statistics in Writing Task 1, but do not overuse.	/ ( ) /	e.g. *in my country (and probably other countries, too)...*

60 UNDERSTAND THE QUESTION TASK

It is important to fully understand the task you must perform in the IELTS Writing Test. The Golden Rule is that you must be sure of the type of answer you are required to give to the examiners, and what you must do with that information to give the answer accurately. (See Basic Hint 7.)

You will probably receive a lower Writing Test Band Score if you fail to...

> ...**write what you are required to write in Task 1**. You will be asked to write a letter in Writing Task 1. You should write in the style appropriate for letter-writing: paragraphs, inclusion of a short concluding paragraph, signature etc.

...**write what you are required to write in Task 2**. You will be asked to write a short essay in Writing Task 2. You should write in the formal style appropriate for course essays.

...**write at least the minimum number of words** requested per task. There is no maximum word limit, but there is a limit to the amount of space in which to write your answers. Of course, you can request more paper, but this takes time – and you need all the time you can get to write.

...**write directly on the given topic**. Once you have accurately determined what the topic is and what questions you are asked about the topic, keep to the topic throughout the entire piece of writing.

...**write for the intended reader**. For instance, if you are asked to write a letter to a bank (in Task 1), your answer should be written using business correspondence language as expected. If you are asked to write your point of view about a particular topic (in Task 2), it is best to use language appropriate for a tutor at college.

It is inappropriate to write in note form in the IELTS test.

It is inappropriate to use **colloquial** or **slang words or expressions** in more formal writing. Also, you should avoid using the word *"thing"*, or words containing the word *"thing"*, such as *"something"* or *"anything"*. Use more descriptive words instead.

It is usually not desirable to use "*etc.*" or "*and so on*" unless you are writing a personal letter. Instead, make a list of at least **3 examples** of what you wish to say, and punctuate as follows:

e.g. *" ... in the water, air **and** soil. "* but *" ... they sat for the test, passed, **and** failed to use their qualifications. "*

Note that the comma after the second last item is usually included **only** if there might otherwise be an unintended confusion of meaning, as in the second example above.

...**write all that is requested in the task**. For instance, if you are asked to give recommendations or advice, make sure that you do. Also, avoid making statements that are too general, too simple, and too obvious. Your answer should be written in some detail.

The Topic and The Topic Question

It is important to know precisely what the **topic** is, and what the **question** is concerning that topic.

❐ Look at the circled topics of Task 2 in Writing Test One and Two:

TEST ONE
(Research) is an essential part of (completing assignments.)
Suggest some good places to obtain useful information.

TEST TWO
Most young people without a partner would prefer to have a boyfriend or girlfriend. Yet (being in a relationship when you are young) is not always a good idea. As part of a class project, write about whether you agree or disagree.

The topic in Test One is "**research (when) completing assignments**". If you wrote at length about whether or not research was essential to assignments, it would be irrelevant. The question clearly asks you to suggest good places to find useful information.

The Test Two topic is "**being in a relationship when you are young**". The question asks you whether you agree that it is not always a good idea. Failure to consider both the advantages and disadvantages of having a partner when you are young will most likely mean a lower score.

61 USE THE "THREE-PART" WRITING APPROACH

Model sentences, paragraphs, essays and reports each consist of 3 basic parts. Even words can consist of three parts:

a **word**:

(prefix) + stem + (suffix)

a basic **sentence**:

subject + verb + complement

a typical **paragraph**:

1 **Topic sentence**: states or refers to the main idea behind the paragraph

2 the **4 "E"s**

- **Explanation** – to make the topic sentence (or key vocabulary within the topic sentence) clearly understood
- **Evidence** – to offer proof of what you are saying as part of an argument
- **Example(s)** – to further illustrate the point you are making
- **Extra detail** – to substantiate the main point of the paragraph

3 **Summary sentence**: concludes the paragraph (optional)

The topic sentence is usually, but not always, the first sentence of the paragraph. (See Reading Hint 42.)

Note also that the "body" of the paragraph consists of one or more, but not necessarily all, of the 4 "E"s (explanation, evidence, example(s), and extra detail).

A Typical Essay:

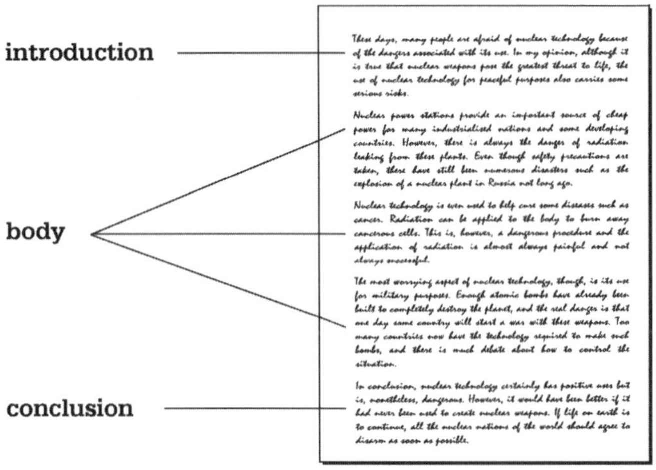

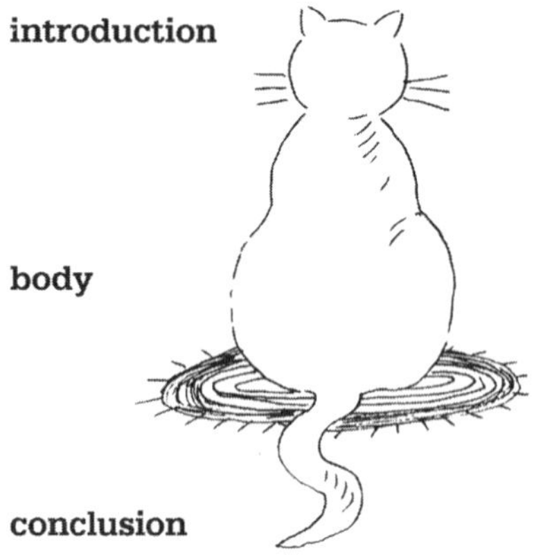

You might like to think of an essay, a report or any formal piece of writing, as being written with the 3-part shape of a cat in the writer's mind. Note the relative sizes of the parts of the cat.

Note that you do not need to place "ears" on the "cat" in the IELTS Writing Tasks. In other words you do not need a title. This is true of the IELTS test, but not of most essays at tertiary level.

62 WRITE INTERESTING SENTENCES

Beware of sentences that are too simple and too obvious. Good sentences inform the reader, and are, therefore, interesting to read. However, do not write unnecessarily complex sentences, and do not use a word unless you are quite sure of what it means. It is better to use simple words correctly than complex words incorrectly. Consider the following topic sentence:

There are many rich and poor countries in the world.

It makes a statement that is much too general in content and is obviously true. Although no-one would argue with the truth of the statement, it is not an informative or interesting sentence to read.

There are many more poor countries than rich countries, yet the latter are in possession of almost all of the world's economic wealth.

Note that the second sentence answers at least **3 wh/how questions**:

Which countries?	...rich and poor
How many (rich and poor) countries?	...many more poor countries than rich
How much (do the rich countries own)?	...almost all of the world's economic wealth.

Who? What? Where? When? Why? Which? How many? How much? How often?

"Answers" to wh/how questions add interest to your sentences.

Try to include the answer to at least 3 wh/how questions in your sentences

63 IMPROVE YOUR WRITING

It is not the aim of this book to provide a detailed course in writing. However, there is a 3-part method you can use to increase your writing power gradually. It might seem simple, but it was the method you used to learn to write in your own language.

1 **Read**

Yes! Read other people's well-written English. That is why people write in the first place – to be read. The more you read, the more you will understand of the structure of English sentences. (See also Basic Hints 2 and 4.)

2 **Copy**

If you should do more reading in English, / why not assist your writing / at the same time? / Simply copy / passages of well-written English / onto paper. / Concentrate as you copy, / thinking about the structure of the sentences / as you write. / Try to remember / the groups of words you copy / in natural phrases / as shown in this paragraph. / Try to remember / more and more words at a time / before checking / to make sure you have copied accurately. / (See Basic Hint 5.)

3 **Write**

There is no substitute for practice. The more you write in English, the easier it will become, and the more accurate your sentences will be. Naturally, it is useful to have your sentences checked by a trained English language teacher, but if that cannot be done, do not worry. If you copy well-written English paragraphs while you are also trying to improve your own sentences, your sentence structures will certainly improve. A large number of exercises designed to improve your writing skills for the IELTS test is included in the companion book *"202 Useful Exercises for IELTS"*.

64 6 COMMON QUESTIONS ABOUT THE WRITING TEST

"What happens if I don't finish the writing tasks in the given time?"

You will be penalised because you will not have fulfilled the requirements of each task. It is, therefore, most important to practise writing for speed a long time before the day of the test, so that you can be sure of finishing in the required time. It is wise to spend only the advised amount of time suggested for each task (20 minutes on Writing Task 1 and 40 minutes on Writing Task 2).

"If I complete only one task, is that better than two unfinished tasks?"

No. You will score very badly. Even if you write an extremely good piece of writing for, say, Task 2, by not attempting Task 1 at all, you will score badly. You must at least attempt both tasks. In addition, Task 2 is worth more marks than Task 1, which is one reason for the longer amount of time advised for Task 2. Another reason is, of course, the greater number of words required.

"How can I improve my writing speed so that I can finish both tasks?"

Practise with a clock. Copy paragraphs of well-written English as quickly as you can, and try to increase your speed gradually. This will help to boost the physical speed at which you write.

Also, use a pen which writes well. It is often faster to write with a pen than with a pencil. It is worth buying a pen with which you are personally able to write smoothly and easily.

Some IELTS Test Centres may not allow the use of pens. (This is true for all centres for writing on the Listening and Reading Test Answer Sheets.) If you must use a pencil in the Writing Test, use a dark lead pencil if possible.

It might be wise to look at the way you hold your pen. Do you grasp it too tightly, as if trying to squeeze out the ink with your fingers? Writing is a physical act, but it should not cause too much physical stress. Your hand should flow easily across the page.

Practise writing smoothly and quickly. Cursive or "running" writing causes less stress than non-cursive writing, and enables the hand to move faster across the page.

If you can take CB IELTS (the computer-based IELTS) in your city, don't waste your time bolding or italicising text on the screen. Use the Modern Method of composing text. (See Writing Hint 59.)

"Do I have to show my writing plans?"

No. Any plans you write are not taken into account when an assessment is made of your work. Therefore, you need not worry about how your plans look. However, you have to be able to understand what you have written. It is always preferable to be neat and tidy than messy.

"What should I do if I have no ideas about the topic?"

You should ask yourself "why not?" Both writing tasks are of general interest, and no special knowledge is required. It is essential that you read about current affairs in your own language as well as in English in order to keep up with what is happening in the world. Join your local library, read English language newspapers and magazines. Watch current affairs programmes on TV, and listen to current affairs programmes on the radio. Do everything you can to become well-informed, especially about the topics that people talk about in English-speaking countries.

"Does spelling count towards the IELTS Writing Band Score?"

Yes, and so does punctuation. All the requirements of good writing are taken into account. However, you should not worry greatly if you make a few spelling errors. Naturally, you should try hard to avoid all errors by leaving time at the end of the Writing Test to check your work for grammatical mistakes, spelling, and punctuation. (See also Writing Hints 59 and 65.)

It is encouraging to remember that your work does not have to be perfect. A non-English-speaking person is not expected to write an essay, or describe a chart or table as well as a native-writer, unless he or she has been speaking, listening, reading, and writing in English for many years.

65 10 POINT GRAMMAR CHECKLIST ☑

☐ 1. Check for missing or incorrect articles:

too late to enrol in course... ✗ *too late to enrol in **the** course...* ✓

☐ 2. Check the 3rd person singular 's' agreement in the present tense:

...she want to go to college... ✗ *...she want**s** to go to college...* ✓

☐ 3. Check that your verbs are correct (in the active tense and passive voice):

In 1788 the First Fleet arrive... ✗ *In 1788 the First Fleet arrive**d**...* ✓

☐ 4. Check that your verb forms are correct:

They have been tried to... ✗ *They have been tr**ying** to...* ✓

☐ 5. Check all your subject-verb agreements:

...poor countries has suffered... ✗ *...poor countries **have** suffered...* ✓

☐ 6. Check your countable and uncountable nouns:

Most student do not wish to... ✗ *Most student**s** do not wish to...* ✓
but *Most peoples in the world...* ✗ *Most **people** in the world...* ✓

☐ 7. Check that your pronouns refer to (previously mentioned) nouns:

***He** wants to go to college...* ✗ ***He** wants to go to college...* ✓
(if *"a student"* is **not** mentioned before) (if *"a student"* **is** previously mentioned)

Note that pronouns **can** come before the nouns they substitute for, but this is not common.

☐ 8. Check that your prepositions are correct:

I am interested at... ✗ *I am interested **in**...* ✓

☐ 9. Check that your parts of speech are correct:

...it was a destruction act... (noun) ✗ *...it was a destruc**tive** act...* (adj.) ✓

☐ 10. Check that your conditional forms are correct:

			likelihood
Zero:	If + present tense	..., + present tense + verb root ...	↑ always
1st:	If + present tense	..., + will (may, might, could etc.) + verb root ...	maybe
2nd:	If + past simple tense / continuous	..., + would (may, might, could etc.) + verb root ...	maybe not
3rd:	If + past perfect tense	..., + would have (may have etc.) + past participle ...	did not occur ↓

Leave up to **5 minutes** at the end of the test to read your work again with this checklist in mind. Whenever you write, in the IELTS test and for practice, you should always check for errors.

There are no direct grammar questions in IELTS, nevertheless grammar is still of great importance in all your answers

66 USE CONNECTIVE WORDS

Connectives, or linking words, are essential in formal (and semi-formal) English writing to link clauses, sentences, paragraphs, and ideas together to form a cohesive unit of written work. Connective words and phrases that are appropriately used count towards a higher Writing Test Band Score.

TABLE OF SOME OF THE MOST COMMONLY USED CONNECTIVE WORDS AND PHRASES

(Refer to an academic writing textbook or teacher for a detailed discussion of appropriate usage.)

First of all, ... * / In the first place, ... * To begin with, ... * First(ly), ... * → Second(ly), ... * → Third(ly), ... * First, ... * → Next, ... → Then, ... → After that, ... → Finally, ...	**Group 1. Sequencing/Listing** Use to catalogue (make a list of items or sequence (place in order) what you say.
Also, ... Besides, ... Furthermore, ... In addition, ... Moreover, ...	**Group 2. Reinforcing** Use to add to and thus strengthen what you have said.
In the same way, ... Likewise, ... Similarly, ...	**Group 3. Equating** Use to indicate similarity with what has been said.
In conclusion, ... * In summary, ... * To conclude, ... * To sum up, ... *	**Group 4. Summarising** Use to introduce a generalisation of or conclusion to what you have said.
For example, ... For instance, ... In particular, ... particularly, ... such as ... — — — — — — ..., that is, ... / ..., that is to say, ..., namely, ...	**Group 5. Referring** (e.g.) Use to indicate you will give (or have given) one or more examples of what you have said. — — — — — — (i.e.) Use to indicate an explanation of what you have said.
As a result, ... Consequently, ... Hence, ... So ... Therefore, ... Thus, ...	**Group 6. Showing Results** Use to express the consequence of what you have said.

- Connectives marked with an asterisk (*) do not usually occur in the middle of sentences.
- Inclusion in a particular group does not mean that the connectives are always interchangeable.

In other words, ... In that case, ... Then, ... — — — — — — (Or) else, ... Otherwise, ...	**Group 7. Inferring** Use to deduce from what you have said. (Either what might or might not have happened, is happening, or will happen.)
Alternatively, ... On the other hand, ... Then again, ...	**Group 8. Giving Alternatives** Use to refer to an alternative to what you have said.
In other words, ... That is to say, ... To put it simply, ...	**Group 9. Restating** Use to express what you have said in another way (usually more simply.)
Conversely, ... In comparison, ... In contrast to this, ... Instead, ... — — — — — — On the contrary, ... , whereas ... ... , while ... / ... , whilst ...	**Group 10. Contrasting** Use to compare or contrast with what you have said.
After all, ... All the same, ... Although ... , Though ... , Even though ... Even if ... However, ... In spite of ... , despite this/that ... Nevertheless, ... Nonetheless, ... Still, ... Yet, ...	**Group 11. Conceding** Use to indicate other ways of considering what you have said.

Key:
Basic Connectives
- ... of the "**and**" type
- ... of the "**or**" type
- ... of the "**but**" type

WRITING TASK 1

The General Training Module Writing Task 1 is the shorter of two writing tasks you are asked to perform. You have exactly 60 minutes to complete both tasks, and, while you can do the tasks in either order, it is generally best to start with Task 1. You are strongly advised to spend no more than 20 minutes on this task because you have only 40 minutes remaining to complete the more demanding Task 2, which carries more weight towards your final Writing Band Score.

67 UNDERSTANDING WRITING TASK 1

Writing Task 1 is designed to test your ability to write a particular kind of letter. It may be a personal letter (semi-formal; i.e. not merely a few notes), perhaps to a friend, a family member, or someone you know or are soon to meet; or it may be a more formal letter, perhaps to a person within a particular institution such as a college, for example. It might also be a business letter, say, to a bank or other company.

Whatever the case, you are asked to respond to a given problem by requesting information or giving an explanation of a situation. The reason for the letter – usually some kind of problem – is clearly given to you in the task. By writing the letter, you will help solve this particular problem.

You should write the letter using complete sentences within paragraphs, that is, not in note form.

The **minimum** number of words you are required to write is 150.

The examiners assess your writing ability according to how well you can do one or more of the following (depending on the task you are given):

- express your wants
- express your requirements
- express likes and dislikes
- give opinions
- explain your reasons
- make complaints
- express your concerns
- ask for or give factual information
- explain how to do something

...and, of course, you are assessed on your ability to construct a suitable letter using the skills required to do so in English.

First of all, you must fully understand the task and what you are asked to do. Spend a minute or two working out what it is you are looking at, and what information you must ask for or include.

68 PLAN THE NUMBER OF PARAGRAPHS

Once you have read the task carefully and you are sure of what to do, you need to plan your answer. Since you have only 20 minutes to complete the task, you do not have time to write a detailed plan on paper. Instead, you should determine the number of **main points** you need to make. This will assist you to determine the number of paragraphs to write before you begin.

❒ Look at the question for Task 1 of Writing Test One on page 105.

You have recently moved into a new flat. Unfortunately, you lost some money the other day, and cannot afford to pay next month's rent when it is due.

Write a letter to the landlord or landlady. In your letter

- ***explain the situation***
- ***say that you will will pay when your parents send you the money***
- ***mention that there are some problems with the flat.***

To begin with, you will need to start with **Dear Sir or Madam,** as indicated in the Writing Task rubric (the instructions). Since you would know if the flat owner was a landlord or landlady, you can choose either.

Notice, the task also tells you **not** to write any addresses.

Then you should note that, in this case, there are **three pieces of information** you must include in your answer:

1. you must explain the situation you are in
2. you must explain that you will pay when your parents send you the money
3. you must mention some problems with the flat.

Let us now look at how the Model Answer (page 155) is constructed:

The Model Answer for Task 1 of Writing Test One is written in 3 paragraphs:

Dear Sir,	
Paragraph 1:	the situation + payment when parents send the money
Paragraph 2:	the problems with the flat
Paragraph 3:	short sentence summary
Yours sincerely,	

You can see that the first two vital pieces of information have been combined in the introductory (first) paragraph. It would have been possible to write a separate paragraph for each piece of information. However, it is sometimes a good idea to put two main points in one paragraph in a short letter like this, especially in the introductory paragraph. A paragraph that contains only one or two sentences might look too short.

You will note that there is a short summary sentence which constitutes the third paragraph. This paragraph is a special case in which it is not necessary to write a long paragraph. The idea is to leave the reader of the letter with a final impression of how you want your letter to be received. It is often written using a "stock" or commonly used phrase (see Writing Hint 72), and a polite stock phrase is usually required in formal letter-writing.

Plan the number of paragraphs before you begin, by noting the main points that you must include in your answer.

69 USE INTRODUCTION "LEAD-IN" PHRASES

Obviously it is wise to make a good start. All letter writers need to "lead-in" to what they wish to say. There are a number of popular ways to start the first sentence of your introductory paragraph when writing a formal or semi-formal letter. Study the following part sentences:

I am writing to you	because...		
	to	let you know advise you	that...
	in reply to your recent letter in which you *(told me something)*		
I am anxious to obtain some information from you about...			
It is with regret that I write to you advising you			that *(something negative)*
I regret to I am sorry to	inform you let you know		
As you are probably already aware, *(I am... / it is... / something is...)*			

Certainly, you should **never** begin the introductory paragraph of a formal or semi-formal letter with "How are you?". Although it is friendly, it is not appropriate to ask about the health or well-being of a person that you do not know very well.

Be careful to use the suggested phrases in the box with the right type of letter or they will not make sense. It is, of course, essential that you are able to complete these part sentences so that they lead in naturally to what you wish to say in the first paragraph.

Practise now by completing the following part sentences taken from the box with ideas of your own to form suitable introductory paragraphs:

1. I am writing to you because ....

   ....

   ....

   ....

2. I am writing to you to let you know that ....

   ....

   ....

   ....

3. I am writing to you in reply to your recent letter in which you ....

   ....

   ....

   ....

4. I am anxious to obtain some information from you about ....

   ....

   ....

   ....

   ....

5. I regret to inform you that ....

   ....

   ....

   ....

7. As you are probably already aware, ...

   ....

   ....

   ....

Ask a teacher to check your sentences. Are they accurate? If they are not quite accurate or they do not make good sense in English, make sure you find out why!

It is very important to start your letter clearly by indicating to the reader the reason for your letter.

Start your letter by using a suitable phrase which leads into an explanation of the reason for your letter.

70 PAY ATTENTION TO THE LAYOUT OF THE LETTER

As you write your letter you should make sure that you are following the correct layout rules for letter-writing. You do not have time (or enough paper without asking for more) to prepare a draft letter and write it out again neatly, so it is essential that you lay out the letter correctly as you write.

❒ Look at the two letters below, which do you think is better organised?

LETTER A

Dear Sir, I am writing to you because I am unable to pay
next month's rent which is due on Saturday. Unfortunately,
the other day I lost my wallet, and there was a large amount of
money inside. I have, therefore, had to write to my parents
to ask them to send me some money urgently. As soon as it
arrives, I ~~would like you to~~ will immediately notify you and
arrange to pay by cash or cheque. I hope that this does not cause
you too much inconvenience. There are also some problems
with the flat that I wish to bring to your attention. First, the cold
tap in the bathroom will not turn off properly, and the
water is dripping constantly. This will need to be fixed
quickly because it is wasting water. Second, one of the
back rings on the top of the oven does not work at all.
I'm sorry that I cannot pay the rent on time, and trust that
you will understand.

Yours sincerely,

Mary Campisi

LETTER B

Dear Sir,

I am writing to you because I am unable to pay next month's rent which is due on Saturday. Unfortunately, the other day I lost my wallet, and there was a large amount of money inside. I have, therefore, had to write to my parents to ask them to send me some money urgently. As soon as it arrives, I will immediately notify you and arrange to pay by cash or cheque. I hope that this does not cause you too much inconvenience.

There are also some problems with the flat that I wish to bring to your attention. First, the cold tap in the bathroom will not turn off properly, and the water is dripping constantly. This will need to be fixed quickly because it is wasting water. Second, one of the back rings on the top of the oven does not work at all.

I'm sorry that I cannot pay the rent on time, and trust that you will understand.

Yours sincerely,

Mary Campisi

Letter A does not look like a real letter at all. It does not have the recognisable shape that all well-written letters in English have. There is no evidence of knowledge of even the basic layout rules of writing. For instance, there are no straight-sided margins, nor is it easy to see where the paragraphs begin and end.

In addition to keeping to the basic layout rules of writing (see Writing Hint 59), make sure that your letter has the same layout features as Letter B:

1. Leave a single blank line after the salutation line (Dear Sir or Madam,)
2. Use either the Traditional or the Modern Method of dividing your piece of writing into paragraphs (see Writing Hint 59).
3. The sign off line (Yours sincerely, / Regards / Yours faithfully, etc.) is usually written on the left side of the page, as is your name below it. This gives your letter a recognisable and neat left-hand sidedness.
4. The final paragraph (the one before the sign off line) is generally shorter than the other paragraphs (see Writing Hint 72).

Note that since you are asked to write at least 150 words, it is best to write two main paragraphs of approximately 60 words each, or three main paragraphs of about 40 words each. The final paragraph should then contain approximately 30 words (or less if your main paragraphs are larger).

It is necessary to know how many words you usually write per line in order to quickly estimate how many words you have written overall (by counting the number of lines and multiplying by your usual number of words per line).

71 MAKE YOUR QUESTIONS RELEVANT AND POLITE

If you are going to write a sentence in question form in your letter, which is quite acceptable and often a good idea, make sure that the question you ask is relevant to the topic and is informative to the reader. However, do not ask too many questions in your letter.

❒ Look at part of the Model Answer to Task 1 of Writing Test Four on page 158.

> First of all, I need to know if it is too late to enrol in the course. Can you write and tell me if there are any places available? I certainly hope that my enrolment is still possible.

Notice that the question is asked after the problem is explained in the first sentence. The question naturally leads on from the statement of the problem. You should avoid asking a question if it is not completely clear why it is being asked.

There is also a sentence following the question which clearly relates to it. The question is, therefore, made completely relevant.

Of course, your question should be relevant to the task topic. It would be foolish (and inappropriate) to ask the recipient of the letter over to dinner in order to appear friendly! It is never a good idea to be too familiar with a person that you do not know well.

It is also better to ask a question using a longer or more polite form than a short direct form:

"Can you write to me and tell me if... ?"	is preferable to	"Are there any places left?"
"Do you happen to know why... ?"	is preferable to	"Why... ?"
"Would you be kind enough to... ?"	is preferable to	"Will you send... ?"

72 USE FINAL PARAGRAPH "STOCK" PHRASES

A formal or semi-formal letter usually ends with a final paragraph that is shorter than the main paragraphs. It often begins with a "stock" or commonly used phrase that is popular, appropriate and acceptable for these types of letters.

Sometimes the final paragraph consists of a single phrase of this type. Other times the stock phrase will introduce a further concluding statement. The stock phrase may also come at the end of the final paragraph:

I look forward to your reply.

I look forward to hearing from you in the future.

I would be very grateful if you would attend to this matter as soon as possible.

I await your reply in anticipation.

Thank you for your co-operation in this matter.

Thank you for your co-operation and **I hope to hear from you shortly.**

Please do not hesitate to contact me if you have any queries about this matter.

I'm sorry to have caused you any trouble and **I trust that you will understand.**

Whichever stock phrase you choose, learn them carefully and reproduce them perfectly. Of course, a stock phrase used incorrectly is not worth as many marks as when used appropriately. Without them, though, a letter will look unfinished and will not be as impressive.

Your final paragraph is usually shorter than the preceding paragraphs, and its role in your letter is to leave the recipient with a final impression of what you had to say or what you want them to do.

As you can see from the Model Answers in this book, the final paragraphs are either short or, if you have not written enough words to complete the task, contain enough words to bring the total of words to at least 150.

73 USE A "SIGN OFF" WORD OR PHRASE

Another important "stock" phrase in a letter is the final word or phrase you use before you sign your name. We shall call them "sign off " phrases in this book.

❐ Look at the sign off phrases for the Task 1 Model Answers to Writing Tests One and Three on pages 155 and 157 respectively.

Yours sincerely,	Regards
Mary Campisi	Mariko Kato

If you sign off with an informal word or phrase (such as *"Regards"*) it is not necessary to follow it with a comma. It is customary to use a comma only if you use a sign off phrase beginning with *"Yours"*... .

Some common sign off phrases appear below:

FORMAL – SEMI-FORMAL	
Yours sincerely,	(use for business/information letters)
Yours faithfully,	– some people distinguish between " ... sincerely" and " ... faithfully" by using " ... sincerely" for persons when the name is known, and " ... faithfully" when the name is not known.
Regards	– "Regards" is less formal, but very commonly used for business.
INFORMAL	
Yours truly,	(use for personal letters to friends in business)
Best wishes	(use for personal letters to friends)
Love *(or* "Lots of Love" *)*	(use for family or close friends – usually to the opposite sex if a friend)

Notice that sign off phrases are not always necessary. The Model Answer to Task 1 of Writing Test Two uses an adjective ("Disgusted") in place of a name followed by the town the writer lives in. This is the accepted way to end a letter to a newspaper. The Model Answer to Task 1 of Writing Test Four uses a short "stock" phrase as the final paragraph, and therefore omits a sign off phrase.

74 PUTTING IT ALL TOGETHER

Let us now consider the complete answer to one of the Writing Task 1 questions.

❐ Look again at the question and Model Answer for Task 1 of Writing Test One on page 105:

You have recently moved into a new flat. Unfortunately, you lost some money the other day, and cannot afford to pay next month's rent when it is due.

Write a letter to the landlord or landlady explaining the situation and that you will pay as soon as your parents send you the money. Also, mention that there are some problems with the flat.

> Note: there is no need to write any addresses (including your own) for IELTS Writing Task 1.

1

Dear Sir,

2 I am writing to you because I am unable to pay next month's rent 6
which is due on Saturday. Unfortunately, the other day I lost my
wallet, and there was a large amount of money inside. I have,
therefore, had to write to my parents to ask them to send me some 7
3 money urgently. As soon as it arrives, I will immediately notify you
and arrange to pay by cash or cheque. I hope that this does not 8
cause you too much inconvenience.

There are also some problems with the flat that I wish to bring to your
attention. First, the cold tap in the bathroom will not turn off properly, 9
and the water is dripping constantly. This will need to be fixed
4 quickly because it is wasting water. Second, one of the back rings
on the top of the oven does not work at all.

I'm sorry that I cannot pay the rent on time, and trust that you will 10
understand.

5 Yours sincerely,

Mary Campisi

> Note: for a non-personal letter, you can, if you wish, include a **subject line** after the salutation:
>
> Re: Rent due Saturday
>
> *("Re" means "Regarding".)*

FORM

1. Begin with the correct title for the person to whom you are writing. If you do not know the gender, use "Dear Sir or Madam,".
2. Write in paragraphs, each dealing with one (or two) main point(s). You may begin the first paragraph (if formal or semi-formal) with

"I am writing to you...	because... *(sth)* "
(or)	in reference to... *(sth)* "

3. Use linking words where appropriate, such as "therefore", "however" and "also".
4. You might also use sequencing words to list the points you make ("First", "Second" etc.)
5. End with "Yours sincerely," for a business letter, or "Best wishes" for a personal letter.

CONTENT

6. Begin by clearly stating the reason for the letter you are writing. If required, write formally, in which case do **not** include personal questions such as "How are you?"
7. Next, state what you have done, and/or (as in this case) what you intend to do.
8. You may wish to write a sentence starting with "I hope..." if a request you make might cause some inconvenience.
9. You must include **all** the points that the question task asks you to make, or you are sure to score lower than expected.
10. Your last (short) paragraph usually restates the main reason(s) for writing or, in a formal letter, may end with "I look forward to hearing from you in the future" or a similar phrase.

75 CAUSE AND EFFECT & COMPARISON AND CONTRAST

In the Task 1 letter or Task 2 essay, you might need to refer to the cause of some particular situation and its effect. Note that, when constructing sentences, either the cause or the effect can be mentioned first.

CAUSE			EFFECT
Crime	causes is the cause of		a considerable number of problems.
	is the reason	behind for	

EFFECT					CAUSE
A number of serious problems	are	caused by due to			crime.
		the	result consequence	of	

			CAUSE	EFFECT		EFFECT
One	effect	of	crime	is fear.		
The	consequence(s) result(s)					
	effect(s)			are fear and suspicion which	result in lead to	disharmony.

CAUSE				EFFECT
Crime is a major problem in big cities.	As a	result consequence	(of this),	fear is widespread.
	Consequently, For this reason, Hence, So, Therefore, Thus,			

CAUSE					EFFECT
As a	result consequence	of	crime,	big cities face	a number of problems.
Owing to			an increase in population,		

Here are some incomplete sentences which need to be put together to indicate cause and effect relationships. Match the phrases on the left with the phrases on the right by linking with a suitable cause and effect phrase in the box. Not all the phrases will make a good match, and some ideas are left for you to complete from your imagination. Check your ideas with an English teacher:

An increase in crime
....
Pollution
....
Drugs in sport
....
Living in a big city
Keeping animals as pets

leads to
is the cause of
is often due to
makes
results in
are the reason why
are often caused by
is because of

....
many illnesses.
a lot of stress.
....
a lack of money.
children more responsible.
....
people are angry.

For some Writing Task 2 essay questions you might need to make comparisons. You can contrast various things by describing their similarities and differences. Even if the question does not specifically ask you to compare or contrast, it may be necessary to do so in order to establish a point of view or opinion.

A is bigger than B. A is more expensive than B.	C is bigger than (both) A and B. C is more expensive than A and B.	C is the biggest. C is the most expensive.

C is	significantly considerably a great deal a lot much	bigger than B.

C is	a little bit slightly		bigger than A.
	just	(a bit) (a little)	

C is	(much) more	important ✓ clever ✓ ~~big~~ ✗	than B.

Whereas While Whilst	B is small, C is large.

C is	extremely really very rather quite	big.	On the other hand,	B is small.
			In / By comparison,	
			In conrast,	

The main difference between One of the differences between	C and B is that C is big,	whereas while whilst	B is small.

A is	different	from to	B.
	unlike		

A and B C and D	are	very quite	different	to from	each other.
			similar	to each other.	

D is	the same *(size)* exactly the same	as	C.
	equivalent *(size)* to		

D is	approximately about almost	the same *(size)* as	C.
	similar *(in size)* to		

A is	not	(nearly) (anywhere near)	as big as C.
	nowhere near		

B is small	compared	with to	A..

Many people think that A and B are similar.	On the contrary,	A and B are quite different.

Practise using the above structures in sentences which make comparisons, or contrast items of your own choice by substituting them for the letters A B C and D in the sentences given above.

You can also refer to the Part 2 sample topic cards given in Speaking Hint 94, and use the ideas in those topics to practise comparing and contrasting.

WRITING TASK 2

76 UNDERSTANDING WRITING TASK 2

Writing Task 2 is more important than Writing Task 1. Writing Task 2 counts more towards your overall IELTS Writing Test Band Score than Writing Task 1. However, you must complete both tasks to get an accurate Band Score. You are strongly advised to spend only 20 minutes on Writing Task 1 before turning your attention to Writing Task 2. It is a mistake to spend longer than the advised time on Task 1. You will definitely need 40 minutes on Writing Task 2, and you should leave some time at the end of the hour to check your work in both tasks. (See Writing Hints 65 and 81.) Note that you do not have to attempt Task 1 first. You can answer Task 2 first if you wish.

The task requirement for Task 2 is that you write not less than 250 words on a given topic of general interest. In this book we shall refer to the task as the writing of an essay. In Task 2, an essay can be either an argument regarding a topic, or an account of a situation regarding a topic. It may seem strange but the task is no longer referred to in the IELTS Handbook as requiring an essay. Although from the examiners' point of view there is probably some good reason for this – "essays" can mean different things to different groups of people – it is still best to write in the traditional formal style required of a short English essay.

This task assesses not only your ability to write, but also your ability to think about and discuss an issue of some kind. It is, therefore, important that you have ideas and opinions on a wide range of subjects of general interest, which means that you should be well-read and informed about most of the popular and controversial issues that are debated in the media these days. Sometimes, the IELTS Writing Task 2 topics are of educational interest, in which case your personal knowledge and experience of the topic may be relevant, but be careful not to write about your personal experiences; use them instead to talk generally and objectively about the topic. In addition, you will need to present your thoughts in an organised and orderly way.

There are five steps in the process of writing an essay for the IELTS Writing Test:

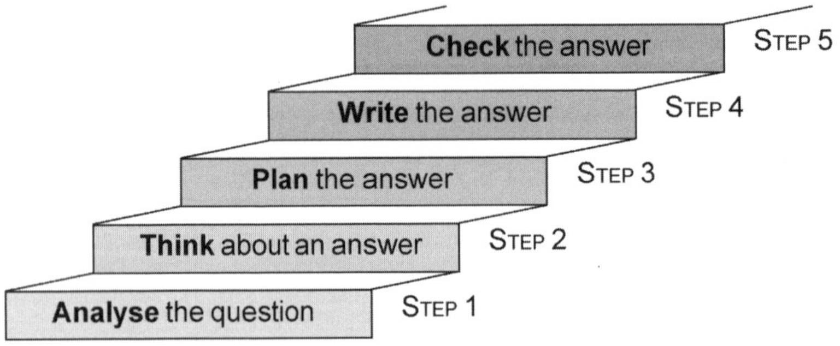

77 STEP1. ANALYSE THE QUESTION (approx. 1 minute)

The Writing Task 2 questions are of 2 basic types. In this book we will refer to them as Type A and Type B questions.

Type A Questions

Firstly, there are questions requiring an **argument** as an answer. Essays that contain an argument are those in which your opinions regarding a topic are essential, as is your understanding and presentation of conflicting opinions. You should consider the argument as having two sides (usually yes/no, or positive/ negative), one of which you support.

If you reduce the argument to a yes/no question, the essay you write will be much like a debate in which you present both sides of the issue: the side you believe in, and the side the opponents of your views believe in. You should support your argument with sufficient evidence in order to prove your point, as well as refute the opposing side of the argument. (See Writing Hint 80.)

Type B Questions

Secondly, there are questions which require an **account** as an answer. Essays of this type ask you to describe and explore the situation regarding the topic, with less emphasis on giving opinions. You should describe the situation regarding the topic, and explore the reasons for the situation being what it is. Although in this case you do not have to support an argument, it is wise to provide evidence of the truth (or otherwise) of the situation.

In both Type A and B questions you may need to make recommendations, offer solutions, or give advice.

❒ Look at the Task 2 questions for all four Writing Tests, and determine the question type, Type A or Type B. Then check with the answers given below:

TEST ONE

Research is an essential part of completing assignments.

Suggest some good places to obtain useful information.

TEST TWO

Most young people without a partner would prefer to have a boyfriend or girlfriend. Yet being in a relationship when you are young is not always a good idea.

Do you agree or disagree?

TEST THREE

A new shopping centre is going to open in your town. At present, nobody knows what kind of shops or facilities are going to be provided for customers. What shops and facilities would you like to see made available to the shopping public?

Make useful suggestions for the shopping centre's management.

TEST FOUR

Some people believe that the world is much less safe today than it used to be. There are still many wars being fought, and high-tech weapons are sold openly to any country that wants to buy them. In cities, violent crime is increasing every year.

It is not a very safe world in which to bring up children. Do you agree or disagree?

Answers:

The topics for Tests One and Three ask for an account of the situation regarding the topic. The topics for Tests Two and Four ask for an argument. (Test Three also asks for suggestions as your solution to the problem.)

Consideration of the Question

It will help when planning your answer to consider the Writing Task 2 questions as being written in either **wh/how**, or **yes/no question form**. The latter is especially helpful when considering a Type A (argument) question because it makes it easier to determine the opposing sides of the argument.

❒ Look at the Task 2 questions for Writing Tests One and Two below:

TEST ONE

...becomes a wh question:

***Where* are some good places to obtain useful information for research when completing assignments?**

TEST TWO

...becomes a yes/no question:

Is being in a relationship when you are young always a good idea?

The question in Writing Test Three is already in wh question form, but can you ask the correct question for Writing Task Four?

....

78 STEP 2. THINK ABOUT AN ANSWER (approx. 2 minutes)

Before you can plan your answer, you need to think of 2 or more main ideas that you will use to support what you have to say in your essay. This step is often referred to as "**brainstorming**". In a true brainstorming session you write down as many ideas and words as you can that come into your head as you think about the topic. Do not judge the worth of the ideas as they come to you – that comes later, after you have put the notes you have made into groups of associated words and ideas.

This preparatory brainstorm session – alone, with a partner, or in a study discussion group – is essential when writing well-constructed essays. It shows the complexity of the task, and reveals what you already know and what you need to know about the topic in order to complete the essay.

Practise brainstorming well in advance of taking the IELTS test. See Speaking Hint 91 for Speaking Test Stage 2 topics with which to practise brainstorming for ideas. Write down on a blank piece of paper as many ideas and words as you can about the topic you choose. Next, put the topic in the middle of an "**Idea Web**" like the one below, and put the words you have brainstormed into groups of associated ideas. You do not have to include all the ideas that you write down.

❒ Look at the following brainstorming session used to create the Model Answer for Task 2 of Writing Test One:

Research

- an essential part of completing assignments

Good places to obtain information:

reading lists from tutor
school libraries
college libraries
teachers
computers - internet
books, magazines, nespapers
sample past exam papers
CD-ROM disks

encyclopaedias
librarian's help
videos
survey people
questionnaires
type of assignments
book titles
(must do research before you start writing)

parents' help
friends?
specialist bookshops

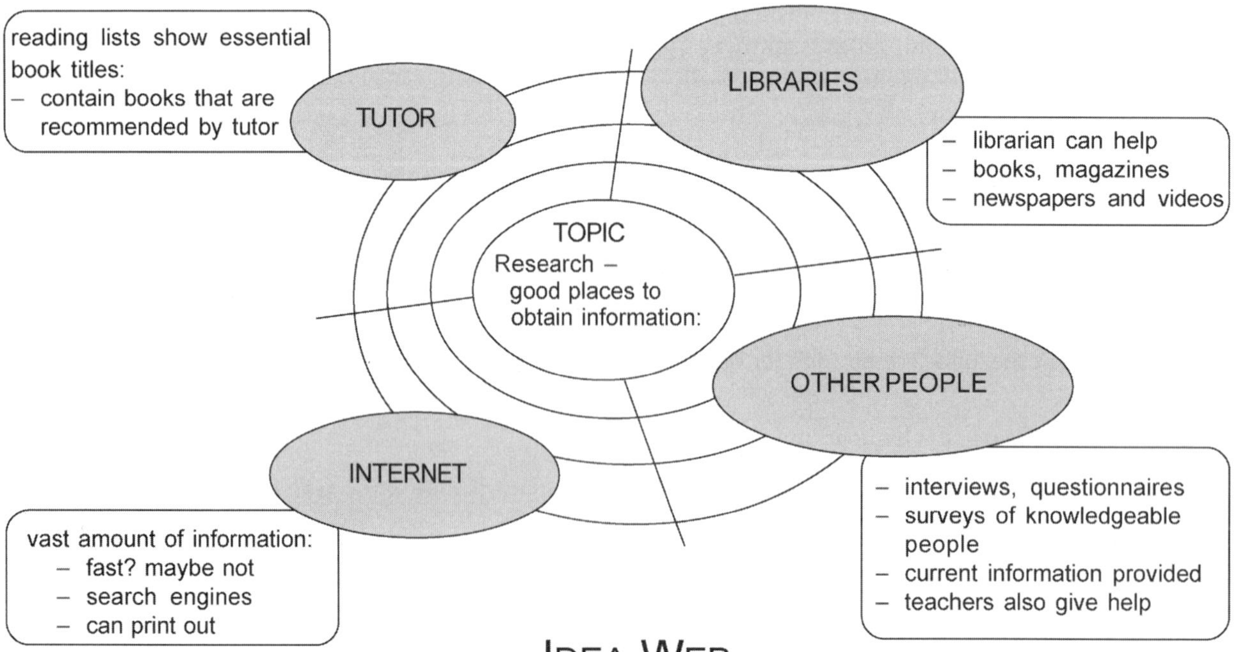

IDEA WEB

Note that you do not have time in the actual test to complete a detailed brainstorming session or "Idea Web" as illustrated above. The method is given for practice only. Nonetheless, you should regularly brainstorm in order to develop the skills necessary to help you think of main ideas for your answer.

With Type A questions, you will only write a successful essay if you can think of a minimum of 2 main supporting arguments for the case you wish to present. Similarly with Type B questions, you will need a minimum of 2 main areas of discussion on which to base your essay about the topic. In each case only 2 to 4 main ideas are necessary because of the length of the task: 250 words.

79 STEP 3. PLAN THE ANSWER (approx. 2 minutes)

You do not have time in the actual test to write a detailed plan like the sample plan shown below. Your plan will need to be much shorter, and perhaps only "written" in your head. (Any written plans in the actual IELTS test are ignored when your writing is assessed.) However, once you have thought of the main ideas that your answer will contain, you do need to **structure and organise** your answer. Evidence of organisational ability counts towards your Writing Task 2 Band Score.

You should only take a few minutes to read and understand the question, and to think of and construct an answer (approximately 5 minutes for Steps 1 to 3). Therefore, it is important to know how to form a well-organised plan quickly and skillfully with the ideas you have "brainstormed".

❒ Look at the plan for the Model Answer for Task 2 of Writing Test One:

PLAN (Test One)

TOPIC: research (when completing assignments)

TYPE B QUESTION: Where are good places to obtain information as part of *(the topic)*?

INTRO: (approx. 40 words)		=	research essential (for written and spoken assignments) – report will discuss best places to look for information
BODY:			
PARAGRAPH 1: (approx. 60 words)	*(TUTOR)*	=	students can get a reading list from the tutor – show essential book titles for written task – contains books tutor recommends
PARAGRAPH 2: (approx. 60 words)	*(LIBRARIES)*	=	try libraries at school or college – wide range of reference material – computers – CD-ROMS on many subjects – spoken assignments could be improved with a video
PARAGRAPH 3: (approx. 60 words)	*(INTERNET)*	=	latest information source – information from all over the world – searches can take a long time – page printouts available – do not need to print out every page of information found
CONCLUSION: (approx. 30 words)	*(OTHER PEOPLE)*	=	interview people with specialist knowledge or conduct surveys
250 words (minimum)			

Note these points about the plan above:

- The plan is composed of 5 parts: topic, question type, introduction, body and conclusion.
- The purpose of the introduction is to express the topic clearly. Also, the writer intends to include both written and spoken assignments in the answer.
- There are 3 main ideas expressed in the body of the report. The body consists of 3 paragraphs each discussing a good place to do research. Note that body paragraph 1 in the Model Answer (on page 155) is shorter than the planned number of words, but body paragraph 2 is longer.
- The conclusion of the report contains one minor point that is not fully developed. Since the task is to write a report, not an essay, there is no need to summarise your main points.
- The total of the proposed minimum number of words for each paragraph is the minimum number of words required to adequately complete the task.

Complete the plans below for Task 2 of Writing Tests Two, Three and Four, by referring to the Model Answers on pages 156, 157 and 158, and the example plan on page 67.

PLAN (Test Two)

TOPIC: being in a relationship when you are young
TYPE.........: Is *(the topic)* not always a good idea?

INTRO:

B *PARA. 1: (PROBLEM)*
O
D *PARA. 2: (PROBLEM)*
Y
PARA. 3: (OPPOSITE OPINION + REFUTATION)

CONC:

PLAN (Test Three)

TOPIC: shops and facilities in a new shopping centre
TYPE.........: What *(the topic)* would you like to see? Make suggestions for the centre's management.

INTRO:

PARA. 1: (SHOPS)
B
O
PARA. 2: (MORE SHOPS)
D
Y
PARA. 3: (FACILITIES)

CONC:

PLAN (Test Four)

TOPIC: a safe world
TYPE.........: Is it *(the topic)* in which to bring up children?

INTRO:

B *PARA. 1: (PROBLEM)*
O
D *PARA. 2: (PROBLEM)*
Y
PARA. 3: (OPPOSITE OPINION + REFUTATION)

CONC:

80 STEP 4. WRITE THE ANSWER (approx. 30 minutes)

Once you have a plan, either quickly written down or in your head, the time comes to actually write the answer. Begin with the introduction – there is no need to write a title, or repeat the question.

The Introduction

❒ Look at the introductions to the Task 2 model answers for Writing Tests One to Four:

TEST ONE **The most important step in the completion of a class assignment is researching the topic.** Some assignments require you to give a written answer, and others require a spoken presentation. However, finding useful information is only possible if you know where to look. This report will describe some of the best places to find information.

TEST TWO **When you are young, there is often a great deal of peer pressure put upon you to be in a relationship.** Although most young people spend a lot of time dreaming about finding the right boyfriend or girlfriend, I believe that early relationships can lead to many problems which young men and women might not be able to solve easily.

TEST THREE **I am glad that a new shopping centre is going to open in our town.** We badly need a good place to shop and meet up with our friends. In my opinion, we need many different kinds of shops, but the centre should also provide us with a number of community facilities.

TEST FOUR **It is unfortunate that the world is becoming less and less safe.** Everyday in the news we read that someone has been murdered, and crime has increased in major cities all over the world. Furthermore, cities are no longer safe places in which to raise children. In my opinion, the main cause of people being unkind to each other is a lack of understanding.

The topic sentence of each introduction (shown in **bold print**) states the main idea of the paragraph, and introduces the theme of the essay itself. The ideas within the paragraphs are joined together with connective or linking words (shown underlined). In all these examples, the topic sentence is the first sentence of each paragraph. It does not always need to be the first sentence, but it makes the paragraph easier to write. (See also Reading Hint 42.) Notice how the topic sentences are clear, simple, interesting and informative. (See also Writing Hint 62.)

Tests Two and Four are answers to Type A questions (argument essays). Note that the writer's opinion is given in the introduction.

In all introductions the sentences following the topic sentence give the reader an idea of how the rest of the essay is constructed. They function similarly to a "map" of the essay, although, as in the examples above, the map need not be complete in a short IELTS Writing Task 2 essay. (See also Writing Hint 68.)

The final sentence of the introduction leads naturally into the first body paragraph

The Body

❒ Look at the first body paragraphs of the Task 2 Model Answers for Writing Tests One to Four:

TEST ONE ***To begin with*, there is the reading list that the tutor gives students in class.** Reading lists show the essential book titles you should read to complete a written task, and are useful because they contain the books that the tutor recommends.

TEST TWO ***Firstly*, having a special friend is a large responsibility.** It takes up a lot of time looking after the needs and interests of another person. It could be better to spend this time studying or playing sport. After all, there will be plenty of opportunity for young persons to share their lives later, when they are grown up.

TEST THREE

***To begin with*, there should be a large food supermarket within the centre.** People must have a good and cheap place to buy their weekly food supplies. *However*, we must also have specialty food shops that supply foods that are hard to get in a supermarket. A large delicatessen would be a good idea. And perhaps we can have an Asian foodstore since Asian food is very popular nowadays.

TEST FOUR

Mankind has always fought wars and probably always will. Yet there have never been so many high-tech weapons available to so many countries before. If the rich countries which supply poorer countries with these weapons understood the problems they create, arms sales would be illegal. I cannot understand why some drugs are illegal, but weapons that kill thousands of people are sold everywhere.

As with the introduction, the topic sentence of each first body paragraph (shown in **bold print**) states or refers to the main idea of the paragraph, and the ideas within the paragraphs are joined together with connective or linking words (shown underlined).

Note the use of the sequencing phrase (*"Firstly"*) in the first body paragraph of Writing Test One. A sequencing word (*"Next"*) is also used in the second body paragraph. Notice that the same sequencing construction is not used repetitively (*"Firstly, Secondly, Thirdly,"*). For this reason, the technique is not used in both of the Model Answers to the writing tasks of Test One.

In each case, the sentences of the first body paragraph are relevant to the main idea or topic of the paragraph. The same is true of all the body paragraphs. The body paragraphs **develop the main idea of the essay**. If a new idea is introduced, it is supported with additional detail or with examples.

If you are developing an argument, you should support each statement you make with appropriate evidence. Note that the statements made can contrast with as well as support the main idea, in order to develop the argument. This can be seen in the first body paragraph of Writing Test Four.

The final sentence of a body paragraph often completes the main idea of the paragraph

Balancing the Argument

❒ Look at the third body paragraph of the Task 2 Model Answer to Writing Test One:

Second, there is the library in the school where you are studying. Most good colleges have libraries containing a wide range of books, newspapers, magazines and reference material. These days, modern, well-equipped libraries have banks of computers with CD-ROM disks on a variety of subjects. Alternatively, if you are researching information for a spoken presentation, you might borrow a video to show your class. If you cannot find the books you need in the school or college library, you can go to the local library and ask the librarian there to help you.

Essays requiring an argument of some kind should be balanced by including a paragraph which either gives an **alternative** viewpoint, or states and **refutes** the opposing side of the argument.

The argument in Task 2 of Writing Test Two is whether or not it is always a good idea to be in a relationship when you are young. The position taken by the writer is that it is not always a good idea. In order to balance the essay, the alternative viewpoint is also considered: *"Some people argue that today's youth are better informed..."*.

However, if you disagree with the other side of the argument, you will need to refute that opinion or position. This means that you first state the opposing side of the argument, and then give reasons why you do not agree. Perhaps the opposing argument is weak, or does not include all the known facts. Or maybe yours is a more compelling argument, in which case you must say why. Of course, you may disagree strongly, mildly, or only partially.

Suggested phrases for refutation paragraphs:

Many people	believe that...	. However, I strongly disagree . Nothing could be further from the truth *(Strong disagreement)*	because... . In fact, ...
Others	may argue that...	. I find it hard to agree . Nevertheless, I cannot agree *(Mild disagreement)*	for the following reasons:
Those who disagree	point out that...	. Perhaps this is true, but it cannot be denied that... . This is partly true, then again, ... *(Concessional disagreement)*	

The Conclusion

❐ Look at the conclusions to the Task 2 Model Answers for Writing Tests One to Four:

TEST ONE **Finally**, people can be good sources of information, too. By interviewing people with particular knowledge, or conducting surveys, you can obtain the information that is most current and suitable for your needs.

TEST TWO **In general**, while it is true that, for young people, being together and in love is wonderful, there are often many difficult issues to cope with in a full-time relationship.

TEST THREE **In conclusion**, I would like to see a lot of free activities and product demonstrations in the new centre, because this will attract customers and make the shopping centre a great success. If the centre contains a lot of office space, it will be a big mistake.

TEST FOUR **To sum up**, we live in a violent world. Bringing up children in a world where violence is regularly shown on television shows and on the news is proof that it is not a safe place. If we do not try to solve this problem, our children's future will suffer.

The conclusion usually begins with a special concluding phrase (see those shown above in **bold**) that links it to the rest of the essay. (See also Writing Hint 66.)

Notice that a conditional sentence can be very effective in the conclusion. One reason for this is that it can refer to what might occur as a result of your suggestions or recommendations. Of course, you can use conditional sentences elsewhere in your essay as well. If you do use conditionals, be sure that the construction of your sentences is grammatically correct. (See Writing Hint 65.)

Also, in a short essay of approximately 250 words the conclusion can be just one or two sentences long. The conclusion should briefly sum up what you have said in your essay, and does not usually contribute a new idea, unless it is a minor point. However, it is a good place to make recommendations or suggestions, or to give advice and offer solutions – if you are asked to do so.

81 STEP 5. CHECK THE ANSWER (approx. 5 minutes)

You should allow up to 5 minutes at the end of the writing task to check your work for grammatical errors and missing or faulty punctuation. Use the "10 Point Grammar Checklist" (see Writing Hint 65) and the "Quick Punctuation Guide" (see Writing Hint 59).

To help you remember what to check for, you might like to learn this short rhyming verse:

First look for missing Articles, and be sure to check the rest,
Third-person present singular Verbs are next, just add an 's'.
Then check the voice and tense of Verbs, Verb forms and Verb agreements,
But after the four Vs come the four Ps or there'll be grievance:
Plurals, Pronouns, Prepositions; check your Parts of speech,
And finally, Conditionals; if uncertain, then check each.

SENTENCE CONSTRUCTION

82 USE A VARIETY OF SENTENCE TYPES

In both writing tasks, and especially Writing Task 2, it is important to avoid using repetitious sentence constructions. You need a variety of ways to express yourself in your sentences. The best way to practise is to observe how other writers construct their sentences and imitate them.

There are 4 basic sentence types: **simple**, **compound**, **complex** and **combination** sentences.

a) Simple Sentences

- with 1 <u>verb</u> and a single *subject*:

  ***Computers* <u>make</u> life easy for many people.**

  ....

  ....

- with 2 <u>verbs</u> and a single *subject*:

  ***Computers* <u>cost</u> a lot of money and <u>require</u> regular maintenance.**

  ....

  ....

- with 2 <u>verbs</u> and a compound *subject*:

  ***Businesses and individuals* <u>buy</u> computers and <u>use</u> them mostly for correspondence.**

  ....

  ....

The sentences above are simple – they consist of one **independent clause**. A **clause** is a group of words containing a subject and a verb. (A group of words without a subject and/or verb is merely a **phrase**.) An independent clause can function as a complete sentence, in which case it ends with a full stop.

b) Compound Sentences

Compound sentences consist of two or more **independent clauses** joined in the following ways:

- with a semi-colon:

  ***Some people* <u>like</u> computers; *others* <u>are</u> afraid of modern technology.**

  ....

  ....

- with one of these 7 conjunctions: and – but – or – nor – for – so – yet (note the comma)

  ***Students usually* <u>write</u> with a computer, but *I* <u>like</u> writing by hand.**

  ....

  ....

- with a conjunctive (joining) adverb: furthermore – moreover – therefore (etc.)

  ***Students usually* <u>write</u> with a computer; however, *I* <u>like</u> writing by hand.**

  ....

  ....

The punctuation in each case is important and counts towards your final IELTS Writing Band Score.

c) Complex Sentences

Complex sentences consist of an **independent clause** and one (or more) **dependent clauses.** A dependent clause is a group of words including a verb which do not form a complete sentence by themselves, and so depend on the existence of an independent clause. There are 3 basic types of complex sentences:

- with a dependent clause functioning as an **adverb**: (beginning with an <u>*adverb*</u>)

  ***<u>Although</u> computers can save time*, they take a long time to understand.**

  ....

  ....

  ....

  [A dependent adverb clause can come before or after the independent clause. The dependent adverb clause is followed by a comma only if it comes before the independent clause.]

- with a dependent clause functioning as an **adjective**: (beginning with a <u>*relative pronoun*</u> or <u>*relative adverb*</u>)

  Database software is essential for companies *<u>which</u> need to maintain records*.

  ....

  ....

  ....

  [A dependent adjective (relative) clause can begin with **who**, **which**, **whose** etc. (relative pronouns) or **when**, **where** and **why** (relative adverbs). The dependent clause adds information to a noun. A comma is required only if the information is not essential to the noun.]

- with a dependent clause functioning as a **noun**: (beginning with <u>*that*</u>, <u>*whether*</u>, or "<u>*wh*</u>" question words etc.)

  Most experts insist *<u>that</u> computers are essential in schools.*

  ....

  ....

  ....

  [A dependent noun clause can function either as the subject or the object (as above) of the independent clause. A comma is, therefore, unnecessary.]

d) Combination Sentences

Combination sentences consist of a combination of compound and complex sentences. They therefore consist of at least two independent clauses and one or more dependent clauses:

When computers first appeared, they were huge, but now they are extremely compact.

....

....

....

Writing informative, varying and accurate sentences takes a great deal of skill and practice.

You are advised to spend some time analysing the dependent and independent clauses in the sentences contained in the Model Answers for both writing tasks on pages 155–158. Also, we refer you to our companion practice book *"202 Useful Exercises for IELTS"*.

SPEAKING TEST HINTS

83 BE PREPARED AND TRY TO RELAX

You should be on time and prepared for the interview. (See also Basic Hint 3.) Remember to have your passport with you to show to the examiner for identification.

The examiner is provided with a list of standardised questions to ask you, and will conduct the interview in a manner that you might not be used to if you have not had some previous practice. The Speaking Sub-test is a formal interview, not an ordinary conversation. In Parts 1 and 2 of the test, the examiner cannot talk to you freely. He or she must follow a strict set of questions that is determined in advance of your test. In Part 3 the examiner can talk with less restriction.

Do not worry about the interview being recorded. Its primary purpose is to make sure the examiner conducts the interview properly, and is usually only used to assess your English if you pay to have your interview scored again. Such a circumstance is generally unadvisable. The second of the two scores will apply – even if it is lower.

First impressions are very important. You should always reply with an answer that is informative and as interesting as possible.

Body language is also important. Sit comfortably and try to show with your body that you are relaxed, but not too relaxed! Remember that the speaking part of the IELTS test is the same for Academic and General Training Module candidates and is formal in style. With your body, aim to create a relaxed impression, and, by what you say, aim to create an intelligent impression.

84 BE WILLING TO TALK AND BE POSITIVE

Do not simply reply yes or no to a question and wait for the next one. Remember, this test is your opportunity to speak. Try to be as helpful and willing to talk as you can. The examiner is there to guide you as to what to say and will do as little of the talking as possible. You should aim to be talking for at least 75–80% of the time. Also, take advantage of every question to show that you are an interesting and informed person.

In order to present yourself in the best way possible you should try to sound positive about your past, present and future. Candidates sometimes think that absolute honesty is always necessary. However, if you are studying in a foreign country, for example, and you are asked what you think of that country, it is unwise to say that you think it is terrible – even if you believe it to be true!

The examiner is expecting to talk to a positive, intelligent and courteous candidate

85 THE EXAMINER FRAME

You have probably heard or been told by your English teacher that the examiner uses what is called a "frame" from which to ask you questions. A frame is simply a set of pre-determined questions on a topic. For example, in order to first get to know you, the examiner will ask a few questions about your background, but he or she will only ask the questions in the chosen frame.

Does this mean you can find out from other students who have previously taken the test what the questions are going to be in your test? Unfortunately, this is not possible! The use of frames does not mean that all students hear exactly the same set of questions. In fact, there are many frames from which the examiner can choose questions.

You might be interested to know that the introduction of standard sets of questions on various topics for all candidates means the accuracy of your assessment is further guaranteed.

Although you do not have to concern yourself about where the questions come from, it is essential to understand that the standardisation of questions means that your answering technique is very important (see Speaking Hint 86).

In addition, you should know that the examiner is giving you a score out of 9 in four areas of speaking ability:

1. **Fluency and Coherence**

   – Does your speech flow? Can you be easily understood?

2. **Lexical Resource**

   – Do you use a reasonably wide range of vocabulary in your speech?

3. **Grammatical Range and Accuracy**

   – Do you use English grammar properly when you speak?

4. **Pronunciation**

   – Do you use English sounds, stress and intonation patterns etc. correctly?

Your final Band Score for the Speaking Sub-test is the average of these four scores.

86 MAKE GOOD USE OF THE QUESTIONS ASKED

If the situation was an ordinary conversation, it would be perfectly reasonable to answer some of the questions with a short one or two word answer, *but this is not an ordinary conversation.*

<u>Ordinary conversation</u>

Question: Where do you come from?

Answer: Germany.

Question: Which part of Germany?

Notice that the questioner has asked a second question to get more detail.

<u>Formal IELTS interview</u>

Question: Where do you come from?

Answer: Germany. Hamburg. It's in the north, you know – a very busy city with a population of over one and half million people. But actually I live about 15 kilometres out of town – on a small farm.

In this case the candidate has given a brief but satisfactory answer that makes full use of the question asked. Remember, especially in Parts 1 and 2 of the test, the examiner cannot ask further questions to find out what you should have told him or her in the first place.

However, do not fall into the trap of trying to impress with large words and complex explanations. A complicated answer is not necessarily better than a simple and concise answer because you can easily become lost for words! The examiner is listening for a level of fluency, and hesitation does not help your overall Band Score.

In general, it is better to give simple and accurate answers than complex, inaccurate answers. Simple answers, however, do not mean one-word answers; this will prevent you from showing the examiner how well you can speak and require the examiner to move on to the next question too soon.

Answer the questions in full when they are given to you – you are unlikely to get a second chance to answer them

87–91 PART 1. INTRODUCTION & INTERVIEW (4–5 minutes)

87 Requirements

You will certainly be asked at least a couple of general questions about your background, so you should have already prepared answers to some basic questions about yourself. For practice, write a short description of your present situation, and imagine the questions a stranger might ask you based on what you have written.

The requirements for effective performance in Part 1 are that you:

- introduce yourself in a relaxed, friendly manner
- produce basic information about yourself simply, accurately, and as fluently as possible
- present yourself as a person who is willing to talk and has interesting things to say about himself or herself.

Remember, Part 1 is mainly concerned with who you are, what you have done, your home or your family, your job or your studies, and your interests

88 What To Do and What Not To Do

✓	✗
1 Show the examiner you are confident by smiling and looking him or her in the eye.	1 Do not tell the examiner that you are nervous, or blink your eyes and move about too much.
2 If the examiner offers to shake your hand, return his or her handshake firmly.	2 Do not shake hands with the examiner as if your extended hand were a cold wet fish!
3 Answer the questions you are asked clearly and in some detail (using at least two or three sentences).	3 Do not cut the interview questions short with one-word or very short answers.
4 Show that you are in control by talking freely about yourself and your past.	4 Do not wait for another question – the examiner wants you to answer each question in full.
5 Make sure you have practised well enough before the test so that the past tenses you use are accurately formed and appropriate.	5 Do not be afraid to correct yourself if you make a grammatical mistake, but fluency is just as important. Your grammar practice should take place in the classroom or at home.

89 Suggested "Opening" Words and Phrases

Practise using the phrases and sentences below with the help of a partner. Ask your partner to ask you some basic "getting to know you" questions.

Good morning. / afternoon. Pleased to meet you.

Where shall I sit? Over here? I'm very well thank you. And you?

As you can see, I come from...

I was born in *(place of birth)* but now I live in...

You can see that I'm *(nationality)* but I've been living in *(your host country)* for *(period of time)*...

I am very close to my family, although I don't live with them any longer.

Recently, I've been studying / working at...

Before that I studied / worked at...

I've been studying English now for *(1 year)*...

At the moment I'm studying / working at ...

90 Part 1 – Background Information Topic Areas:

Your Home and Family

Questions about this topic are fairly common in all English test interviews, including the IELTS. The examiner wishes to find out some general background information about you, and your home and family is a good place to start.

Common questions might include:

Where do you live? Do you live by yourself or with your family? Who do you share with? Is it a nice place? What's it like? Are you here in *(your host country)* alone or is your family with you? Do you like living in *(your host country)*? What do your parents do? * Do you have any brothers and sisters? * i.e. what is their profession or work status?	*You will probably not be asked all of these questions, but be ready to answer these or similar questions clearly and willingly.* *Show as much interest in your own answers as the examiner does listening to the answers you give.* *Try to think of yourself, and sound like, someone special – which, of course, you are!* *Do not take too long to answer each question at this stage – let the examiner guide you. You should sense when he or she wants to move on to the next question.* *Remember to smile!*

Your Jobs and/or Studies

If you have a job (or have had a job in the past), that could be of interest to the examiner. If not, it does not matter – you are probably engaged in study or can talk about your English course. If current work or study does not apply to you, then talk briefly about how you began to learn English and the school in which you studied.

Your Interests

Most students have interesting hobbies or activities that they enjoy doing – make sure that you are prepared to talk about what interests you and what you do in your spare time. Again, make yourself sound as if you are the only person in the world who does these exciting things.

Other Familiar Topic Areas

Refer to the Speaking Game on page 151 for more topic ideas for Part 1.

91 Suggested Words and Phrases *...if you are unsure of the question or how to answer:*

I'm not exactly sure what you mean. Could you repeat the question please?
I'm not quite sure how to answer that question, but (perhaps)...
That's a rather difficult question, but (maybe) I can answer you by saying...

...if you cannot think of what else to say:

I think that is all I can tell you about...	Would you like me to tell you more about...?
Is that all you'd like to know?	I'm afraid that's about as much as I know.
I think that's about it.	I can't think of anything else right now...

92–94 PART 2. INDIVIDUAL LONG TURN (3–4 minutes)

92 Requirements

You will know that Part 2 has begun when the examiner asks you to talk in some detail about a particular topic – a topic which is usually easy for you to find things to talk about. Note that you are only asked to talk about one topic.

The requirements for effective performance in Part 2 are that you:

- talk in some detail about the topic referred to on the card you are given
- try give an organised answer by following the instructions written on the card
- keep talking about the topic – with no help from the examiner – for at least one minute and up to 2 minutes.

Remember, Part 2 is concerned with your ability to speak with little or no hesitation and in some detail about a simple topic

93 What To Do and What Not To Do

✓

1. Use your preparation time to think about your answer – think only about what is written on the card.
2. Organise your reply by following the order of the instructions given on the card. (See Speaking Hint 94.)
3. Be aware of how long you have been talking by practising with a wristwatch before you do the test. (See Speaking Hint 94.)
4. Make sure you have answered all that is required on the card, and be prepared to answer a couple of questions at the end.

✗

1. Do not digress; that is, do not talk of things which are not directly related to the topic on the card.
2. Do not hesitate for too long in your answer. It is better to speak about anything than not to speak at all!
3. Do not be afraid to correct a grammatical mistake, but fluency is just as important as grammar, and too much correction will make it hard for you to be understood.
4. Do not expect the examiner to give you feedback on how well you performed in your talk.

94 Part 2 – What To Do in the Minute of Silence

When the examiner hands you the card your one minute of preparation time has begun. Read the card carefully, noting what the topic is. Since there is no title on the card*, the topic might not be immediately clear, but the topic is given in the very first sentence.

You will see that there are a number of instructions to follow, and all the items of information required are expected to be referred to in your answer. You can certainly add extra information if you think it is appropriate, and you are wise to do so – if you have time – provided that you do not digress (speak "off" or away from the topic).

The best approach is to read the card quickly from beginning to end, and then go back to the first specific instruction after the topic sentence. Think of things to say about each of the instructions in the remaining time you have. Although you are allowed to make notes (and refer to them in your answer), unless you have practised this approach, it is probably best to spend your time thinking rather than writing. But some candidates may wish to ask the examiner for notepaper to write on.

There are usually 3 or 4 instructions to speak about, so aim to speak for 30 seconds on each one.

* the use of card titles in the Speaking Test Game on page 151 is for ease of use in the game

A Sample Topic Card:

> Describe a city or a town that you know well.
>
> You should include in your answer:
>
> – the location of the city or town
>
> – the part of the city or town you are most familiar with
>
> – important landmarks and places to visit
>
> ...and what makes that city or town special to you and to others.

Notice that the topic is there in the very first sentence. Note also that there are 4 further instructions that follow (there may be more or less). If you speak for about 30 seconds on each of these 4 instructions, you will have spoken for about 2 minutes – which is more than adequate. Do not speak for longer than 2 minutes.

The examiner may or may not stop you talking after two minutes, so aim to finish within that period of time. Of course, it is very important to speak for at least one minute, so if you have difficulty speaking for that length of time you will have to practise, practise, practise.

Try using a wristwatch, and time yourself on each part of the topic. Become accustomed to speaking for approximately 30 seconds on one instruction. Then move on to the next instruction. You can look quickly at your watch in the test itself, but we do not advise it. It is much better to practise recognising how long 30 seconds "feels".

When you get better at "feeling" how long you take to speak about parts of the main topic, you can approach the entire answer in a similar way – that is, by estimating how long you have spoken for, and making sure you have included all parts of the answer within two minutes.

So, what specifically can you talk about? Look at a breakdown of the above topic:

the location of the city or town	*Sydney – harbour city – clean – busy*
	on the east coast of Australia
the part of the city or town you are most familiar with	*live in a large older-style house*
	my suburb: wide streets, trees
	sunny weather, blue skies, modern buildings
important landmarks and places to visit	*Opera House, Harbour Bridge*
	One looks like a ship's sails, the other like a coat-hanger
what makes that city or town special to you and to others	*sense of space and freedom*
	people close to water and beaches

Your answer should not only be interesting, it should also be informative.

Look at the following possible answer:

> “I'm going to talk about the city of Sydney – on the east coast of Australia – a very modern and clean city with a beautiful harbour...er...with a population of about six million inhabitants – it gets quite busy in peak hour because just about everyone travels to work by car or train; but it is a great place to live because there are many exciting things to see and do – especially for young people.
>
> I live in the inner-city – in a typical older style building...er...I think it was built about 100 years ago...it's quite spacious, but many people live in modern apartment blocks. Sydney is quite a tall city – skyscrapers etc. – but there are lots of wide streets – often lined with trees. The Australian gum-tree is everywhere, but of course, koalas and kangaroos can only be found in the zoo these days! Because the weather is so warm – most days there are blue skies and sunshine – because of this, people tend to smile a lot – they seem to enjoy their lives.
>
> The Opera House is a favourite place for tourists to visit – it looks like the sails of a ship from a distance. And the Harbour Bridge is also strange – it looks something like a coat-hanger – and it is used very effectively at Xmas and New Year to put on wonderful firework displays.
>
> I think it's the sense of space and freedom that people notice first when they come to this city. It has a mixed population – people come from so many different backgrounds – but there doesn't seem to be as much tension as in other cities. Perhaps people are too busy dreaming about the beach to worry about riots and that sort of thing. Water is always nearby, and the harbour is really one of the most beautiful sights in the world.”

The answer is given in fairly simple English – you should avoid giving a complex answer with difficult vocabulary. It contains all the points written in note-form on the previous page, and is approximately the right length for a good answer. Of course, the speed at which you speak will also determine how much you are able to say. Increase your speaking speed by practising "topic talking" daily and by improving your pronunciation.

Use the sample cards below and in the Speaking Test Game on page 151 to practise writing out an answer of similar length, and ask a teacher to check your work. Then try giving a spoken answer from the notes you have made. It is fine to memorise an answer for practice if it helps to speed up your English, but do not waste your time memorising large pieces of English to speak in the test. The examiner will not be fooled by this approach! Besides, you would be very lucky to guess your topic before the test.

You might be able to make your talk sound more interesting by "lifting" your voice a little higher than when you speak normally

More Sample Topic Cards:

Talk about a holiday you have taken recently or at some time in the past.

You should include in your answer:

- where you went on your holiday
- why you went to this particular place
- what you did and with whom

...and why you enjoyed your holiday or not.

Describe a health problem you once had (or talk about someone else's problem).

You should mention:

- the nature of the health problem
- why the problem occurred
- what you (or the other person) could not do because of the problem

...what you (or the other person) had to do to get better.

95–99 PART 3. TWO-WAY DISCUSSION (4–5 minutes)

95 Requirements

Part 3 of the Speaking Sub-test is the most demanding. Although it is described as a two-way discussion, you will be expected to do most of the talking. The questions or prompts you must answer are linked to the topic you spoke about in Part 2, but they take the topic further away from you and your immediate life and into areas of more general interest.

The discussion is designed to:

- make you think and comment about various issues (within a specific topic area) that concern people living in today's world
- encourage you to give your opinions
- extend your range of responses to include some or all of the following:
  - describing in detail
  - contrasting and comparing
  - discussing situations as they were in the past
  - imagining situations as they might be in the future.

Remember, effective performance in Part 3 requires an ability to respond to questions and prompts about abstract ideas

96 What To Do and What Not To Do

✓

1 Try to talk around a difficult question by speculating (guessing), using simple words if you can to express complex ideas. This is much better than trying to impress with big words that you may use incorrectly.

2 It is not a good idea to just give up; always attempt to answer a question as fully as possible and the best way you can. If you get stuck and cannot continue, the examiner might be able to help you if you say: "Can you ask the question in a different way?"

3 Use a variety of introductory phrases to begin expressing an opinion (see Speaking Hint 97).

4 Use appropriate future forms and phrases to express the possibility of a future situation occurring. (See Speaking Hint 99.)

✗

1 Do not repeat the information you gave in the original talk you gave in Part 2. Although the questions and prompts in Part 3 are connected to the topic in Part 2, it is unlikely that information you gave then will be appropriate now.

2 Do not worry if you cannot answer easily. The examiner is asking more difficult questions in Part 3, and is probably trying to find your "ceiling" – the point at which you cannot communicate easily (for lack of vocabulary or some other speaking skill).

3 If asked to talk about the future, do not overuse the word "will". There are many ways to express the future in English. (See Speaking Hint 99.) The word "will" is often too definite to use to guess about things which, after all, may not happen.

97 Introductory Phrases for Giving Opinions

I think / believe (that)...	In my opinion...	I strongly believe that...
What I think is this: ...	It seems to me that...	In my view ...
As far as I'm concerned...	If you ask me... *	Don't you think that ...

* this phrase is used even when you have been previously asked a question!

98 Part 3 – Practice Topics for Discussion:

Since you cannot know what topic you will be asked to talk about in Part 2 of the Speaking Sub-test, it follows that you cannot know in advance any particulars about the wider topic area that is discussed in Part 3. The following possible discussion topics are for practice only:

- Problems that affect your country
- Financial success and how to achieve it
- Poverty and hunger in the developing world
- Crime and punishment
- Fashion and design
- Public transport
- Youth and the problems they face
- The role of television and radio in society
- The influence of the print media
- Current affairs
- The changing nature of family life
- Nuclear energy
- World economic solutions
- Diet, health and exercise
- The consequences of global warming
- Recreational facilities in modern cities
- Future energy resources
- The relevance of school examinations
- Materialism and the consumer
- Space travel
- Modern medicine
- Censorship and the Internet
- Types of governments in the world today
- Women in the workplace
- The qualities and skills of a good company manager
- The necessity of a strong defence force
- The advantages of an international language
- The design of modern cities
- The influence of sport in society
- Street protests and individual rights
- Religion and the church in the modern world
- The pros and cons of living in a foreign country
- The meaning of happiness
- Living together, marriage and divorce

When you first practise speaking about these topics, try it in your own language. Think about the situation *as it might have been in the past, the way things are now,* and *how things might become in the future.* Make comparisons, give opinions, and try to sound authoritative. Then practise in English!

99 Suggested Phrases for Speaking About The Future

<table>
<tr>
<td>I'm certain that... (something will/is going to happen)
Most probably... (something will/is going to happen)
It's (always) possible that... (something might happen)
I hope that... (something happens or doesn't happen)</td>
<td rowspan="4">(+)

certainly will
bound to
most probably
probably
possibly / maybe it will
(may) might / perhaps

it's 50-50 whether or not ...

possibly / maybe it won't
(may) might / perhaps | not
probably won't
most probably won't
I doubt (very much) if...
surely / definitely | won't

(−)</td>
</tr>
<tr>
<td>(Something) probably | will / won't | ...(happen) in the | short / long | term

(Something) might even... (happen)
Perhaps (something) will even... (happen)
Of course, (something) could always (happen), especially if... *</td>
</tr>
<tr>
<td>There's | a good / a 50-50 / a reasonable / little / not much | chance that... (something will happen)</td>
</tr>
<tr>
<td>Sometimes I wonder | if / whether | (something is going to happen)... *

I'm not sure if it'll... , but... *</td>
</tr>
</table>

* Note the inclusion of first conditional "if clauses", which can be useful when asked to speculate about the possibility of something happening in the future.

100–101 CONCLUDING THE INTERVIEW

100 Requirements

When the examiner has finished the discussion in Part 3, the Speaking Sub-test has come to an end. The examiner will thank you for talking and the interview is concluded.

- remember to thank the examiner for his or her time and say goodbye
- as you leave the room, don't forget to remain positive – the examiner might not have yet completely made up his or her mind about your score, and the final impression you make is important.

If you have questions about the test itself, such as when the results will become available, talk to the person in charge of the day's proceedings

101 What To Do and What Not To Do

✓

1 Relax and remain in control right up until the moment you leave the interview room.

2 Shake hands confidently, if you are invited to do so, and thank the examiner for his or her time.

3 Simply say:

"Thank you very much for your time.
I enjoyed talking with you. Goodbye."

...or a similar concluding sentence or two of your own.

✗

1 Do not tell the examiner how relieved you are the test is over, and there is no need to comment on your performance!

2 Do not overdo your friendliness at the end. Be glad you did your best, smile and leave the room.

3 Do not ask the examiner for your Band Score. He or she is unable to give you that information.

☺ A FINAL WORD

IELTS is a demanding and challenging examination. Because the Band Score you receive is probably of great importance to your future you should a make a serious effort RIGHT NOW to achieve the level of English you require. Don't wait until tomorrow – tomorrow never comes.

Think deeply about what you can achieve with your life if you score well. Think about what you will be able to do later.

Well-placed effort is always rewarded. The hard work you do now will eventually make your life easier. A little pain now for a lot of gain later. That is the secret of success – perhaps the secret of living itself – for learning never ends.

The first time you take any test you are unfamiliar with the way in which it is conducted and will naturally feel slightly nervous. Many candidates take the IELTS test the first time for practice – to get an accurate assessment of their level and to familiarise themselves with the process – before taking it a second or even third time. Each time you must wait for three months before being allowed to take the test again. It takes at least that period of time to increase your overall Band Score by one Band, and requires intensive daily study.

Good luck...and remember the Golden Rule:

NOTES

PRACTICE TESTS

HOW TO TAKE THE PRACTICE TESTS

Note: these tests are graded in level. The early tests are not written at the standard of difficulty you will find in the actual IELTS test. They are intended to:

- introduce students to the question types in context,
- offer examples of the thinking strategies required for certain question types, and
- build students skills towards achieving well on the later, more difficult tests here and in our other books.

For tests of similar standard of difficulty to the actual IELTS test refer to the *"404 Essential Tests for IELTS"* books and CDs.

Before the Practice Tests

Find a quiet room with a desk, and make sure that you have enough time to complete each test and are not going to be interrupted.

You will need a pen* and two photocopies of the Listening and Reading Test Answer Sheet on page 159, and a photocopy of the Writing Test Answer Sheets on pages 160 and 161. You will also need a cassette or CD player for the Practice Listening Tests, a blank tape or speech recording software for the Practice Speaking Tests, and a watch or clock.

** in the actual IELTS test you must only use pencil when writing on the Listening and Reading Test Answer Sheets.*

During the Practice Tests

Follow each test's instructions carefully, and do not spend longer on the examination than the instructions allow. If you spend longer on the Practice Tests than the instructions allow, you will not get an idea of how well you will perform in the real IELTS examination.

When you have finished the Listening Test, allow yourself 10 minutes to transfer your answers onto the Answer Sheet, give yourself a short break, and then go on to the Reading Test.

At the beginning of each reading passage there are suggestions for how long you should spend on the questions. These are included as a guide only and **do not appear in the actual IELTS test.** You might find, however, that you can answer the questions more quickly for the first two reading passages.

At the end of 60 minutes, stop doing the Reading Test and immediately continue with the Writing Test. Then go on to the Speaking Test, and record your responses on a blank tape or to an audio file on disk.

After the Practice Tests

Check your answers to the Listening and Reading Tests with the Answer Keys on pages 152 and 153. Check your answers to the Writing Tests with the Model Answers on pages 155 to 158. Ask a teacher to look at your Writing Tasks and to listen to the tape you recorded for the Speaking Test in order to estimate your scores.

Then use the Score Interpreter on page 154 to discover how well you did in each Sub-test, and how much extra English study you may need to do to improve your score. In the actual IELTS test, your Overall Band Score is the average of the 4 Sub-test Band Scores.

Once you have completed Practice Test One, and have checked with the Score Interpreter, turn to the Hints Section for help with those questions that caused you difficulty. Refer to the Notes for the Listening and Reading Tests at the end of the tests and online. Then continue the test process with Practice Tests Two, Three and Four on pages 108, 127 and 138 respectively.

PRACTICE LISTENING TEST ONE

SECTION 1 *Questions 1 – 10*

Questions 1 – 4

Choose the correct letter from ***A–C****.*

Example: How do George and Lisa get to the airport?

A by taxi
B by train
C by bus ANSWER **A**

1 What are George and Lisa looking for?

A a newsagent
B a café
C the check-in desk

2 Who do they ask for directions?

A a man sitting down with a hat on
B a man on a trolley
C a man at the check-in desk

3 Where is the FrancAir Check-In desk?

A

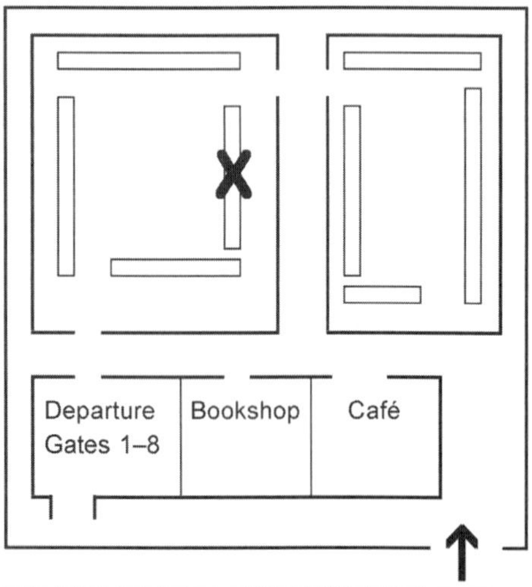

C

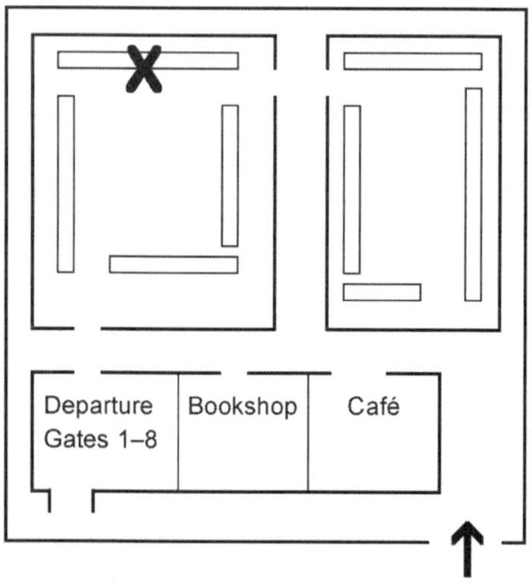

B

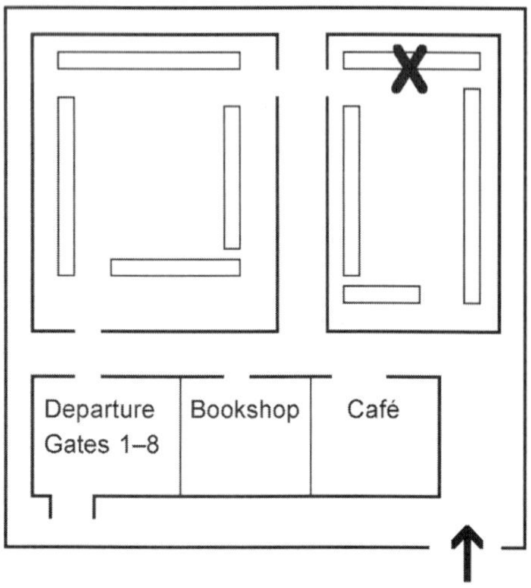

D

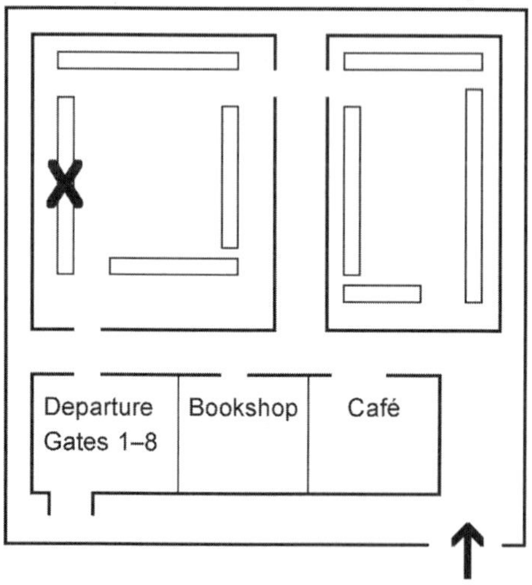

4 What does George want to buy before he catches the plane?

A a book
B coffee
C a couple of things

Questions 5 – 10

Complete the missing information in the form below.

AMOUNT PAID:

(5) ....

Excess Baggage Declaration Certificate

Given Name: ......George..

Family Name: **(6)** ....

Nationality: **(7)** ....

Destination: **(8)** ....

Contact Number: **(9)** ....

Declaration of Contents:

books..

clothes..

(10) ....

SECTION 2 *Questions 11 – 20*

Questions 11 – 13

*Choose **THREE** letters from **A–F**.*

Which **THREE** events have recently taken place?

A an earthquake
B a tsunami
C a giant wave of water
D a chain reaction
E measuring of the earthquake
F airlifting of villagers

Questions 14 & 15

*Choose **TWO** letters from **A–E**.*

Which **TWO** items below describe the previous disaster in Mandaland?

A almost 1000 people killed and large areas devastated
B 2000 buildings destroyed and people killed
C the economy damaged and buildings destroyed
D sea-walls collapsed
E thousands killed and long recovery process

Questions 16 – 20

Complete the notes below.

*Write **NO MORE THAN THREE WORDS** for each answer.*

- ***Building reconstruction***

  – large buildings near the coast including **(16)** ....

  – fast and easy exit to the rooftop is a requirement **(17)** ....

- ***Contact***

  – telephone lines **(18)** .... (so don't phone direct)

  – only contact **(19)** .... on the hotline

- ***Updates***

  – stay tuned for **(20)** ....

SECTION 3 *Questions 21 – 30*

Questions 21 – 25

Write ***NO MORE THAN THREE WORDS*** *for each answer.*

21 Which company does Julie work for?

....

22 What diploma course did Julie take at college?

....

23 What does Julie like most about her job?

....

24 What is Julie's main responsibility when on duty?

....

25 Why does Julie regularly change the time on her watch?

....

Questions 26 – 30

Complete the table below.

Write ***NO MORE THAN THREE WORDS*** *for each answer.*

	Changes	Benefits
seats	**(26)**	to the consumer
entertainment	**(27)**	to the consumer
smoking	restrictions	**(28)** .... **(29)** ....
economy class meals	**(30)**	to the consumer

Table 1. Improvements to Service on British AirWorld

SECTION 4 *Questions 31 – 40*

Questions 31 – 34

*Choose the correct letter from **A–D**.*

31 For each professional area the lecturer discusses

- **A** the professional qualifications necessary.
- **B** the available career opportunities.
- **C** the personal skills needed.
- **D** all of the above

32 The reception desk in a hotel is described as

- **A** impressive at first.
- **B** a switchboard operating system.
- **C** the nervous centre of the hotel.
- **D** the first point of contact with a guest.

33 It is essential in front desk and reception work to have

- **A** a foreign language.
- **B** a good dictionary.
- **C** switchboard operation skills.
- **D** none of the above

34 The lecturer says that a member of a drink and bar service team

- **A** need not have a thorough knowledge of wine.
- **B** must not drink on the job.
- **C** can eventually become a wine maker.
- **D** can eventually manage a cellar dealing only with wines.

Questions 35 – 37

*Choose **THREE** letters from **A–E**.*

Which **THREE** of the following statements are mentioned?

- **A** A love of food is essential in restaurant service.
- **B** You enter restaurant service as a Grade 1 chef.
- **C** The most experienced cook is a Grade A chef.
- **D** It takes time to become a Grade 1 or Chief chef.
- **E** There is a lot of competition in the top hotels.

Questions 38 – 40

*Choose **THREE** letters from **A–E**.*

Which **THREE** items will the lecturer continue with?

- **A** areas of specialisation
- **B** guest relations
- **C** choice of core subject
- **D** answering questions
- **E** introduction to next week's topic

That is the end of Practice Listening Test One.
You now have 10 minutes to transfer your answers to the Answer Sheet.

NOTES ON LISTENING TEST ONE

NUMBERS REFER TO THE QUESTIONS: ***(ANSWERS ON PAGE 152)***

1 George and Lisa are looking for the check-in desk. Notice the background noise on the tape which may be a feature on the actual test tape. You are at a slight advantage if you sit closer to the tape than further away, but unfortunately, this is usually not a decision you can make in the **Test Room.**

2 If they are looking for the check-in desk, they do not ask the man at the desk.

3 This question practically gives the answer to Question 1. Word variables here are **bolded**:

Man: Oh, let me think. I haven't worked here very long. The best way to get there would be to **turn left** at the end here, where the café is, and then **go straight ahead** until you're **opposite** the departure gates entrance...no, no...sorry...um, it might be quicker to **turn right** as soon as you get **past** the café, and **keep going along** the corridor until you come to the sliding doors **at the end**. **On the left**. Yep...that's it. All the check-in counters are in a hall there. I'm pretty sure FrancAir is **directly to your left** as you walk in the hall.

Lisa: Thanks a lot. So, it's **left past** the café, and then **right opposite**...

Man: ...the bookshop.

4 George intends to look around the bookshop but get (i.e. buy) a cup of coffee.

5 The amount George pays is spoken by the desk clerk. Yes, you do need to write the Pound sign (£) on the Answer Sheet.

6–9 Form-filling is generally straightforward, and form answers are given in the order they appear (but this may not be the case with tables and charts).

10 There is only one possible answer to this question. University textbooks are the books that are already mentioned on the form.

11–13 The word *"recently"* in the rubric (instruction) rules out answers B, C and D as possible correct answers. Also, it is clear the intensity of the earthquake was measured because we are told the earthquake was *"6.5 on the Richter scale"*. (See Reading Hint 36 too.)

14–15 The correct answers are obtained by listening carefully for words on the tape which give the **exact** meaning of **all parts** of each choice. In answer choice **A**, only the last part of the choice is correct *"large areas* (were) *devastated"*. In answer **B**, buildings were destroyed but we don't know how many. We do hear the number *"2000"*, but this does not help us get the correct answers.

16 The answer is either *"hotels"* or *"resorts"* or *"hotels and resorts"*. It doesn't matter if you only give <u>one</u> of these as your answer – it still makes sense – but you should make the words plural. It is possible that you could be penalised for not making your answers grammatically correct – especially within clauses and sentences. If teachers tell you it isn't important, they are not telling you how native English-speakers would answer, regardless of whether you will get the right answer in the test or not. It's a bad habit to get into – and you will pay for it sooner or later...in the Writing Test.

17 See the explanation in Basic Hint 10.

18 The question asks for the explanation as to why you can't make a direct call.

19 Some candidates might be tempted to put the telephone number as the answer: 0179–3333. But it says "only contact **(19)** .... on the hotline". The hotline IS the telephone number.

20 The keywords are heard directly. Make sure you observe the three word limit.

21 Julie works for a company called British AirWorld, which is two words (it is written at the bottom of the page), but if you spell it out in three words (or even one word) that would be fine – but you must give your answer in three words or less.

NOTES ON LISTENING TEST ONE CONTINUED

NUMBERS REFER TO THE QUESTIONS:

22–24 These are straightforward questions, the answers to which must obey the three word limit, and, in fact, knowing this helps you because at least one of the answers will have three words Question 22 for instance). Questions 23 and 24 are qualified because they ask you for *"the most"* or *"the main"* something. Julie likes many things about her job, but she chooses one only as the best. Likewise, she has many responsibilities, but only one main responsibility.

25 Julie regularly changes the time on her watch to *"beat jet lag"*, so she says. As you can see, later questions in the test are not so direct. In this case, you have to catch the meaning of the entire answer she gives. The alternative answer *"changing time zones"* is also possible.

26–30 Tables such as this one are common now in the IELTS Listening Test. As long as you use the column and row headings as keywords for the answers, and remember the three word limit, you should have few problems. (See Reading Hint 53 too.)

31 In some multiple choice questions there may be the possibility of all the choices being correct (or none of them). For reasons known only to IELTS, these all or none options are seen less often in more recent tests. We include a few examples in this book because they are excellent for practice, especially since you can replay the tape as many times as you need.

32 The answer to this question is discussed in detail in Hint 30.

33 The keyword here is *"essential"*. Check the tapescript:

Lecturer: The ability to speak more than one language is, naturally, **a great asset** in this job, as is clear diction and familiarity with switchboard operating systems – a technical skill that is taught only in the front desk and reception core option.

Qualifications? Well, ideally, an Associate Diploma with at least one foreign language would be good, but this is **not strictly necessary**. You are encouraged, however, to take up another language.

"A great asset" is good to have but not essential.

34 The lecturer says that a member of a drink and bar service team can eventually do either of two things:

Lecturer: Two of the main avenues open are **cellar management: dealing exclusively with wine** and fortified wines...the, er...selection, purchase, storage, and general upkeep of the hotel cellar, and the other area is working in co-ordination with fine restaurants as a wine manager or consultant.

35–37 You have to choose three items from five, thus two are incorrect. If you have good comprehension of what was said on the tape, you should be able to discover which two items are untrue or not said. You begin as a Grade 3 chef, so answer B is incorrect. There is no mention of a Grade A chef.

38–40 As before, you must eradicate (get rid of) two false items. In this case, the lecturer clearly tells you what he is going to do, but the information comes all at once. The difficulty is with remembering all you have heard.

When practising, be willing to play the recording as many times as you need to hear the right answers, and make good use of the pause button.

Notes for the other Practice Tests in this book are now online at:

http://www.aapress.com.au/101hints/

PRACTICE READING TEST ONE

This is a practice reading test that resembles the International English Language Testing System Reading Test. The test is in three parts. Answer the questions on your Answer Sheet as you progress through the test.

PART 1

Questions 1 – 16

You are advised to spend about 20 minutes on Questions 1 – 16.

Refer to the reading passage on the next page and answer the questions below with the correct ***word, phrase or number****. Write your answers in boxes 1 – 4 on your Answer Sheet.*

Figure 1. Sydney – Facts and Figures

HISTORY

Example: 1788	– First Fleet arrives from England
1933	– Harbour Bridge completed
1956	– Olympic Games held in Melbourne
1988	– Bicentenary celebrations
2000	– Olympic Games held in Sydney

SIZE

Population (2010):	– **(1)** .... million
Area (city & suburbs):	– **(2)** .... square km
Sydney Harbour:	– 57 square km

LOCATION (air distance in km)

	Sydney	Jakarta	Taipei	Hong Kong	Seoul	Tokyo
Tokyo	***7825***	5925	1050	2882	570	–
Seoul	***8332***	5160	732	1040	–	
Hong Kong	***7371***	1602	768	–		
Taipei	***7263***	4392	–			
Jakarta	**(3)**	–				

CLIMATE

Summer:

Mean average temperature	– 21.7° C
Average hours of sunshine (per day)	– 14.5 hours

Winter:

Mean average temperature	– 12.6° C
Average hours of sunshine (per day)	– **(4)** ....

MAJOR FEATURES

Harbour Bridge (height):	– 134 metres
Sydney Tower (height):	– 305 metres
Opera House (cost):	– $85 million
Monorail (length):	– 3600 metres
Sydney Harbour Tunnel (length):	– 2300 metres
No. of surf beaches:	– 34

Studying in Sydney, Australia – An Overview for International Students

Paragraph (i)

Australia has been a popular choice for thousands of international students over many years. Australia's universities and colleges have become increasingly recognised overseas for their exceptionally high standard. In addition, Australia is conveniently close to South-East Asia (Jakarta, the capital of Australia's closest Asian neighbour, Indonesia, is only 5506 kilometres from Sydney). Revised entry procedures for overseas students have made it possible for an increasing number to study in Australia. Sydney, the largest Australian city, is the principal port of call for international airlines with services operating to Australia.

Paragraph (ii)

Named after an ex-Governor of New South Wales, Sydney is the State's capital city. Located on the south-east coast of Australia in the temperate zone, it enjoys a mild climate, averaging 14.5 hours of sunshine per day in summer and 10.25 hours in winter. It is also the largest, oldest, and perhaps most beautifully situated city in Australia. First established by the British as a convict settlement in 1788, it is a modern cosmopolitan city that has developed into one of the nation's major industrial, business, and manufacturing centres.

Paragraph (iii)

Sydney is home to nearly 4.9 million people (as of 2010). The suburbs reach out from the city centre and harbour some 55 km to the north, 35 km to the west and 30 km to the south, creating a metropolitan area of about 3000 square kilometres. The 57 square kilometre harbour is one of the largest in the world, and famous for the unmistakable 134 metre high arch of the Harbour Bridge and the graceful sails of the Opera House. It is a busy waterway with ferries, freighters, hydrofoils and pleasure craft.

Paragraph (iv)

Not far from the city centre are the attractive old residential suburbs of Balmain, Glebe, and Paddington, where many people live in smart terraced houses. Art galleries, pubs, and restaurants abound in the cosy streets that tend to be quite narrow, whereas the suburbs surrounding the city's colleges and universities consist mainly of family homes and multi-unit blocks - an ideal situation for students looking for a homestay, or to rent. Sydney's newer suburbs now have a large multicultural population, and local shopping centres reflect the influences of many cultures.

Paragraph (v)

Sydney is home to the State Art Gallery of New South Wales, the State Conservatorium of Music, the Australian Opera, the Sydney Dance Company, and the Australian Ballet. The world-class Sydney Symphony Orchestra offers superb classical music all year round. Local theatre is innovative and well supported, and large-scale overseas productions tour regularly.

Paragraph (vi)

As well as scores of cinemas and theatres throughout the city and suburbs, there are numerous clubs which appeal to people of all ages, and cater for all tastes. Pubs are the venue for smaller modern bands, while the big-name popular music artists, both local and international, attract capacity audiences at the huge Entertainment Centre in the heart of the city.

Dining Out

In Sydney, a vast array of ethnic and local restaurants can be found to suit all palates and pockets. In summer, café patrons often sit outside at tables under umbrellas, and enjoy the passing parade of shoppers. Students who prefer to cook at home can choose from several large weekend markets, where fresh fruit, fish, and vegetables may be bought more cheaply than at the local supermarket. Sydney also has its own Chinatown.

Shopper's Delight

In the heart of the city are several big department stores linked by enclosed over-the-street crossings and underground walkways. Most noticeable are the towering Centrepoint complex and the Queen Victoria Building, both containing many shopping arcades, coffee shops and restaurants. Out of town, in the suburbs, there are huge regional shopping centres. At the weekend markets, bargains can be had when shopping for clothing as well as for a wide range of assorted goods.

Sporting Facilities

Australia is recognised as one of the most sports-conscious nations in the world. Sydney boasts an impressive number of facilities for all types of indoor and outdoor sporting activities. Wherever one goes, there are golf courses, cricket pitches, football ovals, tennis and squash courts, and, of course, indoor and outdoor swimming pools. Avid ice-skating and ten-pin bowling fans will find that these activities are also popular and inexpensive.

Conclusion

Whatever a student is interested in, it is certain to be available somewhere in Sydney. Outside the colleges and universities the scope for filling the leisure hours is enormous, while on campus the choice is equally varied.

Questions 5 – 9

*Choose the most suitable heading from the list of headings below for the first six paragraphs (**I – VI**) of the reading passage. Write your answers in boxes 5 – 9 on your Answer Sheet.*

List of Headings

A	Sydney – Location and History
B	Residential Inner-City Suburbs
C	Australia – Attractive to International Students
D	Entertainment for Young and Old
E	The Harbour and Surrounding Suburbs
F	The Cultural Climate

Example: Paragraph (i) ..C..

5 Paragraph (ii) ....

6 Paragraph (iii) ....

7 Paragraph (iv) ....

8 Paragraph (v) ....

9 Paragraph (vi) ....

Questions 10 – 16

Use the information given in the reading passage.

Write	***TRUE***	*if the statement is true*
	FALSE	*if the statement is false*
	NOT GIVEN	*if the information is not given in the text.*

Write your answers in boxes 10 – 16 on your Answer Sheet.

Answer

Example: Sydney is a popular destination for overseas students. TRUE

10 Sydney was first established as a settlement for convicted criminals. ....

11 Sydney Harbour is the largest in the world. ....

12 The streets of Paddington are not very wide and contain houses arranged in rows. ....

13 The Entertainment Centre is only for international popular music artists who attract large audiences. ....

14 There is now a greater variety of restaurants to choose from in Sydney than in the past. ....

15 Some department stores in Sydney are joined by walkways above and below the ground. ....

16 Australians are sports-minded people, but this is not realised by the rest of the world. ....

Part 2

Questions 17 – 29

You are advised to spend about 20 minutes on Questions 17 – 29.

WORKING IN AN ENGLISH-SPEAKING COUNTRY – A GUIDE TO BEHAVIOUR

Most newly-arrived immigrants to a foreign country will have thought long and hard about how to support themselves before they leave home. The majority will have jobs in place that have been secured as a means to be allowed into the country. Modern economies are always acquiring the skills of individuals who were born overseas but want to start a new life in another culture.

The most obvious requirement for immigrant workers in countries such as the U.K., Canada, the U.S, Australia and New Zealand is to speak the language; not only so they can perform their tasks to the standards required of them, but that they may take full advantage of the opportunities the workplace might provide.

Proficiency in a language does not end with a score in a language test. Sharpening one's English skills – on a continual basis – is an essential part of "getting on" at work. And, as many "newbies" quickly realise, it is often the colloquial language that has them "foxed". A smart worker will purchase a dictionary of colloquial words and slang – and especially idioms – for the particular country they are living in. It is unfortunate, but English learnt at school will no longer be enough to fully grasp what is being spoken around you.

The English language is not the only obstacle to communication. Even native speakers who were not born in the country they find themselves working in may notice that cultural barriers can get in the way of being accepted in the workplace. Since sport is a universal way of helping to break down those barriers, it pays immigrant workers to quickly take up an interest in the sports their co-workers regularly follow. Perhaps surprisingly, in some English-speaking countries, women can be even more fanatical than men about their favourite team.

If sport is not the prevailing discussion in the office or factory, it will be wise to work out what else "makes the other man or woman tick". By this we mean taking note of what one's workmates are thinking and doing apart from work. The better you know the people you work with – your boss included – the more likely you are to get on well with them. And in the final analysis, forming fruitful relationships is key to your success at work.

Naturally, one of the most important factors for success is to be competent at what you are asked to do. If you make a mistake, don't try to cover it up or make excuses – or, worse still – blame someone else; instead, accept that you are on a learning curve and mistakes will inevitably occur. Listen carefully to any advice you are given and do your best not to repeat the same mistake twice.

Another often overlooked factor in performing well at your new job, especially if you are an immigrant, is time management. Everyone at work must learn to manage his or her time

1. Unpunctuality
2. Argumentativeness
3. Laziness
4. Losing your temper
5. Intolerance
6. Harrassment
7. Being aloof or superior
8. Gossipping
9. Making accusations
10. Blaming others

Results of a survey into the Top 10 Ways to Offend at Work

well, but it is all too easy to perform tasks either too slowly or too quickly depending on the work culture in your own country. This is a mistake. If you work too slowly, because that is how things are done in your workplace at home, then you will inevitably find yourself unappreciated by your boss and others, regardless of how well you actually do the job. And if you complete your assignments too soon, and continually show everyone else up, your co-workers might resent you even more.

Lastly, it is a good idea to learn to sometimes "bite your lip". There will be occasions when you will want to say what you know you should not and you will have to learn restraint. Take our advice and keep some things to yourself. In fact, if you are wise, you will learn to give a wide berth to those two divisive topics "religion" and "politics" altogether.

Colloquialisms, slang terms and idioms:

getting on	– succeeding; being accepted
a newbie	– a person new to something
to be foxed	– to be puzzled
to bite your lip	– to stop yourself saying something you might regret
to show someone up	– to do something which makes someone ashamed or embarrassed
to give a wide berth to	– to keep far away from someone or something

---

Questions 17 – 21

*Choose the correct letter from **A–D**. Write your answers in boxes 17 – 21 on your Answer Sheet.*

Example: Most new arrivals in English-speaking countries have

A a lot of money.
B little or no English.
C higher skills than native speakers.
D jobs to go to. ANSWER **D**

17 Language proficiency is

A the result of taking a test.
B likely to "fox" new immigrants.
C a never-ending requirement in the workplace.
D colloquial words, slang and idioms.

18 Cultural barriers affect

A all immigrants.
B women more than men in the workplace.
C the way in which workers are treated.
D all of the above

19 Immigrant workers are encouraged to

- **A** follow a popular sport.
- **B** take an interest in their co-workers.
- **C** relate well to others.
- **D** all of the above

20 When asked, people tend to

- **A** be offended by workers who are unsociable.
- **B** dislike immigrants who make excuses.
- **C** dislike immigrants who repeat mistakes.
- **D** agree that immigrants are unpunctual.

21 According to the author it is a good idea to

- **A** work at your own pace.
- **B** not talk too loudly.
- **C** avoid discussing controversial topics.
- **D** none of the above

Questions 22 – 29

Read the following memo and complete the summary on the following page.

Write your answers in boxes 22 – 29 on your Answer Sheet.

MEMO TO ALL BRANDON WEBB EMPLOYEES

Date: September 25th
From: Jack Zeno, CEO

RE: Updated health and fitness policy

It has come to my attention that existing company policy guidelines regarding the fitness level of our employees are not being followed by all staff. As you are aware, it is a condition of your employment – working for the top Health & Lifestyle company in the country – that your level of health and fitness be continually monitored by our in-house medical practioners and maintained by our personal trainers. As of December 1st, it will no longer be excusable for any staff member under 60 years of age to avoid Monday morning gym classes without a medical examination.

Additionally, all staff will now be required to fill out timesheets to show they have adhered to the minimum number of hours of training per week according to their employment contracts. It will be the responsibility of department managers to collect these timesheets at the end of each week and ensure that the work is being done to the satisfaction of the trainer in charge.

I recognise that our staff are almost without exception dedicated to living healthy lifestyles, but it is acknowledged that certain individuals have recently and regrettably transgressed the law. Consequently, Brandon Webb has voluntarily agreed to impose mandatory random drug-testing of all staff for a trial period of two years to commence early next year.

Although these changes will require a high degree of co-operation and commitment, I have no doubt that we will all benefit from living up to our obligations, not just to the company, but to ourselves, and that we will continue to provide our clients – and I refer especially to our young sporting clients – with the role models they deserve both on and off the field and in and out of the gym. Further details regarding the new policy will be announced in the coming weeks.

Thank you, Jack Zeno

Questions 22 – 29

*Choose the correct **word or phrase** from those given in the box below the summary.*

Write your answers in boxes 22 – 29 on your Answer Sheet.

*Note: **you may use each word or phrase once only.***

New Health and Fitness Policy

Company policy will change as of ***Example:*** ...December 1st..... . Not all of Brandon Webb's employees are currently maintaining their **(22)** .... Employment contracts require that all staff have their health and fitness levels regularly **(23)** .... by the company's own doctors. Under new policy **(24)** .... , it will become **(25)** .... for staff who do not **(26)** .... the Monday gym class to undergo a medical examination. However, this does not apply to staff over 60 years old.

Department managers will now ensure that employees fill out timesheets every week to **(27)** .... that they have **(28)** .... the minimum training required of them. In addition, random drug-testing will come into being for a trial period of two years.

The changes will mean staff will need to work together and remain committed to setting good **(29)** .... to the young sportspeople they serve.

check	avoid	mandatory	contracts
assessed	December 1st	complete	guidelines
necessity	undertaken	attend	fitness levels
healthy lives	role models	examples	proof

Part 3

Questions 30 – 40

You are advised to spend about 20 minutes on Questions 30 – 40.

THE *QUIK-FRY*™ ELECTRONIC WOK

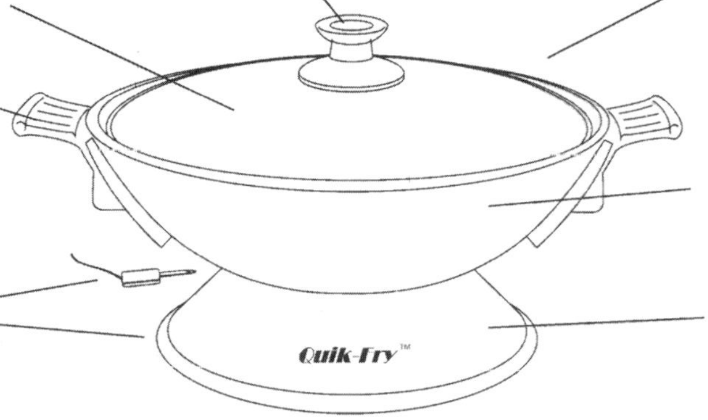

Instructions for Use:

It is most important that you read this instruction booklet carefully before first using the *Quik-Fry*™ wok. Until you become familiar with the product, we advise that you keep the booklet handy and refer to it when required.

IMPORTANT SAFEGUARDS

In order to prevent the risk of electric shock, DO NOT IMMERSE the cord or the probe in water or any other liquid.

Whenever the wok is used near children, it is essential that close supervision takes place. Never leave the appliance unattended if in use.

Before disassembling the wok for cleaning, SWITCH OFF AND REMOVE THE PLUG from the power source.

DO NOT USE THE *Quik-Fry*™ WOK OUTDOORS.

Avoid touching hot surfaces; instead use the heat-resistant handles on the wok or the heat-resistant plastic knob on top of the glass lid.

DO NOT COVER the *Quik-Fry*™ wok with the lid while using it to deep fry foods. Failure to comply will cause condensation to drip onto the oil and lead to splattering.

DO NOT OPERATE NEAR HOT SURFACES such as electric hotplates, gas burners or in a heated oven.

DO NOT ATTEMPT REPAIR of the *Quik-Fry*™ wok. If the cord becomes damaged, or if the appliance is malfunctioning, do not operate. Return the appliance to the nearest authorised service centre for repair. DO NOT OPEN THE BASE OR TOUCH THE ELECTRICAL COMPONENTS INSIDE. Tampering with the base will void warranty.

Manufactured for operation only from a standard domestic power source.

How to Use the *Quik-Fry*™ Electronic Wok:

Be sure to season the wok before using it for the first time. Assemble the wok and heat to the highest setting (6). Rub the non-stick inner surface of the wok with 1 tablespoon of oil. Use thick paper towelling, being very careful to avoid contact with the hot surface.

Cooking Methods:

Cooking Method	Heat Required	Food Preparation	Action Required	Time
Stir Frying [1 2]	very high	cut into uniform dice or small shreds	use tossing motion in a small amount of oil [3]	2–3 minutes
Braising	very high	as for stir frying	add liquid after stir frying, then simmer until cooked	5–10 minutes
Deep Frying [4 5 6]	high [7]	wipe moisture from food [8]	cook only a few pieces at a time [9]	< 5 minutes
Shallow Frying	high [7]	pre-cook food	as for deep frying, but use only 2 tbsp of oil	< 5 minutes

[1] blot meat dry to avoid stewing of food in excess liquid
[2] add ingredients in order of length of time required for cooking
[3] use up to 1 tbsp of oil only
[4] never use more than 6 cups of oil (maximum depth - 5cm)
[5] allow oil to cool before removing from wok
[6] never cover with the lid
[7] enough for the oil to simmer without smoking
[8] to avoid splattering
[9] to ensure crispness

Questions 30 – 34

Answer the following questions with the correct ***words or phrases*** *from the text. Write your answers in boxes 30 – 34 on your Answer Sheet.*

Write ***NO MORE THAN THREE WORDS*** *for each answer.*

Example: What is the first thing you must do before using the *Quik-Fry*™ wok?

........read the instructions........

30 What reason would you have to take the *Quik-Fry*™ wok apart?

....

31 What type of electrical power source is the wok designed for?

....

32 What will definitely happen if you open the base?

....

33 After assembly, and before your initial cooking session what should you do?

....

34 Which method of frying involves reducing liquid to ensure safety?

....

Question 35

*Choose the correct letter from **A–D**. Write your answer in box 35 on your Answer Sheet.*

35 The wok must never be operated

A by hand.
B by children.
C outdoors.
D all of the above

Questions 36 – 39

*Complete the following notes. Write your answers in boxes 36 – 39 on your Answer Sheet. Write **NO MORE THAN THREE WORDS** for each answer.*

- The **(36)** .... cooking method requires food to be cooked twice.
- The lid should never cover the wok when deep frying in order to prevent **(37)** ....
- The **(38)** .... of the wok make it ideal for deep frying.
- The least amount of oil is used when **(39)** ....

Question 40

Write your answer in box 40 on your Answer Sheet.

40 Which thorough cooking method requires pieces of food ready for cooking to be of similar size?

....

That is the end of Practice Reading Test One.

NOTES ON READING TEST ONE

NUMBERS REFER TO THE QUESTIONS: ***(ANSWERS ON PAGE 152)***

1 *"Sydney is home to nearly 4.9 million people (as of 2010)." (para. (iii): line 1).*

2 *"...creating a metropolitan area of about 3000 square kilometres." (para. (iii): lines 1–3).*

3 *"...Indonesia, is only 5506 kilometres from Sydney." (para. (i): line 4).*

4 *"...a mild climate, averaging... ...10.25 hours in winter." (para. (ii): lines 2–3).*

5–9 See Basic Hint 9 and Reading Hints 45 and 46.

10 See Reading Hints 43 and 46.

11 See Basic Hint 11.

12 See Reading Hint 48.

13–14 See Basic Hint 11 and Reading Hint 44.

15–16 See Reading Hint 49.

17 *"Sharpening one's English skills – on a continual basis...is...essential..." (para. (iii): lines 2–3).*

18 *"...cultural barriers can get in the way of being accepted in the workplace." (para. (iv): lines 4–6).*

19 Para. 4 advises to follow a sport; Para. 5 advises to take an interest in others and relate well.

20 The Top 10 list gives survey results which show that unsociable behaviour is likely to offend. It is not a survey about attitudes towards immgrants in the workplace. See Reading Hint 54 too.

21 *"...give a wide berth to those two divisive topics "religion" and "politics" altogether." (para. 8: line 6–8).*

22–29 See Reading Hint 55.

30 *"detachable base and probe for easy cleaning"* Check the diagram for information and be sure to comply with the instruction to use NO MORE THAN THREE WORDS in your answer.

31 *"Manufactured for operation only from a standard domestic power source." (last line of safeguards notice).* Again, comply with the number of words restriction.

32 *"Tampering with the base will void warranty." (last paragraph of safeguards notice).* This will definitely happen; electric shock or any other consequence may happen only.

33 *"Be sure to season the wok before using it for the first time." (first para. of page 102).*

34 Deep frying is the only cooking method referring to a safety issue: *(column 3 – row 4 and footnote 8).*

35 "DO NOT USE THE *Quik-Fry*™ WOK OUTDOORS." *(Fourth safeguard).* Even though children should not use the wok, the reading passage does not say this.

36 The answer to this question is found by consulting the table: *"add liquid after stir frying, then simmer until cooked" (column 4 – row 3).*
Shallow frying is correct too: *"pre-cook food" (column 3 – row 4).* Only one answer is required.

37 *"DO NOT COVER the Quik-Fry™ wok with the lid while using it to deep fry foods. Failure to comply will cause condensation to drip onto the oil and lead to splattering." (Sixth safeguard and footnote 8).*

38 *"tall sides make the Quik-Fry™ wok perfect for deep frying" (Sixth safeguard).* Check the diagram.

39 The answer to this question is found by consulting the table: *"use tossing motion in a small amount of oil".* Footnote 3 confirms "stir frying" as the answer.

40 Braising is the only thorough cooking method *"5–10 minutes"* requiring the food to be *"cut into uniform dice or small shreds"* as for stir frying.

Notes for the other Practice Tests in this book are now online at:

http://www.aapress.com.au/101hints/

UPDATES: http://www.aapress.com.au/updates/

PRACTICE WRITING TEST ONE

Writing Task 1

You should spend about 20 minutes on this task.

You have recently moved into a new flat. Unfortunately, you lost some money the other day, and cannot afford to pay next month's rent when it is due.

Write a letter to the landlord or landlady. In your letter

- ***explain the situation***
- ***say that you will will pay when your parents send you the money***
- ***mention that there are some problems with the flat.***

Write at least 150 words.

You do NOT need to write any addresses.

Begin your letter as follows:

Dear Sir or Madam,

Writing Task 2

You should spend about 40 minutes on this task.

Write about the following topic:

Research is an essential part of completing assignments.

Suggest some good places to obtain useful information.

Give reasons for your answer and include any relevant examples from your own knowledge or experience.

Write at least 250 words.

That is the end of Practice Writing Test One.

☺ PRACTICE SPEAKING TEST ONE

Practise answering the questions below, giving answers that are at least one or two sentences long or more. If possible, practise with another person – taking it in turns to answer the same question – and compare your responses.

(Please note that the following questions are only a guide to the type of questions you might be asked in the actual test. For practice purposes we include more questions than you are likely to be asked.)

Part 1

Come in and sit down over here. First, let me take a look at your passport.

... it's required for security purposes.

Thank you. My name is (interviewer's name). What would you like me to call you?

You come from (your country). Tell me about your country.

Do you live with your family? Why or why not?

Is your family large or small?

What do your parents do?

Would you like to do the same job as your mother/father?

(If you live overseas...) How long have you been in (your host country)?

Tell me about your accommodation in (your host country).

Do you work at the moment? Tell me about the work you do.

Have you ever had any other jobs?

Are you studying now? Describe the course you are studying.

Tell me about your teacher or your boss.

What are your main interests?

What (other) indoor activities do you enjoy?

What do you like to do on the weekend?

Are there any special places you like to go when you go out?

Do you have any English-speaking friends?

How would you describe your lifestyle?

Part 2

Thank you. Now I'd like you to take this card. I want you to speak for one or two minutes about the topic written on this card. Follow the instructions. I will give you one minute to prepare before I ask you to give your talk. You can make some notes to help you if you wish. All right?

> Describe an organised event that you have attended (for example: a concert, a show, a sports match etc.).
>
> You should include in your answer:
>
> when you attended the event and what you saw
>
> where the event was held
>
> why you chose to see this event
>
> ...and what you remember most about the event.

(follow-up questions)

Did you go to the concert with anyone? What did they think of it?

Are there any kinds of concerts or events that you wouldn't like to go to? Why?

Part 3

Thank you. Please give me back the card. Entertainment is a very important part of our lives. Most people listen to the radio or watch television, and young people love dance parties.

How did people entertain themselves before these things came into existence?

Do you think radio and television has had a positive effect on the world?

Has television stopped family members from communicating with each other?

Outdoor concerts and sports events are very popular. But violence at these events is on the increase. Why is this do you think?

Will people stop attending sports events in the future if they become too dangerous?

What should authorities do to prevent violence taking place at sports events?

Is there too much violence on television and in the cinema these days?

Does violence on television or on video contribute to violence in society?

Do you think video games are too violent for children?

That is the end of the interview. Thank you and goodbye.

That is the end of Practice Speaking Test One.
Check your answers to Practice Test One with the Answer Key on page 152.

PRACTICE LISTENING TEST TWO

SECTION 1 *Questions 1 – 10*

Questions 1 – 2

*Choose the correct letter from **A–D**.*

Example: Jon has to be at the college

A tomorrow
B this morning
C this afternoon
D next year   ANSWER **C**

1 Which timetable does Ewa decide upon for Friday?

A	B	C	D
MORNING:	**MORNING:**	**MORNING:**	**MORNING:**
Reading Skills	Vocabulary	Writing Skills	Grammar
Writing Skills	Speaking Skills	Reading Skills	Reading Skills
Pronunciation	Reading Skills	Grammar	Writing Skills
AFTERNOON:	**AFTERNOON:**	**AFTERNOON:**	**AFTERNOON:**
Listening Practice	Grammar	Listening Practice	No Electives
Speaking Skills	Writing Skills	Vocabulary	

2 What time does Ewa's special English class start?

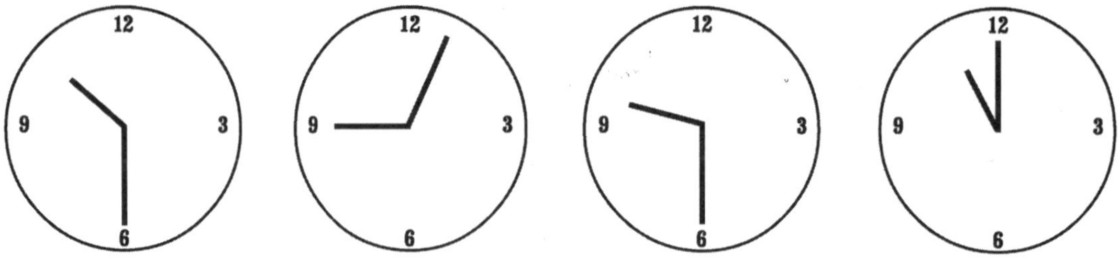

A **B** **C** **D**

Questions 3 – 5

Write ***NO MORE THAN THREE WORDS*** *for each answer.*

3 How long has Jon been studying at the college?

....

4 Why is the Student Centre large?

....

5 Name a club that Jon belongs to at the college:

....

Questions 6 – 10

Complete the missing information in the form below.

NATIONAL BUSINESS COLLEGE

ORIENTEERING CLUB: REGISTRATION FORM

Given Name:		Ewa
Family Name:	**(6)**	....
Nationality:	**(7)**	....
Student Number:	**(8)**	....
Present Course:		Advanced Programming
Years of Experience:		two years
Blood Type:		A +
Day of Session:	**(9)**	Sat AM / PM Sun AM / PM
Home Phone No.:	**(10)**	....

SECTION 2 *Questions 11 – 20*

Questions 11 – 15

Complete the sentences below.

11 Estonia is only .... square km in size.

12 Estonia is about .... the size of Scotland.

13 The percentage of native Estonians is ....

14 Tallinn is the .... city of Estonia.

15 Tallinn is located in the .... of the country.

Questions 16 – 20

Complete the summary below.

Write ***NO MORE THAN THREE WORDS*** *for each answer.*

Estonia is a small, flat country in Europe dotted with numerous islands and lakes. The manufacture of agricultural machinery and **(16)** .... are the major industries, with **(17)** .... and vegetables the main **(18)** ....

Once a part of Greater Russia, the nation is now an independent **(19)** .... Although many people speak Russian, the official language is Estonian. The weather in Estonia in summer is **(20)** ....

SECTION 3 *Questions 21 – 30*

Questions 21 – 26

Write ***NO MORE THAN THREE WORDS*** *for each answer.*

21 Who does Anna currently work for?

....

22 Which area did Anna originally wish to work in?

....

23 How does Anna describe her job?

....

24 What showed Anna she was doing the wrong course?

....

25 To increase her English vocabulary, what does Anna listen to?

....

26 According to Anna, what do you need to increase your energy?

....

Questions 27 – 30

Complete the table below.

Anna's Future Plans	short-term	long-term
council	gain **(27)**	~
hospital	**(28)** .... than present job	~
own business	~	open an **(29)** .... providing **(30)** ....
return home	~	improve the diet of my people

SECTION 4 *Questions 31 – 40*

Questions 31 – 34

The speaker discuss the computer lab rules. Classify the rules below:

Write ***A*** *if the rule prevents problems occurring*
B *if the rule assists with machine maintenance*
C *if there is no given reason for the rule.*

31 Rule 1: ....
32 Rule 2: ....
33 Rule 3: ....
34 Rule 4: ....

Questions 35 – 36

Choose the correct letter from ***A–C****.*

35 The Macintosh computer network

A can only be used by second and third year students.
B can be used by some first year students.
C is reserved for third year student use.

36 The computer lab opens on weekdays at

A 8:00 a.m.
B 9:00 a.m.
C 3:30 p.m.

Questions 37 – 39

Choose ***THREE*** *letters from* ***A–F****.*

Which **THREE** methods of obtaining help are mentioned?

A on screen
B consult a manual
C use your computer lab card
D ask a lab assistant
E ask your tutor
F online support

Question 40

40 How many computer lab rules does the speaker discuss?

....

That is the end of Practice Listening Test Two.
You now have 10 minutes to transfer your answers to the Answer Sheet.

PRACTICE READING TEST TWO

This is a practice reading test that resembles the International English Language Testing System Reading Test. The test is in three parts. Answer the questions on your Answer Sheet as you progress through the test.

Part 1

Questions 1 – 14

You are advised to spend about 20 minutes on Questions 1 – 14.

Refer to the reading passage on the next page "The Recreation and Sports Association" and answer the questions below. Write your answers in boxes 1 – 6 on your Answer Sheet.

Write ***NO MORE THAN THREE WORDS OR A NUMBER*** *for each answer.*

Example: What two main types of activity are promoted by the RSA?

....Recreation and Sports..

1 How many clubs are there on the college campus?

....

2 What does a member of the Recreation and Aquatic Centres need to show when requested?

....

3 Do students pay member rates for facilities at the Centres?

....

4 At what time does the Recreation Centre usually open on public holidays?

....

5 How many netball courts are available for hire?

....

6 What telephone number should you ring for general information?

....

THE RECREATION AND SPORTS ASSOCIATION

Welcome! The Recreation and Sports Association (RSA) provides recreational and sporting activities for students, staff, and the community. Students and staff have access to a wide variety of programmes ranging from meditation to whitewater canoeing. Our Association offers all students and staff an opportunity to forget the rigours of college life, and involve themselves in healthy and enjoyable activities.

The RSA continues to forge links with the community through auxiliary membership to any of the 25 clubs on campus, or access to our many facilities including the Aquatic Centre, Synthetic Hockey Centre, and the Recreation Centre.

Membership All students and staff are automatically members of the Recreation and Aquatic Centres. Membership entitles students and staff to all facilities and programmes at member rates. In addition, members are eligible to join any of our constituent clubs.

Types of Membership Cost

Students: Paid from enrolment fees		*Staff*: Nil	*Auxiliary*: $90
Graduates: $76		*Life*: After 6 years of fees, $15	

Membership cards must be produced upon request, or non-member rates will apply.

Recreation Facilities The Recreation Centre comprises the Indoor Recreation Centre, the Aquatic Centre, and a variety of playing fields and tennis courts.

Hours of Operation

During Session	Monday / Thursday	–	7.30 a.m. – 11 p.m.
	Friday	–	7.30 a.m. – 9 p.m.
Out of Session	Saturday - Sunday	–	8.30 a.m. – 6 p.m.
Public Holidays	(unless otherwise notified)	–	9.30 a.m. – 6 p.m.

The Recreation and Sports Association now has

- **new pool changing rooms**
- **an expanded sports lounge**
- **2 new cricket nets**
- **4 new tennis courts**
- **a new aerobics room**

The Squash Centre has

- **4 glass-backed squash courts.**

Bookings can be made by telephone (9371 - 7689), or by calling in person to the Centre.

The Sports Hall is a multi-purpose facility catering for a broad range of indoor activities including:

- **Badminton** (6 courts)
- **Basketball** (2 courts)
- **Volleyball** (2 courts)
- **Hockey** (1 court)
- **Soccer** (1 court)
- **Netball** (2 undersize, 1 international court)

Aerobics / Conferences: Space is available for long-term hire or on a casual basis, depending on your requirements. Call into the Recreation Centre and see the range of activities available.

Gymnasium: The Unigym is located upstairs in the Recreation Centre. A variety of equipment is available for the weight and circuit-training enthusiast.

Sports Lounge: The Lounge is available on a casual basis for students to sit and have lunch when unoccupied. It can be booked for parties, conferences, lectures, or any other activity suited to moderate-sized groups. This facility is utilised by some of our sporting clubs as a canteen/kiosk area, but can be adapted to suit a variety of uses. It also links to the pool area for an extensive "Pool Party/ BBQ", if you desire. Why not organise a party, BBQ, or social function? The Lounge caters for up to 100 people. All are welcome.

Outdoor Facilities

Aquatic Centre: This magnificent 50 metre outdoor heated aquatic facility is available to anyone. Come and see for yourself! See the Aquatic Centre section of this booklet for details of operating hours and programmes.

Hockey Centre: The region's first synthetic hockey surface is a sight to behold! Gone are the problems of being washed out for half the season. Available for a variety of uses, including competitions, training, and lunchtime sports.

Tennis Courts: The **new** tennis courts are finally here! Two magnificent artificial courts excellent for serve/volley exponents, or two synpave courts ideal for baseliners. All 4 courts are available for hire, and bookings can be made at the Recreation Centre reception. Excellent value for money on permanent bookings.

Ovals and Cricket Nets: The Recreation Centre takes **all** bookings for use of the ovals. We currently have 3 ovals for a variety of uses, including club training sessions, lunchtime sports, and casual student use. The 2 new cricket nets mean we now have a total of 5 practice nets available to all.

Other Information

The Aquatic Centre is a multi-use facility providing pool space for a large variety of university and community sporting and recreational groups. Although we do provide for these alternative sporting groups, we also cater for the lap swimmer, recreational swimmer, and those who just want to laze around, or simply stand and splash in the water. Lap swimmers have priority over all other swimmers, and can always be assured of available swimming lanes. The best times to swim laps are 8.30 a.m. – 12.00 p.m., 3.00 p.m. – 4.00 p.m., and 6.00 p.m. – 7.30 p.m. However, at times the pool may be completely booked.

Please read the signs in the pool passage, and take a copy of the "Timetable of Pool Use". The Recreation and Sports Association's own newspaper – *Sports Unillustrated* – will keep you up-to-date on any changes to timetables.

For further enquiries phone: 9371 –4356 during office hours.

Questions 7 – 14

Complete the student's notes below with information from the reading passage. Write your answers in boxes 7 – 14 on your Answer Sheet.

Notes on the Recreation and Sports Centre

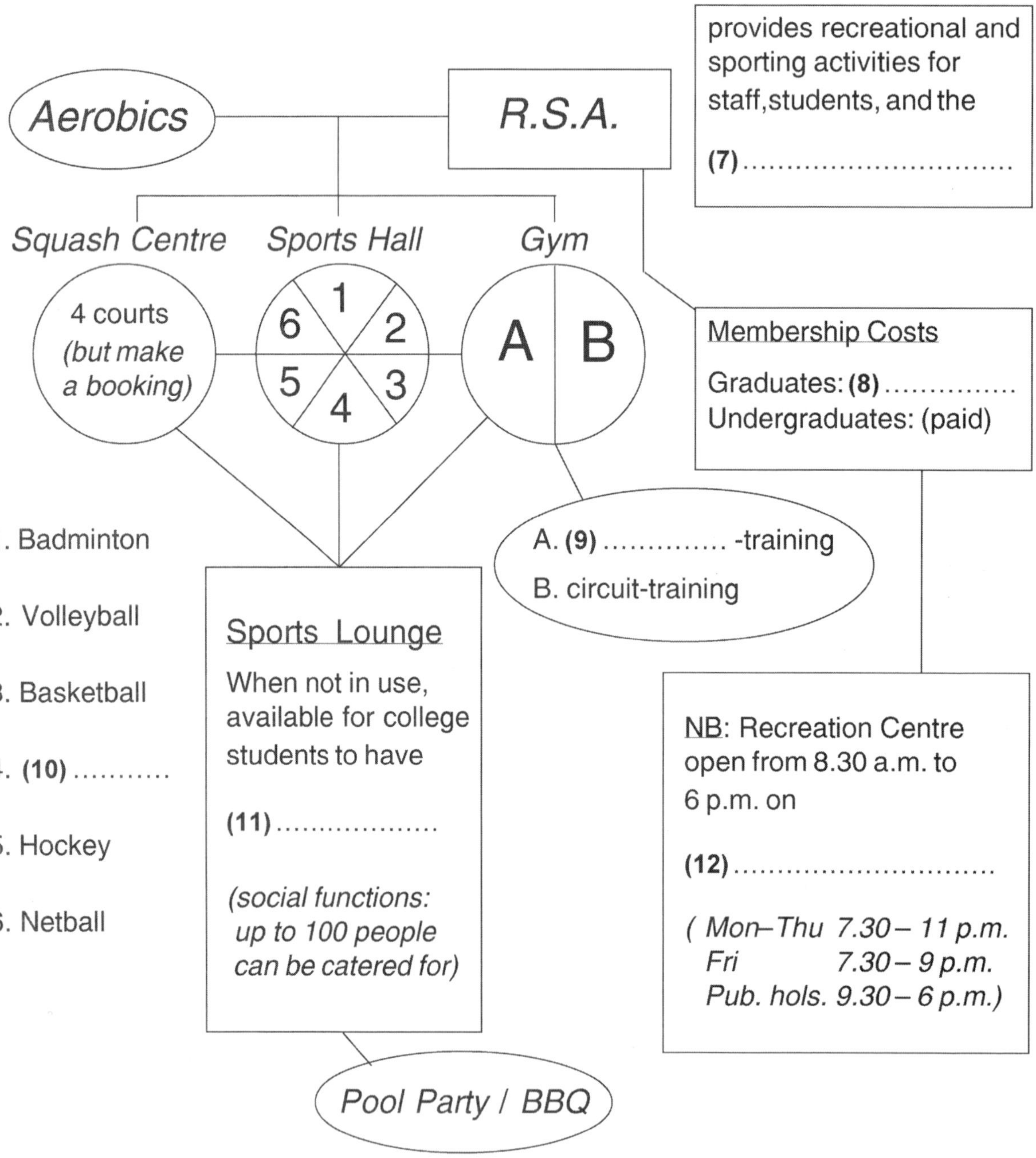

- Lap swimmers are always provided with **(13)** ....
- The Sports Association's newspaper has current information about the **(14)** ....

Part 2

Questions 15 – 27

You are advised to spend about 20 minutes on Questions 15 – 27.

JOB SEARCH ASSISTANCE *from the Human Resources Dept.*

Economic woes

The recent downturn in the economy has meant that some of our employees will soon be seeking employment elsewhere. Our company is committed to assisting staff in the search for a new position whenever and wherever we can. Please read the following tips and tools for effective job searching:

1. Be organised.

First and foremost make sure you are planning your attack on the job market in an organised and professional manner. Apply your talents to the cause for a fixed minimum number of hours per day. Keep records of everything you do. Obtain as much information as possible from reliable sources online and off, and be sure to keep a job search diary. Do not procrastinate. Always return calls when they are made to you, and follow up opportunities the moment they present themselves.

2. Work on your résumé.

The importance of a well-presented, accurate and comprehensive résumé cannot be overemphasised. Creating and composing a professional document is essential, but not everyone has specific experience about what and what not to include nor the requisite design skills. To show yourself in your best light, pay someone to perform this task for you. A quality résumé can be worth a hundred times what you spend on it.

3. The importance of references.

Use relevant references from as many reputable persons and establishments you have worked for in the past as you can. Although current policy forbids the disclosure of reference details, retrenched staff members can expect fair treatment and positive referrals from managers at this company when dismissal is due to unavoidable downsizing.

4. Use a variety of search options.

Use a job search agency to get the best jobs (you should not have to pay up front for this – or usually at all, since a commission is obtained later from your employer). Peruse ads online and in the daily papers, both local and statewide. Contact companies direct, and make it known that your talents are for hire. Social media websites, including Twitter and Facebook can help. Ask us how.

5. Get networked.

It can help a great deal to get others involved in your search. The moral support of friends in a similar position to you will combine with your help towards them and create a synergy that opens doors and moves mountains!

6. Dress well for the interview.

Job applicants do not always look the part. A prospective employer can easily be turned off by a scruffy person with good qualifications. Package yourself as you would a top product, for that is how you must present yourself. Incidentally, women are not advised to wear too much jewellery or make-up to an interview.

7. Send a thank you note.

Once your interview is over, and if you know it went well, consider sending a thank you note to the interviewer. The job application is not over when you walk out the door. This small step can help resurrect your chance if the number of candidates for the job is large. Surprisingly, few people take advantage of this opportunity to be remembered.

8. Keep a positive outlook.

It is all too easy to become discouraged after failing to secure a job after a number of attempts. Try to learn something from each interview experience so that your failures will count towards your eventual success. Mock interview sessions can be arranged in the evenings between managerial and floor staff. Contact Joan Blackwell on 0402–969–465 or speak directly with your manager.

9. Things to avoid.

Don't imagine that get rich quick schemes or gambling with your payout funds will help you through the lean times. Job scams are an unfortunate fact of working life. If the job sounds too good to be true, it probably is. Never hand over money to a prospective employer in the hope that his or her offer of training will result in employment. More often than not, the job will fail to materialise.

Questions 15 – 17

Complete the following sentences with suitable ***words or phrases*** *from the text above. Write your answers in boxes 15 – 17 on your Answer Sheet.*

Write ***NO MORE THAN THREE WORDS*** *for each answer.*

Example: The economic downturn is the reason that some staff members will be

.............................*seeking employment*.. .

15 When an opportunity arises follow it up immediately; in other words,

....

16 It is not possible to .... the need for a quality résumé.

17 When staff lose their jobs due to downsizing, they will receive

....

Questions 18 – 20

Choose the correct letter from ***A–D****. Write your answers in boxes 18 – 20 on yourAnswer Sheet.*

Example: A good résumé should include references

A regardless of their relevance.
B only if they are relevant.
C from all sources.
D both positive and negative. ANSWER **B**

18 The Human Resources Dept.

A keeps the content of references private.
B always gives a good reference to past employees.
C advertises in the daily papers.
D will contact companies directly for you.

19 Paying a job search agency is

- **A** only necessary once you have landed the job.
- **B** not often the obligation of the job-seeker.
- **C** an option to choose if you wish to get the better jobs.
- **D** all of the above

20 At the interview session, you are advised

- **A** to dress well but not to overdo the accessories.
- **B** to take something positive from the interview.
- **C** not to accept costly training that might result in you being hired.
- **D** all of the above

Question 21

*Choose **THREE** letters from **A–G**. Write your answer in box 21 on yourAnswer Sheet.*

Which **THREE** of the job search tips below are **NOT** mentioned in the text?

- **A** be regular in your job-seeking efforts
- **B** be selective when you record events in your job search diary
- **C** send your résumé to as many companies as possible
- **D** team up with other job-seekers
- **E** sharpen your interview skills with role-plays
- **F** follow up on potentially successful interviews
- **G** upgrade your job skills while looking for work

Questions 22 – 27

*Read the text below and answer **Questions 22 – 27**.*

 to  ? Working Overtime ~ Facts and Fiction...

Working overtime for no pay has become standard practice in most offices and factories throughout the U.K., the U.S., and even Australia and New Zealand - countries where Workers' Unions once ruled supreme. Gone are the days when union bosses could and would order workers to down tools and strike if employers so much as requested a minute of voluntary unpaid work time. What has gone wrong? Or right, depending on your viewpoint?

The financial crisis that overwhelmed the world in September 2008 has been labelled the villain that finally put to rest any notion of compensation for overtime. Airline crews have regularly worked 15-hour shifts for many years with no such luxury. Restaurant staff starting at lunchtime can easily put in 12 hours a day with no expectation of extra pay for their trouble. The difference is that now, right across the board, workers are being asked to stay back at work or run the risk of not being asked to return. It might not be legal just yet, but it is happening.

In Australia, a new National Employment Standard says "an employer must not request an employee work more than 38 hours unless the additional hours

continued...

are reasonable". But how does an employee argue that additional hours are unreasonable? Unreasonable for whom and why? What exactly constitutes an unreasonable request to work back late? Working more than 50 hours a week is considered the uppermost limit before work starts to affect your health – according to the International Labour Organisation – but many workers are expected to work as many or more hours to satisfy the ever-increasing consumer demand for a shop or business to stay open and compete in the modern economy.

This situation does not come as news to most older Asian workers who have long been used to working vast numbers of hours per week for little or no extra monetary reward; however, there is a recent argument that is hard not to accept: worldwide living standards have increased to very high levels for many millions of consumers in the West, and large parts of Asia are fast catching up.

In China and India for example, once considered slow growth economies, the reward for exceptionally hard work is beginning to pay off, with millions of people now able to afford cars and whitegoods that were once luxuries enjoyed only in the West.

The fact is that working long and hard pays dividends; if not in the pay packet, then at the pump or at the local supermarket where prices are kept well within reasonable limits while living standards climb slowly higher for the benefit of all. Workers find it difficult to argue for higher wages for more work achieved when consumer rewards are already being felt across the entire world economy. At the same time, the boss can extract more and more hours from staff without having to pay for it. Paid overtime is becoming a distant memory.

Questions 22 – 27

*Look at the following statements (**Questions 22 – 27**).*

Write	***TRUE***	*if the statement is true*
	FALSE	*if the statement is false*
	NOT GIVEN	*if the information is not given in the text.*

Write your answers in boxes 22 – 27 on your Answer Sheet.

Answer

Example: The Workers' Unions no longer have the power they once had. TRUE

22 Unpaid overtime is limited to the airline and restaurant industry. ....

23 Workers who refuse to perform unpaid overtime can be lawfully sacked. ....

24 Working back late is bad for your health. ....

25 Asian workers now spend more than Western workers. ....

26 Living standards across the globe are steadily increasing. ....

27 Paid overtime may not be necessary when living standards are high. ....

Part 3

Questions 28 – 40

You are advised to spend about 20 minutes on Questions 28 – 40.

THE ENDANGERED NEW ZEALAND KIWI

Paragraph A

The kiwi is synonymous with New Zealand, so much so that Australians endearingly refer to New Zealanders as "kiwis" – people from the Land of the Kiwi. This unique bird, recognisable by its short squat body and elongated beak, is under threat. Its small, clawlike wings render the kiwi flightless; it must of necessity live on the ground. The kiwi is thus easy prey to marauding enemies such as humans and mammals.

Paragraph B

When the great land mass of the south split 75 million years ago, the kiwi and many other ground-living bird species became separated from predatory mammals within what was later to become known as New Zealand. The birds were able to multiply and flourish because there were very few mammals landlocked within the islands. Kiwis have evolved certain mammalian characteristics over time, living on the ground and free as they were from attack by mammals.

Paragraph C

However, when the Polynesians arrived about 1000 years ago bringing with them dogs and rats, the kiwi population and other vulnerable bird species soon suffered a severe reduction in numbers. The coming of the Europeans in the eighteenth century brought even more determined predators, including the cat and, especially, the stoat – a kind of weasel introduced to control rabbits. The stoat is a very vicious and efficient killer of kiwis.

Paragraph D

There are six types of kiwi, and all six are threatened. Two are "critically endangered" because they have populations of less than 250 mature birds. Two are "endangered" meaning that it is estimated that within three generations their numbers will have declined by 50%. The other two are designated "vulnerable" – one because its habitat is shrinking, the other because it is potentially under threat from stoats and other mammals.

Paragraph E

100 years ago there were more than 5 million North Island Brown Kiwis. Today, there are probably around 30,000, and the population is decreasing at a rate of 6% a year. Only the Little Spotted Kiwi is increasing because of successful attempts to transfer the creature to predator-free offshore islands. There are further reasons for hope. Trapping predators and rearing baby chicks for later release into the wild can have a dramatic effect on kiwi numbers; but it will be necessary to do so on a large scale.

Paragraph F

It would be tragic if New Zealand were to lose its national symbol, the kiwi. Surely the strangest bird in existence, unable to fly, it sniffs out its food with a remarkably strong sense of smell. Its legs are powerful and muscular, for the kiwi is a burrower living in dens – some species even preferring tunnels, yet another similarity it shares with some mammals. But it cannot share its habitat with them without eventually losing the battle for survival.

Questions 28 – 32

*Choose the most suitable headings (**I–VIII**) for each paragraph of the reading passage from the list below. Write your answers in boxes 28 – 32 on your Answer Sheet.*

*Note that **you will not need to use all of the headings.***

List of Headings

	I	Survival of the National Symbol
	II	Preventing the Kiwi Decline
	III	Reasons for Concern
	IV	Explanation for Large Bird Populations
	V	The North Island Brown Kiwi
Example:	**VI**	Land of the Kiwi
	VII	Why Kiwis are Flightless
	VIII	The Introduction of Predators

Example: Paragraph A ..*VI*....

28 Paragraph B ....

29 Paragraph C ....

30 Paragraph D ....

31 Paragraph E ....

32 Paragraph F ....

Questions 33 – 35

*The reading passage "The Endangered New Zealand Kiwi" contains 6 paragraphs. Which paragraphs (**A–F**) contain the following information? Write your answers in boxes 33 – 35 on your Answer Sheet.*

		Answer
Example:	The number of types of kiwi:	...*D*.....
33	Examples of kiwi types:	....
34	The reasons for the mammal-like behaviour of kiwis:	....
35	A method of stopping kiwi predators:	....

Questions 36 – 40

Complete each gap in the summary of the reading passage by choosing the best ***word, number or phrase*** *from the box below the notes. Write your answers in boxes 36 – 40 on your Answer Sheet.*

Note that ***you will not need to use all the choices given****.*

The kiwi, a unique bird native to New Zealand, is under ***(Example:)*** ..threat... . For millions of years kiwis flourished on the islands free from predatory mammals and from **(36)** ....

The arrival of the Polynesians some 1000 years ago was a disaster for all **(37)** .... birds because they brought with them dogs and rats – the natural enemies of ground-living creatures such as kiwis. But it was the introduction of the **(38)** .... that caused the kiwi population to drop to its present level of around 30,000 birds. A particularly vicious killer, this weasel-like mammal was brought in to control rabbits.

The kiwi, with its short squat body, long **(39)** .... and powerful sense of smell, is one of the strangest of all the world's birds. Unless decisive action is taken soon to control the number of unfriendly mammals within the kiwi's **(40)** .... , New Zealanders could lose their national symbol.

nose	stoat	flightless	30,000
5 million	threat	beak	Europeans
habitat	rabbit	mammals	clawlike wings
endangered	humans	legs	dens

That is the end of Practice Reading Test Two.

PRACTICE WRITING TEST TWO

Writing Task 1

You should spend about 20 minutes on this task.

> ***The local council has decided to build a block of flats on the park opposite the place where you are living.***
>
> ***Write a letter to the editor of the local newspaper. In your letter***
>
> - ***explain why you are writing***
> - ***protest the development of this beautiful and necessary green space in your town***
> - ***make suggestions for what people can or should do to stop the development.***

Write at least 150 words.

You do NOT need to write any addresses.

Begin your letter as follows:

Dear Sir or Madam,

Writing Task 2

You should spend about 40 minutes on this task.

Write about the following topic:

> ***Most young people without a partner would prefer to have a boyfriend or girlfriend. Yet being in a relationship when you are young is not always a good idea.***
>
> ***Do you agree or disagree?***

Give reasons for your answer and include any relevant examples from your own knowledge or experience.

Write at least 250 words.

That is the end of Practice Writing Test Two.

☹ PRACTICE SPEAKING TEST TWO

Practise answering the questions below, giving answers that are at least one or two sentences long or more. If possible, practise with another person – taking it in turns to answer the same question – and compare your responses.

(Please note that the following questions are only a guide to the type of questions you might be asked in the actual test. For practice purposes we include more questions than you are likely to be asked.)

Part 1

Please come in and take a seat. Do you have your passport with you?

... I need to look at it for security purposes.

Thank you. My name is (interviewer's name). What would you like me to call you?

You are (nationality of the candidate). Which part of (your country) are you from?

Describe your home town to me.

Do you live close to your family? Tell me about your family members.

Where does your father work? And your mother?

What kind of place are you living in at the moment?

Who do you live with and why?

Are there any disadvantages of living where you are at present? What are they?

What does your study room look like? Please describe it to me.

Do you work or study at the moment? Tell me what you do at work or in your course.

What are the best things about where you work or study?

What do you dislike most about your work or study?

What are your main interests?

Why do you enjoy this activity/these activities?

Do you watch much television? What do you like to watch on TV?

How would you describe your lifestyle?

Do you like travelling? What interesting places have you visited?

What method of transport do you use most and why?

Part 2

Thank you. Now, please take this card. I want you to speak for one or two minutes about the topic written on this card. Follow the instructions on the card. You have one minute to prepare before you give your talk. You can make some notes to help you if you wish. All right?

> Talk about a machine that you have bought recently or in the past.
>
> You should say:
>
> what the machine looks like and what it can do
>
> when you bought it
>
> why you bought that particular machine
>
> ...and how that machine has affected your life

(follow-up questions)

Are there any other machines you would like to buy?

Do we really need these machines to live a good life, do you think?

Part 3

Please hand me the card. Thank you. Machines are so important these days. Almost everyone has a car, a telephone and a computer. How would you describe the lifestyle of people living before these machines were invented?

What did they use instead of the car, the telephone and the computer?

What are the advantages of using modern technology?

Are there any disadvantages of using these machines? If so, please explain.

Is your country technologically advanced? In what way?

Can you compare modern cars with the older style models?

How have mobile phones changed our lives?

Do you think computers have changed the way we live?

What do you think computers might be able to do in the future? How do you think computers themselves might change?

Do you think computers are useful in education? How are they useful (or not useful)?

That is the end of the interview. Thank you and goodbye.

That is the end of Practice Speaking Test Two.
Check your answers to Practice Test Two with the Answer Key on page 152.

PRACTICE READING TEST THREE

This is a practice reading test that resembles the International English Language Testing System Reading Test. The test is in three parts. Answer the questions on your Answer Sheet as you progress through the test.

Part 1

Questions 1 – 15

You are advised to spend about 20 minutes on Questions 1 – 15.

Look at the advertisements below for accommodation wanted or available, and answer the questions on the next page:

A

Accommodation Now Available

Park Hotel

Clean Safe Rooms for Gents

Weekly, monthly, long term

From $60pw

242 Carraville Rd Dellaworth

B

Share Accommodation

We require a non-smoking female of between 17 and 25 years to share our newly-established house in Hopetown.

'We' are 2 gals and a guy (and a cute little dog called 'Bobo').

You'll have your own room and, of course, you have to share the basic costs of food and telephone etc.

Rent: $100 per week *Tel: 9268-7354*

PS: Sorry no vegetarians need apply

C

Looking to share?

Sagittarian male aged 32 seeks compatible sharemate (in existing premises or to find) willing to accept this econut's ongoing obsession with the environment, computers, politics, and the Web. Male or female OK :)

REPLY CODE 34254

D

To Let **$360 p.w.**

Ashford New 2 brm security apartment, open living area, fully timbered kitchen, 1½ bathrooms, spa, remote security/ LUG.

5 mins to shops and station.

Apply **Gannon & Berle**

Office open 7 days

(02) 9678-34576

E

Good Home Wanted

My name is Young Hee (female from Korea) and I will be in Wellington from April to December, studying at the North Island Business College.

I'm looking for a family to live with for 8 months, maximum rent $200 a month, and in return I am willing to babysit, cook, clean, and do other housekeeping jobs.

If you are interested in my offer, please write.

F

Residential College Accommodation

Vacancies available March 26 for enrolled students only.

References required.

Stanford Bridge College of Applied Kinesiology, Melb.

Questions 1 – 5

*Look at the six advertisements on the previous page. Answer the questions below by writing the appropriate letters (**A–F**) of the advertisements in boxes 1 – 5 on your Answer Sheet.*

Answer

Example: Which advertisement offers hotel accommodation? ...A.....

1 Which advertisement is for a room to let in a house? ....

2 Which advertisement might interest a family with young children? ....

3 Which advertisement claims the accommodation is convenient and safe? ....

4 Which advertisement offers students accommodation in the near future? ....

5 Which **TWO** advertisements offer accommodation for a male? ....

Questions 6 – 10

*Look at the notice below. Answer the questions that follow using **NO MORE THAN THREE WORDS**. Write your answers in boxes 6 – 10 on your Answer Sheet.*

O P E N D A Y

Plus ***GIANT*** second-hand text book sale* at the

Saturday 5 December (10am - 6pm)

LEVINGTON COLLEGE OF THE ARTS

Graphic Design – Room 32 **Sculpture** – Main Hall **Still Photography** – Room 10
Jewellery Design – Room 16 **Textile Design** – Lecture Theatre **Ceramics** – Foyer
Electronic Arts – West Gallery **Glass** – Courtyard **Painting** – East Gallery

[All exhibitions are free. Second (final) year students' works are for sale where indicated. First year students' works are on display in the Stanley Buck Auditorium. Please note that it is not possible to purchase first year students' works.]

* in the Library

6 Where might you see examples of bracelets and brooches?

....

7 Where might you see an exhibit which included a short black and white film?

....

8 Your friend is a second year student who designs book covers. Where can she sell her designs?

....

9 Your friend is a sculptor who will continue at the college next year. Where can you see his works?

....

10 Which **TWO** places would you visit to see if you could buy a vase to display flowers?

....

Questions 11 – 15

Below is an extract from the results of a search made on the Internet for the words 'english colleges australasia'. Read the extract and answer the questions on the next page:

english colleges australasia | **Search**

EduSeek **found 56,040 Web pages for you.**

1. **Institute of Languages – UNSW (Sydney, Australia)**
   International and migrant students can learn English at one of the largest university language centres in Australia.
   URL: *www.lang.unsw.edu.au/*
   Last modified 3-Apr-09 – page size 6K – in English [Translate]
2. **SELC – Sydney English Language Centre**
   Intensive English courses: General English (9 levels), English for Academic Purposes, Business English, High School Bridging Program, English for the Internet, Test Preparation...
   URL: *http://www.selc.com.au/*
   Last modified 30-May-09 – page size 3K – in English [Translate]
3. **Australian English Colleges**
   English Colleges list. New South Wales: A.G. Mate Academy, Alpha Beta Colleges, Access Language Centre, Aspect International Language Schools, Australian...
   URL: *http://students.idp.com/english/study/*
   Last modified 30-Oct-09 – page size 3K – in English [Translate]
4. **English Colleges in New Zealand**
   Unique international study destination, how to get there, where and what to study...
   URL: *http://www.englishnewzealand.co.nz/*
   Last modified 26-Dec-09 – page size 3K – in English [Translate]
5. **St. Mark's International Colleges – Perth & Sydney**
   Part of the GEOS (Global Educational Opportunities & Services) group. Our two Australian colleges...
   URL: *www.geos-sydney.com.au*
   Last modified 03-Jul-09 – page size 3K – in English [Translate]

*Answer the questions below by writing the appropriate **numbers** in boxes 11 – 15 on your Answer Sheet.*

Example: Which search result gives information about New Zealand?

....

11 Which search result gives the name of a college offering computer classes?

....

12 Which **TWO** search results give information about more than one Australian college?

....

13 Which search result gives the names of colleges in alphabetical order?

....

14 Which search result says the country offers a language learning experience that is like no other?

....

15 How many webpages did the search engine find for the user?

....

Part 2

Questions 16 – 28

You are advised to spend about 20 minutes on Questions 16 – 28.

USING THE NETWORK COMPUTERS page 25

How to Send and Receive an Email

Our computer network is well-equipped with the latest software from Microsoft to enable you to easily send and receive email. Our fast and permanent Internet connection and multiple email mailboxes – one for each employee – will enable you to download (receive) your own email, provided you have logged on with your given password.

Loading up the email program

First, you should load up the browser* (click on the Internet Explorer icon** on the Desktop with the left button of your mouse), and look at the Menu Bar at the top for the **Mail** icon. Click on the **Mail** icon, and click again on the **Read Mail** entry in the drop-down menu. This will load the email program.

1. RECEIVING (downloading) your emails

To read your mail, you need to click on the **Send and Receive** icon at the top of the Menu Bar. This will do two things. It will send any emails you have written which are waiting to be sent, and it will download any emails that have been sent to you.

If you have had an email sent to you, the message header (containing the sender's name and the subject of the email) will appear in the **Inbox** folder message window at the top right of the screen. If you want to read the contents of the email, double-click it with the left button, and the email message will appear full-size on the screen.

2. SENDING (uploading) your emails

a) To reply to an email that someone has sent to you, double-click on the message header in the **Inbox** folder message window at the top right of the screen. This will make the email appear full-size on the screen. Now click on the **Reply** icon at the top left of the Menu Bar. This will bring up the *new mail message* window with the email address of the person you are replying to already there at the top.

Type your reply just like you would for an ordinary letter. When you are ready to send your email, click on the **Send** icon top left. That's all there is to it! Next time you click on the **Send and Receive** icon in the email program, your email will be sent.

b) To compose a new email (without replying to one sent to you), click on the **New Mail Message** icon at the top left of the Menu Bar. This will bring up the *new mail message* window.

You will now need to do 3 things:

(i) Put the address in the little information box to the right of the **[To...]** button. Let's say, john@ozemail.com.au

(ii) Put the subject of the email in the little information box to the right of the word **Subject:** let's say, < < Hello John > >

(iii) Type your letter and, when you're finished, click on the **Send** icon top left.

[* browser – program for looking at pages on the Internet ** icon – small picture]

Questions 16 – 22

*Refer to the reading passage "Using the Network Computers", and look at the statements (**Questions 16 – 22**) below.*

Write	***TRUE***	*if the statement is true*
	FALSE	*if the statement is false*
	NOT GIVEN	*if the information is not given in the text.*

Write your answers in boxes 16 – 22 on your Answer Sheet.

Answer

Example: The page is from a company's computer network guidebook. TRUE

16 All employees use the same password. ....

17 Employees without a password cannot download their own email. ....

18 You can only load the email program from within the browser. ....

19 Clicking on the Send and Receive icon will upload your emails. ....

20 Replying to an email is simple. ....

21 The new mail message window appears full-size on the screen. ....

22 When you have finished writing your email, clicking on the Send icon will send it immediately. ....

Questions 23 – 28

Read the extract on the next page from a company's work and safety publication and answer Questions 23 – 28 below.

*Write the correct letter (**A–F**) in boxes 23 – 28 on your Answer Sheet.*

NOTE: you may use a letter more than once.

Answer

23 Which case might include replacing equipment that is not faulty? ....

24 Which case refers to management of behaviour outside the workplace? ....

25 Which case deliberately targets an abuse of power? ....

26 Which case specifically mentions actions which may result in manslaughter charges being laid? ....

27 Which case discusses the result of non-physical harm that might go unnoticed for years? ....

28 Which case discusses harm that may have an effect on someone who is not an employee or employer? ....

PREVENTING HARM IN THE WORKPLACE

Workers have the right to a healthy and safe workplace. If the workplace does not comply with all sections of the Occupational Health and Safety Act, it is the employer's responsibility to redress the situation or face serious consequences, which may involve the employee seeking substantial financial compensation. It may even require sentencing by law in the case of manslaughter charges being laid where a person has died as the result of injury at work.

CASE A

It is extremely important to protect workers from the hazards of the many thousands of dangerous chemicals produced and used in workplaces statewide. It is acknowledged that workers can be exposed to chemical agents which may seriously affect their long-term health and even their reproductive ability – not to mention the health of unborn children in pregnant women. As well, these and other chemicals may, of course, cause immediate damage to skin tissue if inappropriately handled.

CASE B

Alcohol and illegal substance abuse at home and at work causes major problems in the workplace. Alcohol-related injuries are on the rise, but all recreational drug use can have harmful consequences – not only for the user, but for co-workers who have to deal with the effects of the lack of attention and concentration of drug abusers. Misuse of prescription drugs can also be a factor in harmful situations at work. Absenteeism due to substance abuse costs the economy billions of dollars a year.

CASE C

Failure to heed company warnings, and to adhere to the safety practices legislated by the Occupational Health and Safety Act will inevitably result in injury and/or death. Loss of hearing, loss of sight, loss of limbs and loss of life can and does occur when safety practices are repeatedly ignored. All workers should be made aware of the OHSA requirements at every available opportunity.

CASE D

Repetitive strain injuries may occur over time unless strict policies are in place to reduce the amount of time workers are required to perform the same movements. In addition, ergonomically-friendly furniture, keyboards and monitors, tools, machines and spaces in the workplace environment are essential if harm is to be avoided. Legal compensation may be sued for by those workers who are put at risk.

CASE E

Responsibility for fire safety in the workplace belongs with employers. They must make their workplaces comply with state fire laws. This involves the placing of a suitable number of fire extinguishers in easily accessable places, as well as the constant monitoring of fire exits, and regular fire drills.

CASE F

Harm in the workplace also includes deliberate employee and employer-directed abuses towards others; such abuses may involve harassment of various types and even instances of abuse of trust. For example, failure to reward over long periods of time, or to comply with the agreed upon terms of a contract. Long-term psychological abuse is often more difficult to pinpoint and thus eradicate, but is no less harmful than, say, physical sexual harassment.

Part 3

Questions 29 – 40

You are advised to spend about 20 minutes on Questions 29 – 40.

INTERNATIONAL STUDENTS 'DOWN UNDER'

Section (i)

A recently published analysis of a major survey taken of international students in Australia is providing up-to-date data for teachers and marketers of English language training programs.

Section (ii)

The major regions of student representation in the survey were Asia with 73.4% of students, Europe 10.2%, Pacific 0.5%, and Other 7%.

Japanese students formed the largest national group, representing 34% of the student population. Other national groups represented, in descending order, were Taiwan, Korea, Indonesia, Switzerland, Hong Kong, Thailand, other European countries, China, and Iran.

Increases in arrivals since the early 1990s have occurred from all major source countries, except China, with an increase of almost 50% from Western Europe.

Section (iii)

Approximately one-third of the students questioned were 20 years and under, and almost three-quarters were 25 and under. Only 8% were aged over 30, and fewer than 3% were over 35.

Almost half of all students aged between 31 and 35 were students in Australia on student visas. As expected, a very high proportion (79%) of working holiday visa holders were aged between 21 and 25. Tourist visa holders ranged from under 20 to 31.

The oldest students were from Iran, with 60% aged over 30 and 25% over 35. Students from China also tended to be older than other nationalities, with 25% in the over 30 age bracket.

More than half the Korean students were in their early 20s, with only a few over 25. Students from Hong Kong were also predominantly young, with over half aged under 20. At least 20% of students from all major national groups, except Korea and China, were under 20 years of age. Indonesian students were the youngest, with over 60% under 20.

The Japanese, Swiss, Taiwanese, and Thai profiles followed quite closely the overall student age profile.

Section (iv)

Overall, female students outnumbered male students in the survey. However, there were more males than females from four countries: Iran, Indonesia, Korea, and, to a lesser extent, China. Females accounted for 60% of students from Taiwan, Switzerland, and Japan. Gender differences concerning the responses to questions were noticed, but varied widely according to nationality.

Section (v)

A very high proportion (87%) of students had completed senior high school or better. Just under one-third had completed a university degree, and 5% had completed a postgraduate degree. Over a third had at least completed high school, and over 20% had completed a technical diploma or junior college.

Students with a maximum middle school education formed less than 7% of all respondents, and came predominantly from Hong Kong, Indonesia, and Taiwan. Iranian students were among the highest educated, with more than half having already completed a postgraduate degree.

Koreans, Thais, and Chinese were also particularly well educated, with over 60% of each national group having completed at least a first university degree. Almost half of the Japanese and more than half of the Swiss respondents had completed education to senior high school level or less.

Section (vi)

While student visa holders took either 10–29 week or 40 week courses, most students on working holiday and tourist visas took courses of less than 10 weeks, or from 10 to 19 weeks in length.

More than 50% of all students were taking courses of between 10 and 29 weeks, with the proportion fairly evenly divided between the 10–19 week and 20–29 week ranges. A large proportion of students were taking courses of at least 40 weeks in length, and only a few students indicated enrolment in courses shorter than 10 weeks.

There were noticeable differences between nationalities, with Koreans, Japanese, and Taiwanese taking longer courses than other nationalities, and Swiss and other European students taking much shorter courses.

Section (vii)

Interest in further education differed significantly from country to country. Students from Iran (94.8%), Hong Kong (88.7%), China (88.4%), Thailand (88.3%), and Indonesia (85.4%) registered high levels of interest, whereas lower interest was shown by respondents from Japan (42%) and Korea (62%). There was much lower interest in further study among students from Switzerland (13%), and other European countries accounted for (26%).

Questions 29 – 34

*Choose the most suitable heading from the list of headings (**A–L**) below for each of the seven sections of the reading passage. Write your answers in boxes 29 – 34 on your Answer Sheet.*

*Note that **there are more headings than sections, so not all will be used**.*

List of Headings

A	Further Study	**E**	Major Student Survey	**I**	Student Age
B	Length of Courses	**F**	Student Source	**J**	Visas
C	High School	**G**	Educational Background	**K**	Gender
D	University Degrees	**H**	Asian National Groups	**L**	Female Students

Example: Section (i) ...E...

29 Section (ii) ....

30 Section (iii) ....

31 Section (iv) ....

32 Section (v) ....

33 Section (vi) ....

34 Section (vii) ....

Questions 35 – 40

Complete Table 1 below with the appropriate ***countries*** *according to the information in the reading passage "International Students 'Down Under' ". Write your answers in boxes 35 – 40 on your Answer Sheet.*

Table 1. INTERNATIONAL STUDENTS STUDYING IN AUSTRALIA

	Source of Students	**Under 20 years old**	**20–29 years old**	**Over 30 years old**	**Interest in Further Studies**
75–100%	–	–	–	–	Iran / Hong Kong / China / Thailand / Indonesia
50–74%	–	**(35)**............ and Hong Kong	**(36)**............	**(37)**............	**(38)**............
25–49%	*(Ex:)* Japan	–	–	**(39)**............	**(40)** .... / European countries (not including Switzerland)
0–24%	–	–	–	–	Switzerland

Example: ...Japan.........

35 ....

36 ....

37 ....

38 ....

39 ....

40 ....

That is the end of Practice Reading Test Three.

PRACTICE WRITING TEST THREE

Writing Task 1

You should spend about 20 minutes on this task.

You are taking a holiday in a place recommended by your local travel agent, and you are having a wonderful time. You promised to write and let the agent know what you think of his or her suggestion.

Write a letter to your travel agent. In your letter

- ***let your agent know what you have been doing***
- ***say what you are going to do before the end of your holiday***
- ***explain why you think the agent made the right choice for you.***

Write at least 150 words.

You do NOT need to write any addresses.

Begin your letter as follows:

Dear Sir or Madam,

Writing Task 2

You should spend about 40 minutes on this task.

Write about the following topic:

A new shopping centre is going to open in your town. At present, nobody knows what kind of shops or facilities are going to be provided for customers. What shops and facilities would you like to see made available to the shopping public?

Make useful suggestions for the shopping centre's management.

Give reasons for your answer and include any relevant examples from your own knowledge or experience.

Write at least 250 words.

That is the end of Practice Writing Test Three.
Check your answers to Practice Test Three with the Answer Key on page 153.

PRACTICE READING TEST FOUR

This is a practice reading test that resembles the International English Language Testing System Reading Test. The test is in three parts. Answer the questions on your Answer Sheet as you progress through the test.

PART 1

Questions 1 – 14

You are advised to spend about 20 minutes on Questions 1 – 14.

Look at the following page from the Green Pages® telephone directory below:

ANGUS

DRIVING SCHOOL

helping to drive Australia in 2000

HEAVY VEHICLE DRIVER TRAINING

for over 60 years

- ☑ No Previous Experience Required
- ☑ Truck & Bus Class LR, MR, HR & HC
- ☑ Training Programs for Corporations
- ☑ Certificate and Evaluation Report

9648-7244

Driving Schools (Cont'd)

Green Pages®

Consumer Help

24 hours a day, consumers can get further information on learner driving - Call 1200 35 2334 then enter the following codes:

- 6129 Choosing a School
- 6137 Passing the Written Test
- 6145 Safety on the Roads

Alsley Motor School

ALSLEY

Driving School Established 1968

Professional Service

7 DAYS

9366 5777 or **9366 5778**

Amber Driving School 9665 8234
Amberley Driver Training
77/344 Little Grnacre 9844 0823

Amtex Driving School
12/145 Riddle Mrbra 9349 1747
Andy's Driving School 9879 4053
Andrews Driving School
Rydalmere 9643 8300
Hornsby 9765 7388
Mosman 9211 2965
Ballys Driving School
28 Forth Croydon Park 9649 9967

B C S Pty Ltd

NATION WIDE

All over Australia, you can learn to drive a heavy vehicle, bus or coach at

AFFORDABLE RATES

INQUIRIES WELCOME

Let BCS put you right...

Head Office: (NSW)
8 Elisabeth Street, Sydney
Tel: 9212-5555
Fax: 9212-5544

Green Pages® directory is the best place to advertise if you want to attract new customers

Ring NOW Tel: 14 8888

Yes, you can pass first go!

(to find out how - ring Head Office: 9515 7445)

L **PRATT**

Our first-class instructors will enable you to pass the test quicker and with less stress, saving you (time) + ($) !!

In your local suburb NOW

Eastern Suburbs	9314 6129
Burwood	9798 4486
Crows Nest	9437 8144
Liverpool	9600 2721
Ryde	9871 0987
Sutherland	9545 6008
Wentworthville	9635 1209

L ook
L isten &
L earn

http://www.pratt.com.au

ADTA Member since 1973

Western Suburbs Driving School

from this L *to this* P

We give you the confidence you need

- ***overseas conversions***
- ***automatic/manual cars***
- ***RTA licensed instructors***
- ***male/female instructors***
- ***all cars dual controlled***

9838 - 7555

SPECIAL PRICES - 50TH YEAR IN BUSINESS

67 KINGS HEAD ROAD, MT. DRUITT

Questions 1 – 6

Refer to the Green Pages® telephone directory page and answer the questions below. Write your answers in boxes 1 – 6 on your Answer Sheet.

What telephone number do you call if...

Example: ...you want a female instructor to help you learn to drive? ...9838-7555.....

1 ...you want to learn to drive in Mosman?

....

2 ...you have a driving licence from another country?

....

3 ...you want help with a road safety question? (include the extension)

....

4 ...you do not want to take the driving test more than once if possible?

....

5 ...you want to learn to drive a car at the driving school with the most experience?

....

6 ...you want to find out how much it costs to place an advertisement in the Green Pages®?

....

Questions 7 – 14

As part of a class assignment, you recently conducted a survey about television habits. Look at one of the returned questionnaires below:

TELEVISION HABIT SURVEY - DATE: ..Monday 4/8/08.

Name: ..Peter Golding.......

1. What time did you turn on the TV last night? ..6.00 pm................
2. Do you watch the news? (Yes) / No but only on Channel 9
3. What kind of movies do you like? .action movies (especially Kung-Fu).....
4. If you had to choose, would you watch a) a cartoon series or (b) a drama?
5. Do you like watching music videos? ..Yes, but only old hits.............
6. What's your favourite show on TV? ..The Karrington Kids...............
7. Do you ever watch quiz shows? ...occasionally - if there's nothing else on...
8. Which TV show host do you prefer (a) Joe Diver or b) Carol White?
9. What was the last documentary you watched? .1st episode of 'Chinese Doll'...
10. Do you like shows that feature animals?.............................
11. What sports shows do you watch? ..tennis, cricket, golf (in that order).....

*The text below summarises what Peter watched on TV on Sunday. Complete each gap in the text by choosing the appropriate **word, phrase or number** based on the information in the questionnaire and in the TV Guide on the next page.*

Write your answers in boxes 7 – 14 on your Answer Sheet.

Peter turned on the TV at 6.00 p.m. to watch the ***Example:*** ..**Channel 9 News**. Unfortunately, it was mostly political news, and so he changed channels to **(7)** .... On this channel, there was a **(8)** .... hosted by a person he liked, and he watched the show until 7.00 p.m.

He could not easily decide what to see next because nothing particularly interested him. He finally settled on **(9)** .... but only until **(10)** .... when his favourite show began. After that, Peter really wanted to look at **(11)** ...., but his wife chose the Bugs Bunny re-runs. At 8.30 p.m. he insisted on watching **(12)** ...., which she agreed was the best movie on TV that night despite what the movie reviewer recommended.

His wife went to bed at 10.00 p.m., but Peter decided he would stay up to watch **(13)** .... until the late news at 11.30 p.m. This was followed by highlights of the Victoria v NSW cricket match, which he enjoyed. However, the next day he realised he should have watched the **(14)** ....

Television Guide for Sunday 3/8/08

Channel 7

6.00 Be My Guest! Talk show with the ever popular host Joe Diver. *73246892*

7.00 Eve of Discovery. The Renaissance woman - helped or hindered by religion? *90975*

7.30 World Sport. Highlights. Football post-mortem. *9883456*

8.30 Movie: Smuggler's Cove (87, Rpt) Greg Rowe stars in this laboured piece about LA cocaine racketeers. ***= Thumbs down (Matt White)*** *233657*

10.00 Video Hits. Classic hits of the past. Moldy gold from the 'Best of ... Series'. *09375*

11.30 Fashion Watch. *484356*

11.40 Late Movie: King Fisher (PG, 77). *664533*

Channel 9

6.00 News. *667554*

7.00 Crocodile Hunter (Rpt). Shoot or be killed. *54504*

7.30 Boy's Town (99, MA). Drama about a young boy learning about life in a small town. *854332*

8.30 Movie: Kung-Fu God (93, Rpt). Lou Dong takes on the Lords of the Temple. *43984*

10.00 News Update. *5675056*

10.05 Weather. *137502*

10.10 Chinese Doll. Episode 3 Documentary series about footbinding of Chinese women in the nineteenth century. (98, Rpt). *432521*

11.30 News. *611293*

11.45 Sport Shorts. Cricket highlights - Victoria v NSW from the MCG. *47433789*

Channel 10

6.00 News Report. Current affairs with Carol White. *87865*

6.30 The Meanies. Comedy show. *9801*

7.00 Dollar Dazzle. Trivia quiz hosted by Kip Truman. *340833*

7.30 Cartoon Capers. (Rpt) Bugs Bunny and friends. *523224*

8.30 Movie: Never Say Never Again (M, 83, Rpt, S) James Bond attempts to thwart SPECTRE. Sean Connery, Kim Basinger. ****** Best viewing (Matt White)*** *76740023*

10.45 Late News. *666545*

11.00 Top 40 Hits (M). *776383*

11.40 Weather. *8761*

11.45 Tennis. U.S. Open. Live by satellite. Round 3. Commentator John Newcombe *295329*

Ch. 13 (Cable)

5.30 Hollywood Celebrity. Find out what your favourite TV/movie stars are doing. *431102*

6.30 He's My Man. Sitcom with Rachel Hardcourt. *2801*

7.00 CNN News. World roundup and commentary on daily news events. *886509*

7.15 The Karrington Kids. (PG) The family goes on holidays to Darwin. *85213*

7.30 Media Message. Political discussion. *85213*

8.30 Movie: Jesus Freak (M, 95, Rpt) Interesting spoof on religious TV show quackery. Jason Keel ***** Recommended (Matt White)*** *03344467*

10.50 News. *64225*

11.40 Weather. *7153*

11.45 Sport. Golfing tips with the Shark. *3061*

PART 2

Questions 15 – 28

You are advised to spend about 20 minutes on Questions 15 – 28.

Look at the information below about employees at a travel agency in New Zealand:

Jack Johnson (A)

Born in France of English-speaking parents, Jack has travelled extensively for the past 10 years (to over 35 countries), working in both French and English-speaking countries and also in Russia and China! He intends to open his own travel agency one day. His hobbies are golf, fishing, reading, and writing poetry.

Guy Harvey (B)

Guy was born in Munich, Germany and migrated to Adelaide, Australia when he was a child. Majoring in Hospitality and Tourism, Guy still has a strong desire to travel abroad. His pastimes include doing crosswords and visiting art museums. He is often found doodling with pen and ink.

Sue Clark (C)

Sue first chose acting as a career, but soon quit and turned to the travel industry. Her parents come from Noumea, but she has never travelled overseas. Sue is yet to complete her tourism studies; she works at her Distance Learning Course in the evenings most weekdays, and so has little time for a hobby.

Amber Martin (D)

Hailing from Capetown, Amber has always enjoyed keeping fit. A physical fitness fanatic, at the weekend she plays netball for the Christchurch netball team – helping to keep them at the top for over two years. Her hobbies are watching movies, listening to audiobooks, and learning about the tourist industry.

Venus Marlowe (E)

Venus, from London, England, taught Tourism Management at Luton University for five years. Recently, she decided to work her way around the world and insists that travel is her first love. This is despite an active interest in making short films. She hopes to direct a full-length movie one day.

Chee Fong (F)

At the age of 18, Chee, born in Singapore, originally hoped to become a concert pianist! Unfortunately for him, although he was skilled, it did not work out and eventually Chee joined his family's travel business. He says he is made to work harder than his colleagues because of this! Interests include chess and cooking.

Questions 15 – 18

*Write the answers (**A–F**) in boxes 15 – 18 on your Answer Sheet.*

		Answer
Example:	Which employee loves music?	...F......
15	Which employee was not born overseas?	....
16	Which employee is probably the least artistically creative?	....
17	Which employee is unlikely to stay long with the travel agency?	....
18	We can conclude that only two of these employees have travel industry qualifications. Which **TWO** employees are they?	....

Questions 19 – 22

Refer to the text about the employees on the previous page, and look at the statements below.

Write	***TRUE***	*if the statement is true*
	FALSE	*if the statement is false*
	NOT GIVEN	*if the information is not given in the text.*

Write your answers in boxes 19 – 22 on your Answer Sheet.

Answer

Example: Sue Clark wanted to be a teacher at first. FALSE

19 Jack Johnson likes travelling more than Guy Harvey. ....

20 One of the employees does not want to always work for a boss. ....

21 One of the employees is given preferential treatment at the travel agency because of family connections. ....

22 Venus Marlowe would like to become a professional film director. ....

Questions 23 – 28

Read the extract below from a large company's Who's Who register:

Who's Who at MADISON McCAIN'S page 39

Sophie Hardcastle (Finance Department / Accounts)

Background in business studies and accounting. Has been with the company since it began trading in 1988. Has a strong track record of assisting staff members to get the best from their superannuation packages and retirement payouts. Available for consultation on Wednesdays and Fridays after 3.00 p.m.

Orrin Simons (R & D laboratory)

Orrin's job description is to interpret the current science and turn ideas into reality. He is responsible for the work of over 30 engineers and is currently managing over a dozen new scientific research projects. By appointment only.

Kate Millar (Accounts / Computing)

Recently completed a training course in software certification. Attention to all Office software questions (for hardware problems contact Luke Fuller). Also assists Sophie with employment of accounting staff; contact sessions only during early shift (until 12.30 p.m.)

Bessie Hoyle (Workplace Grievance Officer)

Counselling of personal problems, private matters, resolution of workplace complaints. Hours: after 2.30 p.m. (except Fridays) (Currently on maternity leave until September.)

Frederick Collins (Personnel Dept.)

Speaks four languages including Mandarin. Helps staff with Chinese language issues. Assistance with contracts. (Will assist with queries in place of Ms Hoyle.)

Questions 23 – 28

Look at Questions 23 – 28 below and decide which employee would be able to help you.

Write **SH** if the person to see is **Sophie Hardcastle**
OS if the person to see is **Orrin Simons**
KM if the person to see is **Kate Millar**
BH if the person to see is **Bessie Hoyle**
FC if the person to see is **Frederick Collins**
LF if the person to see is **Luke Fuller**

Write your answers in boxes 23 – 28 on your Answer Sheet.

		Answer
23	you need immediate assistance with a matter you need to discuss in strict confidence	....
24	you are a new employee uncertain about how to interpret part of your job description	....
25	you urgently need advice this morning regarding your interview this afternoon for an accounting position	....
26	you work in the marketing department and would like to discover what the company was like in its early days	....
27	the on-switch of one of the network computers is broken and requires attention	....
28	you have an idea that, if developed, might make Madison McCain's a lot of money	....

PART 3

Questions 29 – 40

You are advised to spend about 20 minutes on Questions 29 – 40.

Read this article from a magazine, and answer the questions on the next page.

CRIME PREVENTION MEANS YOU !

Paragraph 1

It is a sad fact of life that crime is everywhere – in cities, in suburbs, in country towns; committed by the poor, the desperate, the greedy, and, yes, by the rich, too. We must accept that the level of crime in society is inversely proportional to the vigilance with which we fight it. Policing the streets and chasing criminals is just part of the solution. The police can only do so much to prevent crime. It is up to every individual to make the difference, and there is plenty that you and I can do.

Paragraph 2

First of all, we can support the force that is in charge of controlling crime. People who criticize the splendid performance of most policemen and women are, in reality, merely expressing their fear of authority. A police force can only be strong and successful in its fight against crime if it is well resourced. Do all you can to make sure the police have the power to carry out their duty effectively. Politicians will only respond to further requests for finance from the police force if we follow suit and petition them for adequate funding against crime.

Paragraph 3

Secondly, the police force itself must be honest and beyond reproach if it is to earn our respect and do its job well. One simple, yet sure way to make certain of this is for the public to be positive and supportive of the police whenever the opportunity arises. Eventually, the level of community respect for the police will increase, and, in turn, a better class of young persons will choose to join the force.

Paragraph 4

Prevention of crime is also the immediate responsibility of the individual. In other words, one should not commit crime oneself. The obvious injustices within all societies are not justifications for being dishonest. Any crime one commits, however small, only adds to the injustice that we see all around us. Set good examples to your children and your friends, help them to distinguish between right and wrong, and sleep at night with a good conscience.

Paragraph 5

There are many practical ways, too, in which we can help prevent crimes before they occur. What follows is a 10 point guide to personal crime prevention:

1. Get into the habit of always securely locking up your house, your office, your car. Don't make it easy for criminals to break in.
2. A good burglar alarm is definitely an effective robbery deterrent.

3. Mark your expensive possessions for easier identification later, and show stickers to advertise that you have done so.
4. Be aware of what is happening in your neighbourhood; keep watch for your neighbours – report anything suspicious to them and they will do the same for you.
5. Be observant – if you see someone acting strangely or breaking the law, take a quick visual note of what you see, and commit it to paper as soon as you can; write down car numbers, clothing, personal descriptions etc.
6. Most crimes are solved because of information the police receive from the public – don't be a silent witness, tell the police what you know.
7. Keep guns out of sight and under lock and key.
8. Avoid places in your community where you are likely to get into trouble. Don't place yourself in danger!
9. Petition your community leaders to do all they can to prevent crime. If you live in a poorly lit street, write a letter; don't wait for someone else to act.
10. Smile! Don't live with fear and worry – it only attracts problems. Speak prosperity and goodwill to all, and that too will make for a better society.

Paragraph 6

Crime is the outward expression of the weaknesses within a society. Criminals are either the cause of the problem or victims themselves, depending on your point of view. But one thing is certain, the social cost is high and we all become victims if we, as individuals, do not act responsibly and constantly to reduce the level of crime. Crime prevention is up to us all.

Questions 29 – 31

*Choose the correct letter from **A–D**. Write your answers in boxes 29 – 31 on your Answer Sheet.*

Example: Unfortunately, crime is committed

A in cities.
B in suburbs.
C in country towns.
D all of the above ANSWER **D**

29 The more we do to fight crime,

A the more criminals there are.
B the fewer police we need.
C the less crime is committed.
D the more police there are on the streets.

30 People who fear the police

- **A** are criminals.
- **B** may be critical of them.
- **C** think they are dishonest.
- **D** should join the police force.

31 Individuals can prevent break-ins by

- **A** remembering to lock all doors and windows.
- **B** displaying signs indicating that goods can be identified.
- **C** observing local activity.
- **D** all of the above

Questions 32 – 35

The reading passage contains 6 paragraphs. Which paragraphs contain the following information?

*Write the appropriate paragraph number (**1–6**) in boxes 32 – 35 on your Answer Sheet.*

*Note that **you may use any paragraph number more than once**.*

	Answer
Example: The public should support the police.	......3......
32 More crimes are committed in some areas than in others.	....
33 The police should be given the means to do their job well.	....
34 Some people believe that social injustice forces people into a life of crime.	....
35 Crimes are not only committed by the poor.	....

Questions 36 – 40

Refer to the reading passage "Crime Prevention Means You!".

Write	***PF***	*if the information applies to* ***the Police Force***
	I	*if the information applies to an* ***Individual***
	B	*if the information applies to* ***both*** *the Police Force and to an Individual*
	N	*if the information applies to* ***neither*** *the Police Force nor to an Individual.*

Write your answers in boxes 36 – 40 on your Answer Sheet.

		Answer
Example:	"in charge of controlling crime"	PF
36	"must be honest"	....
37	"needs to ask the government for funding"	....
38	"should catch people who are breaking the law"	....
39	"should only use guns with a lock and key"	....
40	"should deter robbers with an alarm"	....

That is the end of Practice Reading Test Four.

PRACTICE WRITING TEST FOUR

Writing Task 1

You should spend about 20 minutes on this task.

You wish to enrol in a course (of your choice) at an Australian college. You have already written a letter to the college asking for information but have received no reply.

Write a letter to the college. In your letter

- ***express your concern because the course will start in less than two months***
- ***find out if you can still enrol***
- ***ask for further information about the course, including the cost.***

Write at least 150 words.

You do NOT need to write any addresses.

Begin your letter as follows:

Dear Sir or Madam,

Writing Task 2

You should spend about 40 minutes on this task.

Write about the following topic:

Some people believe that the world is much less safe today than it used to be. There are still many wars being fought, and high-tech weapons are sold openly to any country that wants to buy them. In cities, violent crime is increasing every year.

It is not a very safe world in which to bring up children.

Do you agree or disagree?

Give reasons for your answer and include any relevant examples from your own knowledge or experience.

Write at least 250 words.

That is the end of Practice Writing Test Four.
Check your answers to Practice Test Four with the Answer Key on page 153.

Instructions for Speaking Test Board Game

(see the board for setup instructions)

PART 1: A player lands on a square and chooses one of the other players to ask him or her a question about the item on that square. The other players can ask further questions if necessary.

Important! If the other players consider the answer(s) given too short or not appropriate, they can appeal to a student chosen as a referee, who must decide if the answer is good enough for the player to stay on the square. Otherwise, the player must go back to the square he or she came from.

PART 2: A player landing on a "Topic Talk" square uses the indicated topic talk card (A–F) and is given 1 minute to prepare a short talk for 1–2 minutes. The other players should each ask ONE further question at the end. Note: Only one "Topic Talk" is required of each player, and when the talk is completed, he or she waits on the star square ("Wait Here After Topic Talk") until the next turn.

PART 3: The **KEY** below is for squares 33-35-37-39-41-43-45. Choose a prompt for the "Topic Talk" given.

33	Talk A ...	Discuss the role of movies in society today.
	Talk B ...	Discuss the role of advertising in modern culture.
	Talk C ...	Discuss how important tourism is in your country these days.
	Talk D ...	Discuss the importance of role models for the youth of today.
	Talk E ...	Discuss whether you think books are too expensive to buy.
	Talk F ...	Discuss what you think makes a good school.
35	Talk A ...	Compare movies made in your country with movies made in America.
	Talk B ...	Compare products made in your country with those made overseas.
	Talk C ...	Compare travel in the past, say a hundred years ago, with travel today.
	Talk D ...	Compare the differences between students in your own country and those from overseas.
	Talk E ...	Compare the differences between reading a book in your own language and in English.
	Talk F ...	Compare the education system in your own country with that of your host country.
37	Talk A ...	How often and where do you go to the movies? Describe the cinema you usually go to.
	Talk B ...	How do products made these days compare with those made in the past?
	Talk C ...	How might the tourist industry in your country change in the future?
	Talk D ...	How can students improve their performance at school?
	Talk E ...	How useful are books translated from English or from other languages into your language?
	Talk F ...	How have schools changed in the last hundred years?
39	Talk A ...	What are the advantages of being a movie star or director?
	Talk B ...	What are some of the advantages of advertising?
	Talk C ...	What are some of the advantages of travel?
	Talk D ...	Are there any advantages of being popular at school?
	Talk E ...	What are the advantages of a book compared with a movie version of a book?
	Talk F ...	What are some of the advantages of doing well at school?
41	Talk A ...	What are the disadvantages of being a movie star or director?
	Talk B ...	Are there any disadvantages of seeing advertisements everywhere?
	Talk C ...	What are the disadvantages of the increased popularity of tourism?
	Talk D ...	What are the disadvantages of being unpopular at school?
	Talk E ...	Are there disadvantages of making books out of paper? Are there any alternatives?
	Talk F ...	In what ways does a bad teacher disadvantage students?
43	Talk A ...	Do you think television has helped to make the world a better place to live in?
	Talk B ...	Do you think banning advertisements for alcohol and smoking is worthwhile? Why?
	Talk C ...	What do you think is the best way to plan a holiday? Why?
	Talk D ...	Do you think it is harder to study when you are young or when you are older? Why?
	Talk E ...	In what ways do you think being a writer might be an interesting job?
	Talk F ...	What sort of equipment do you think is useful in a language school? Why?
45	Talk A ...	Explain what you think movies might be like in a hundred years from now.
	Talk B ...	Explain some of the differences between a consumer society and a primitive society.
	Talk C ...	Explain what we can do to protect nature in the future.
	Talk D ...	Explain the most effective methods of punishment for bad students.
	Talk E ...	Explain why you cannot learn English only from a book.
	Talk F ...	Explain how schools might look in the future.

- Speaking Test Board Game -

No. of Players: 2 or more players per game. If there are 4 or more players, one member of the group can volunteer to be the referee. He or she does not go around the board but decides if the answers given are suitable (for the IELTS).

Equipment: Counters or coins and one die

Object of the Game: Players take turns to throw the die, advancing around the board from START to FINISH. Players must also successfully 'speak' their way around the board. First player to land on the "FINISH" square is the winner. It must be with an exact throw.

Special Squares: Players landing on "Go To" or "Go Back" squares must go to the square indicated.

Players landing on "Free Turn" squares can throw the die again.

Part 1 – Introduction & Interview

- START
- 1 Your parents
- 2 Your brothers & sisters
- 3 Your home town
- Go Back to Start
- 5 Your present home
- 6 The area you now live in
- 7 Your friends
- Free Turn

Part 1 – Continued...

- 9 A job you have now or once had
- 10 An occupation you might enjoy
- 11 Your boss or your teacher
- 12 Your educational background
- 13 Your English study
- 14 The best study methods
- 15 Your hobbies or interests
- Go To 9
- 17 Your favourite sport or game
- 18 The music you enjoy listening to
- 19 What you like to read
- 20 A TV program you have seen
- 21 What you do in your spare time
- 22 Countries you have visited
- 23 Your best friend
- Free Turn

Part 2 – Topic Talk

- 25 Topic Talk F
- 26 Topic Talk E
- 27 Topic Talk D
- 28 Topic Talk C
- 29 Topic Talk B
- 30 Topic Talk A
- Wait Here After Topic Talk

Part 3 – Discussion

- Go To Square 37
- 33 Discuss ... (see Key)
- Go Back 1 Square
- 35 Compare ... (see Key)
- Go To 39
- 37 How ... (see Key)
- Go Back 3 Squares
- 39 Advantages (see Key)
- Free Turn
- 41 Disadvantages (see Key)
- Go To 43
- 43 What do you think? (see Key)
- Go Back 3 Squares
- 45 Explain ... (see Key)
- Go To 33
- FINISH Say goodbye and thank you

A Classmate

Talk about a particular classmate that you admire in some way.

You should speak about:

who that person is and where he or she comes from

when you first met each other

what you have done together

... and why you admire this person.

A Book

Talk about a favourite book that you have read.

You should include:

where and when you read it

some brief information about the book, the story and the characters

why you read this particular book

... and how much you enjoyed reading it.

Your School

Describe a school you attend now or attended in the past.

You should talk about:

where the school is and what it looks like

the other people in the school

the subjects you studied or are studying

... and how the school has affected your life.

A Favourite Place

Describe a favourite place that you like to visit.

You should include in your answer:

where it is located

when you first went there

why you like it there

... and what you have done there in the past.

A Product

Talk about a product you buy regularly.

You should include in your answer:

a description of the product

when and where you buy that product

what you do with it

... and why you buy that particular product

A Movie

Talk about a movie that you have seen recently.

You should say:

where and why you saw this particular movie

who is acting in the movie

what happens in the movie

... and why you like or dislike this movie.

ANSWER KEYS

NB: i) answer words in brackets are optional
ii) alternative answers are separated with a stroke (/)

PRACTICE TEST ONE
Listening Test One

Section 1

1 C
2 B
3 A
4 B
5 £40
6 L A V I L L I E R S *(must be correctly spelt)*
7 Swiss
8 Paris / Sèvres
9 3 3 1 – 9 8 6 1 – 4 5 3 7
10 computer disks

Section 2

11 A
12 E
13 F
(Answers to 11–13 may be in any order)
14 C
15 E
(Answers to 14–15 may be in either order)
16 hotels / resorts / hotels and resorts *(plural only)*
17 of/by law / for/of high buildings
18 (are) jammed
19 (the) authorities
20 (further) development(s)

Section 3

21 British AirWorld
22 Hospitality and Tourism
23 meeting (new) people
24 passenger comfort
25 beat jet lag / changing time zones
26 bigger / more comfortable
27 recent (release) blockbusters / recent (release) films
28 atmosphere more pleasant
29 fire risk reduced
30 offer more / vegetarian meals / two hot meals / interesting / exotic/gourmet food

Section 4

31 D
32 D
33 D
34 D
35 A
36 D
37 E
38 B
39 C
40 D
(Answers to 35–37 and 38–40 may be given in any order)

PRACTICE TEST ONE
Reading Test One

Passage 1

1 (nearly) 4.9 (million)
2 (about) 3000 (sq. km)
3 5506 (km)
4 10.25 (hrs. per day)
5 A
6 E
7 B
8 F
9 D
10 TRUE
11 NOT GIVEN
12 TRUE
13 FALSE
14 NOT GIVEN
15 TRUE
16 FALSE

Passage 2

17 C
18 C
19 D
20 A
21 C
22 fitness levels
23 assessed
24 guidelines
25 mandatory
26 attend
27 check
28 undertaken
29 examples

Passage 3

30 for (easy) cleaning
31 standard domestic
32 void (the) warranty
33 season the wok
34 deep frying
35 C
36 braising / shallow frying
37 condensation / splattering
38 tall sides
39 stir frying
40 braising

PRACTICE TEST TWO
Listening Test Two

Section 1

1 C
2 D
3 one year
4 500 students / many students / lots of students
5 Table Tennis Club / Orienteering Club
6 Z A L E S K A *(must be correctly spelt)*
7 Polish
8 3 4 9 6 8 – A P
9 Sat PM / Saturday afternoon
10 0 1 2 2 2 – 5 6 5 2 4 8

Section 2

11 45,227 (square km)
12 three-fifths
13 64.2%
14 capital
15 north-west
16 electric motors
17 grain
18 crops *(answer must be plural)*
19 (democratic) (parliamentary) republic
20 mild

Section 3

21 (the local) council / Chief Dietician
22 advertising
23 demanding / she likes it
24 (her/first) examination (result)
25 radio / talk-back programmes / radio interviews
26 good/balanced breakfast / higher metabolic rate
27 more experience
28 more challenging
29 agency
30 nutritional advice / consultations

Section 4

31 B
32 B
33 A
34 A
35 B
36 A
37 A
38 B
39 D
40 five / 5

ANSWER KEYS

NB: i) answer words in brackets are optional
ii) alternative answers are separated with a stroke (/)

PRACTICE TEST TWO

READING TEST TWO

Passage 1

1	25
2	(a) membership card
3	yes
4	9.30 a.m.
5	3 / three
6	9371 – 4356
7	community
8	$76
9	weight (-training)
10	soccer
11	lunch
12	Saturday / Sunday / Saturday and Sunday / (the) weekends / the weekend
13	swimming lanes
14	(changes to) timetables

Passage 2

15	do not procrastinate / (always) return calls / be organised
16	overemphasise
17	fair treatment / positive referrals
18	A
19	B
20	D
21	B, C, G
22	FALSE
23	FALSE
24	NOT GIVEN
25	NOT GIVEN
26	TRUE
27	TRUE

(Answers to 27 may be in any order, but all 3 answers must be given)

Passage 3

28	IV
29	VIII
30	III
31	II
32	I
33	E
34	B
35	E
36	humans
37	flightless
38	stoat
39	beak
40	habitat

PRACTICE TEST THREE

READING TEST THREE

Passage 1

1	B
2	E
3	D
4	F
5	A, C
6	Room 16
7	West Gallery
8	Room 32
9	Stanley Buck Auditorium
10	Foyer, Courtyard
11	2
12	3, 5
13	3
14	4
15	56,040

(Answer to 5 must include both answers)

(Answer to 10 must include both answers)

(Answer to 12 must include both answers)

Passage 2

16	FALSE
17	TRUE
18	NOT GIVEN
19	TRUE
20	TRUE
21	NOT GIVEN
22	FALSE
23	D
24	B
25	F
26	C
27	F
28	A

Passage 3

29	F
30	I
31	K
32	G
33	B
34	A
35	Indonesia
36	Korea
37	Iran
38	Korea
39	China
40	Japan

PRACTICE TEST FOUR

READING TEST FOUR

Passage 1

1	9211 2965
2	9838 7555
3	1200 35 2334 (ext.) 6145
4	9515 7445
5	9838 7555
6	14 8888
7	Channel 7
8	talk show
9	Dollar Dazzle / Channel 10
10	7.15 p.m.
11	Boy's Town / Channel 9
12	Kung-Fu God
13	Video Hits / Channel 7
14	tennis / U.S. Open

Passage 2

15	C
16	D
17	E
18	B, E
19	NOT GIVEN
20	TRUE
21	FALSE
22	NOT GIVEN
23	FC
24	FC
25	KM
26	SH
27	LF
28	OS

(Answer to 18 must include both answers)

Passage 3

29	C
30	B
31	D
32	5
33	2
34	6
35	1
36	B
37	B
38	PF
39	N
40	I

SCORE INTERPRETER

↓ Number of Your Correct Answers (out of a possible score of 40)

Your Score	Test One		Test Two		Test Three	Test Four
	Listening	Reading	Listening	Reading	Reading	Reading
0–2	Well Below Average	Well Below Average	Well Below Average	Well Below Average	Well Below Average	Well Below Average
3–4	Well Below Average	Well Below Average	Well Below Average	Well Below Average	Well Below Average	Well Below Average
5–6	Well Below Average	Well Below Average	Well Below Average	Well Below Average	Well Below Average	Well Below Average
7–8	Well Below Average	Well Below Average	Well Below Average	Well Below Average	Well Below Average	Below Average
9–10	Well Below Average	Well Below Average	Below Average	Well Below Average	Below Average	Below Average
11–12	Below Average	Well Below Average	Below Average	Below Average	Below Average	Below Average
13–14	Below Average	Below Average	Below Average	Below Average	Below Average	Below Average
15–16	Below Average	Below Average	Below Average	Below Average	Below Average	Below Average
17–18	Below Average	Below Average	Below Average	Below Average	Below Average	Average
19–20	Below Average	Below Average	Average	Below Average	Average	Average
21–22	Average	Below Average	Average	Average	Average	Average
23–24	Average	Average	Average	Avorago	Average	Average
25–26	Average	Average	Average	Average	Average	Above Average
27–28	Average	Average	Above Average	Average	Above Average	Above Average
29–30	Above Average	Average	Avove Average	Avove Average	Above Average	Above Average
31–32	Above Average	Above Average	Above Average	Above Average	Above Average	Above Average
33–34	Above Average	Above Average	Above Average	Above Average	Above Average	Well Above Average
35–36	Above Average	Above Average	Above Average	Above Average	Well Above Average	Well Above Average
37–38	Above Average	Above Average	Well Above Average	Well Above Average	Well Above Average	Well Above Average
39–40	Well Above Average	Well Above Average	Well Above Average	Well Above Average	Well Above Average	Well Above Average

Key: *(a satisfactory score is taken to mean a tertiary institution entry level Band Score of between 5.5 and 6.5)*

Well Below Average	It is clear you require a great deal more practice before you attempt the IELTS test. It would probably take at least 48–60 weeks of intensive practice to achieve a satisfactory score in the actual IELTS test.
Below Average	You do not yet fully understand the strategies required to do well in the IELTS test, nor how to apply them. At present, you are only likely to hear or find answers with a teacher's help. It would probably take at least 36–48 weeks of intensive practice to achieve a satisfactory score in the actual IELTS test.
Average	You need to read all the hints in this book, and know how to apply them before you attempt the actual IELTS test. Perhaps you would be capable of hearing the answers in the listening test if it were played more than once. You most certainly need more time to complete the reading test. It would probably take at least 24–36 weeks of intensive practice to achieve a satisfactory score in the actual IELTS test.
Above Average	Your score indicates that you understand how to apply most of the hints in this book. However, if you take the actual IELTS test now, you might be disappointed with your result. It would probably take at least 12–24 weeks of intensive practice to achieve a satisfactory score in the actual IELTS test.
Well Above Average	You appear to understand the strategies involved in the listening and reading tests in this book. It may take 6–12 weeks of intensive practice to achieve a satisfactory IELTS Band Score. Take a short approved IELTS course at an English college, or alternatively, you might wish to purchase more practice books.

☞ Please note that the tests in this book are not written at the same level of difficulty; they become progressively more difficult as you work your way through the book. Therefore, it is not possible to give an accurate Band Score indication.

MODEL ANSWERS

GENERAL TRAINING MODULE – WRITING TEST ONE

The Model Answers below are given as examples only. This standard of written English can only be achieved with much practice.

Task 1

Dear Sir,

I am writing to you because I am unable to pay next month's rent which is due on Saturday. Unfortunately, the other day I lost my wallet, and there was a large amount of money inside. I have, therefore, had to write to my parents to ask them to send me some money urgently. As soon as it arrives, I will immediately notify you and arrange to pay by cash or cheque. I hope that this does not cause you too much inconvenience.

There are also some problems with the flat that I wish to bring to your attention. First, the cold tap in the bathroom will not turn off properly, and the water is dripping constantly. This will need to be fixed quickly because it is wasting water. Second, one of the back rings on the top of the oven does not work at all.

I'm sorry that I cannot pay the rent on time, and trust that you will understand.

Yours sincerely,

Mary Campisi *(168 words)*

Task 2

The most important step in the completion of a class assignment is researching the topic. Some assignments require you to give a written answer, and others require a spoken presentation. However, finding useful information is only possible if you know where to look. This report will describe some of the best places to find information.

To begin with, there is the reading list that the tutor gives students in class. Reading lists show the essential book titles you should read to complete a written task, and are useful because they contain the books that the tutor recommends.

Second, there is the library in the school where you are studying. Most good colleges have libraries containing a wide range of books, newspapers, magazines and reference material. These days, modern, well-equipped libraries have banks of computers with CD-ROM disks on a variety of subjects. Alternatively, if you are researching information for a spoken presentation, you might borrow a video to show your class. If you cannot find the books you need in the school or college library, you can go to the local library and ask the librarian there to help you.

Additionally, the Internet allows us to obtain information from a huge number of sources all over the world. It might take a long time to search for what you want, but once you find it you can print out only the pages you require.

Finally, people can be good sources of information, too. By interviewing people with particular knowledge, or conducting surveys, you can obtain the information that is most current and suitable for your needs.

(266 words)

MODEL ANSWERS

GENERAL TRAINING MODULE – WRITING TEST TWO

The Model Answers below are given as examples only. This standard of written English can only be achieved with much practice.

Task 1

Dear Sir or Madam,

I am writing to your newpaper to protest about the proposed development of Newtown Park opposite where I live.

The local council has written to us saying that they are going to build a huge five-storey block of flats on the park next year. I strongly object to this proposal, and so do my neighbours.

There are too many flats in this area already, and, although it is true that people have to have a place to live, they have to have a place to play as well. If the council goes ahead and builds this block of flats, where will our children play? We only have one park in this part of town. The next park is over three kilometres away.

We need this park, and we need the trees and the green space that it provides. If you agree that we must save our lovely park, write to this newspaper and tell the council how you feel about their development plans. Write to me and perhaps we can ask people to sign a petition to stop the project.

Disgusted

(Newtown) *(183 words)*

Task 2

When you are young, there is often a great deal of peer pressure put upon you to be in a relationship. Although most young people spend a lot of time dreaming about finding the right boyfriend or girlfriend, I believe that early relationships can lead to many problems which young men and women might not be able to solve easily.

Firstly, having a special friend is a large responsibility. It takes up a lot of time looking after the needs and interests of another person. It could be better to spend this time studying or playing sport. After all, there will be plenty of opportunity for young persons to share their lives later, when they are grown up.

Next, there is the financial situation to consider. Some activities are cheaper to do together but most are not. Often one partner has more money than the other and must pay for both when, for instance, they go to the movies or to a restaurant. Also, young people love to buy each other gifts, and may try to impress by spending more than necessary.

Some people argue that today's youth are better informed than their parents were and, therefore, might be more capable of making a relationship succeed. This may be true, but young people today still have many emotional problems to face; in a relationship it is more difficult. For instance, it is hard to have complete trust in someone without a strong commitment. Jealousy can be very destructive, especially at an early age.

In general, while it is true that, for young people, being together and in love is wonderful, there are often many difficult issues to cope with in a full-time relationship.

(284 words)

MODEL ANSWERS

GENERAL TRAINING – WRITING TEST THREE

The Model Answers below are given as examples only. This standard of written English can only be achieved with much practice.

Task 1

Dear Jim,

At last I have time to write to you as promised. Surfers' Paradise is a great place for a holiday, and I'm so glad you suggested it to me. The beach really is as good as you said it would be, and your choice of hotel was excellent.

As you know, the hotel is right next to the beach; in fact, my room overlooks the water. The weather has been marvellous so far. Every day I've been swimming, and I am starting to get a great tan. It's a fantastic place for a holiday.

Last week I went to Sea World and saw the dolphins on display. They really are very clever. Yesterday, I met some other hotel guests from my country, and we had dinner together. It was a most enjoyable evening, and we made plans to go out on a day cruise this Saturday. I'm looking forward to it very much.

I think you made an excellent choice of holiday for me because it is so easy to meet new friends here and have a good time. Thank you once again. I'll come in and see you when I return.

Regards

Mariko Kato *(193 words)*

Task 2

I am glad that a new shopping centre is going to open in our town. We badly need a good place to shop and meet up with our friends. In my opinion, we need many different kinds of shops, but the centre should also provide us with a number of community facilities.

To begin with, there should be a large food supermarket within the centre. People must have a good and cheap place to buy their weekly food supplies. However, we must also have specialty food shops that supply foods that are hard to get in a supermarket. A large delicatessen would be a good idea. And perhaps we can have an Asian foodstore since Asian food is very popular nowadays.

Next, we need an all-purpose store such as K-Mart. If possible, I would like this store to be quite large and with a lot of checkout aisles because it is boring when you have to wait a long time to be served. Homeware stores are a good idea, too, since there are many young homemakers in our area.

Of course, we must have all the usual shops such as a hairdressers', a butchers', a chemist, a post office, and various clothes shops. But most importantly we need a lot of places to sit down and eat. Mothers with small children will require special areas for them to play in, and there should be plenty of clean rest rooms as well.

In conclusion, I would like to see a lot of free activities and product demonstrations in the new centre because this will attract customers and make the shopping centre a great success. If the centre contains a lot of office space, it will be a big mistake.

(288 words)

MODEL ANSWERS

GENERAL TRAINING – WRITING TEST FOUR

The Model Answers below are given as examples only. This standard of written English can only be achieved with much practice.

Task 1

Dear Sir or Madam,

I am anxious to obtain information about the college's Graphics Design course which begins in less than two months. Actually, I wrote four weeks ago, but I have not yet heard from you. Perhaps you did not receive my letter.

First of all, I need to know if it is too late to enrol in the course. Can you write and tell me if there are any places available? I certainly hope that my enrolment is still possible.

I need to have more information about the course before I decide to apply, but I realise that I do not have much time. Would you be kind enough to send your reply by express mail? Especially, I need to know the cost of the course, and whether the certificate you offer at the end of the course will be sufficient qualification for me to apply full-time to one of the Graphic Design colleges in your city.

I look forward to your reply.

John Smith *(165 words)*

Task 2

It is unfortunate that the world is becoming less and less safe. Everyday in the news we read that someone has been murdered, and crime has increased in major cities all over the world. Furthermore, cities are no longer safe places in which to raise children. In my opinion, the main cause of people being unkind to each other is a lack of understanding.

Mankind has always fought wars and probably always will. Yet there have never been so many high-tech weapons available to so many countries before. If the rich countries which supply poorer countries with these weapons understood the problems they create, arms sales would be illegal. I cannot understand why some drugs are illegal, but weapons that kill thousands of people are sold everywhere.

It is sad that politicians cannot be trusted to stop fighting wars. People follow their leaders' examples. In big cities people steal from and sometimes even murder their fellow citizens. Is it getting worse than it used to be? I think it is, and, furthermore, I think it will get worse in the future because we are not learning from our mistakes.

Of course, some people argue that the news services are much better these days, and therefore we hear more bad news than before. However, I disagree because my parents tell me that when they were young they could walk the streets safely at night, and people were much kinder to each other.

To sum up, we live in a violent world. Bringing up children in a world where violence is regularly shown on television shows and on the news is proof that it is not a safe place. If we do not try to solve this problem, our children's future will suffer.

(291 words)

IELTS TEST ANSWER SHEET

Name: ....

Question Number:	Answer:					Question Number:	Answer:			
1		▭	1	▭		22		▭	22	▭
2		▭	2	▭		23		▭	23	▭
3		▭	3	▭		24		▭	24	▭
4		▭	4	▭		25		▭	25	▭
5		▭	5	▭		26		▭	26	▭
6		▭	6	▭		27		▭	27	▭
7		▭	7	▭		28		▭	28	▭
8		▭	8	▭		29		▭	29	▭
9		▭	9	▭		30		▭	30	▭
10		▭	10	▭		31		▭	31	▭
11		▭	11	▭		32		▭	32	▭
12		▭	12	▭		33		▭	33	▭
13		▭	13	▭		34		▭	34	▭
14		▭	14	▭		35		▭	35	▭
15		▭	15	▭		36		▭	36	▭
16		▭	16	▭		37		▭	37	▭
17		▭	17	▭		38		▭	38	▭
18		▭	18	▭		39		▭	39	▭
19		▭	19	▭		40		▭	40	▭
20		▭	20	▭			Total:			
21		▭	21	▭			Band Score			
							Marker's Initials			

~ For use with the 101 Helpful Hints Practice Tests for IELTS ~

IELTS WRITING TEST 1 2 3 4 ANSWER SHEET

Name: ....

....

....

....

....

....

....

....

....

....

....

....

....

....

....

....

....

....

....

....

....

....

....

....

~ For use with the 101 Helpful Hints PracticeTests for IELTS ~

LISTENING TEST TAPESCRIPTS

PRACTICE LISTENING TEST ONE

Narrator: Listening Test One. This is a practice listening test which resembles the International English Language Testing System Listening Test. The test consists of four sections. Answer the questions as you listen to the recording. Note that the recording is played once only. Please turn to Section 1.

Section 1

Narrator: Section 1. George and Lisa are overseas students studying in Britain. They are returning home for the summer holidays. First, look at Questions 1 to 4.

(20 second pause)

You will see that there is an example already done for you. For this question only the conversation relating to the example will be played first.

Taxi Driver: That'll be £23. Right. There's your change. Have a nice trip. Oh, I'll just get your bags out of the boot.

Lisa: Thank you very much.

The taxi driver said that he would get the bags out of the the boot of his taxi, so the correct answer is A.

Now we shall begin. You should answer the questions as you listen because you will not hear the recording a second time.

Now listen carefully and answer Questions 1 to 4.

Taxi Driver: That'll be £23. Right. There's your change. Have a nice trip. Oh, I'll just get your bags out of the boot.

Lisa: Thank you very much. Now, George, let's find the check-in desk.

George: Yes, but with all the changes they have made here at the airport, I'm not sure where the check-in desk is.

Lisa: I know. It's strange isn't it? Why don't we ask for help?

George: Good idea. What about that man sitting down over there?

Lisa: Which one? The one with the hat on?

George: But what about the man with the blue uniform and the cap sitting on the trolley? He's bound to know. He looks like he works here.

Lisa: OK, I'll ask him. Excuse me, could you tell me where the check-in desk for FrancAir is please?

Man: Oh, let me think. I haven't worked here very long. The best way to get there would be to turn left at the end here, where the café is, and then go straight ahead until you're opposite the departure gates entrance...no, no...sorry...um, it might be quicker to turn right as soon as you get past the café, and keep going along the corridor until you come to the sliding doors at the end. On the left. Yep...that's it. All the check-in counters are in a hall there. I'm pretty sure FrancAir is directly to your left as you walk in the hall.

Lisa: Thanks a lot. So, it's left past the café, and then right opposite...

Man: ...the bookshop. You can't miss it.

George: Come on then, Lisa. We don't want to be late, and I want some time to get a cup of coffee and look around the bookshop.

Lisa: OK, George, but I want to go and wash my hands first. I'll meet you at the check-in desk.

Narrator: George now speaks to the clerk at the check-in counter. Listen to the conversation, and fill in the information on the Excess Baggage form in the spaces numbered 5 to 10. First, you have some time to look at the form.

(10 second pause)

Now listen to the conversation, and answer Questions 5 to 10.

Clerk: Good morning. Can I help you?

George: Yes. I would like to check in for flight FA-492.

Clerk: Very good. Can I have your ticket and passport please?

George: Yes, here you are.

Clerk: OK. Thanks...er...if you could just put your suitcase on the scales...

George: Oh, I also have this extra box that I want to take as well.

Clerk: OK. Well, that's extra luggage, so I'll have to get you to fill out an Excess Baggage Declaration Certificate. It'll cost extra, I'm afraid. Let's see...er...£40 exactly.

George: Oh well, what's the form for?

Clerk: It's just a form you have to fill out, so if there are any problems, we'll know where you are and how to contact you. So, if you can give me a few details, I'll key in the information. OK then. Now, your passport says your name is...Lavilliers. Is that right?

George: Yes. George Lavilliers.

Clerk: George...er...L-A-V-I-L-L-I-E-R-S. Good. Now, nationality: French. No, wait a minute. It's a Swiss passport.

George: Well, yes, I live in France, but I was born in Switzerland.

Clerk: Swiss. Very good. Flight number: FA–492. Destination is...

George: ...Paris.

Clerk: Are you connecting with any other flight in Paris, or will you be staying there?

George: No, I'm spending my holiday in Paris. Well, Sèvres, just outside Paris.

Clerk: OK, so what's the phone number there?

George: Um...let me think...the country code for France is...er...33, and the number is...1 – 9 8 6 1 – 4 5 3 7.

Clerk: Right. So that's...3 3 1 – 9 8 6 1 – 4 5 3 7.

George: Yes, that's it.

Clerk: And can you tell me briefly what you have in the box?

George: Well, there are some books – just university textbooks from last term – some clothes, and...oh yeah, my computer disks.

Clerk: OK. Thank you. And what would be the approximate value of the contents?

George: Oh, quite a bit actually. About...yes, about £150.

Clerk: That's all. There's your receipt for the box, your passport and ticket, and here's your boarding pass. Gate 7.

You can board the plane in about 35 minutes. Have a nice flight.

Narrator: That is the end of Section 1. You now have 30 seconds to check your answers to Section 1.

(30 second pause)

Now turn to Section 2.

Section 2

Narrator: Section 2. You will now hear a short news item. First, you have some time to look at the questions.

(20 second pause)

Now listen to the news item, and answer Questions 11 to 20.

Trent: Good morning. We have just received word of a major earthquake off the coast of Mandaland in the Pacific Ocean.

At present, scientists are unsure if the quake – registering 6.5 on the Richter scale – will cause a tsunami, a giant wave of water, because it is not known yet at precisely what depth the earthquake took place.

The geographical location of the earthquake is in a mountainous undersea region of the Pacific Ocean which has not been fully and accurately explored.

Scientists are also concerned that the quake might set off a chain reaction of events in the earth's crust.

Meanwhile, on all the islands within a radius of 1000 kilometres of the earthquake, and on the mainland of Mandaland, authorities are urging everyone to leave their homes and make their way up the mountains where they will be safe if a tsunami occurs.

On islands where there are no high levels of land, army helicopters from Australian bases in Mandaland are airlifting villagers to safety.

The last major earthquake in this region caused a tsunami which devastated large areas of Mandaland and killed over 2000 people. The economy of the country was seriously damaged and it took more than twenty years for public buildings and people's homes to be completely rebuilt.

It is hoped that this time, if another tsunami does occur, the warnings given will prevent large scale destruction of life, although it has proved impossible to build sea-walls that can withstand such giant waves of water and attempts to do so on Mandaland were soon abandoned.

However, the reconstruction of all large buildings near the coast – including hotels and resorts – was undertaken with the threat of a tsunami in mind. The availability of fast and easy exit from all lower floors to the rooftop was made a requirement for every building over two storeys high by law.

If you have relatives or persons you wish to contact on Mandaland, it is suggested you do not phone direct – all lines are currently jammed – but contact the authorities on the hotline shown on your screen; that number is 0 1 7 9 3 3 3 3.

Stay tuned for further developments as they come to hand. This is Trent Dunwell for the Channel 4 News Team. The time is now four thirty. After the break – sports news with Jim McKenna.

Narrator: That is the end of Section 2. You now have 30 seconds to check your answers to Section 2.

(30 second pause)

Now turn to Section 3.

Section 3

Narrator: Section 3. Next, you will hear an interview on the radio. First, you have some time to look at the questions.

(20 second pause)

Now listen to the interview, and answer Questions 21 to 25.

Sue: Good afternoon and welcome to "Working Lives". My name is Sue Holt. This week we continue our series by looking at a job that is often thought of as adventurous, exotic, and highly desirable. We're going to take a behind-the-scenes look at the airline hospitality industry. What is the reality behind the smart uniform and ever ready smile of the flight attendant? We're lucky enough to have in the studio Julie Nevard, who works for British AirWorld, and is a senior member of the cabin crew staff. Thank you for finding the time to speak to us. I know that you must have a busy schedule.

Julie: My pleasure. Yes, it is a very full-time job, but I think you realise that very early on in your career.

Sue: How long have you been involved in in-flight hospitality?

Julie: Well, I trained for a year at the British AirWorld Training School, and...I'd already taken a Diploma in Hospitality and Tourism after I left school so, all in all, ... about 5 years...no, more like 6 years.

Sue: So your training was at college?

Julie: Well, yes, the preliminary training, but then the British AirWorld Training course in Manchester was a more specialised hospitality course. I suppose you could call the Diploma my major professional qualification.

Sue: I see. Now tell me, is the job as glamorous as most people believe?

Julie: Absolutely not! Oh, of course, there are many good things about the job. You know, you never know where you might be going. For example, I still get excited when I see the new roster for the first time. Knowing I'll soon be off somewhere I haven't been before, on a new route. The best thing, of course, is that all the time I'm meeting new people. But people don't realise that what I get to see most of is the inside of hotel rooms, and most hotel rooms are pretty similar. Also, it's like, I'm working, but the majority of my passengers are on holiday. Sometimes it's hard to deal with all their demands. There are times you just want to shout, "I'm doing my best, I've got a job to do, leave me alone!", but that doesn't happen very often.

Sue: Then tell me, what is your main responsibility during a flight?

Julie: That's hard to say really. Well, we're responsible for all the needs and demands of each and every passenger, for up to 10 hours on some long haul flights. Not to mention the safety of the plane and all the passengers. I suppose, if I have to come up with a single answer, it'd be passenger comfort.

Sue: Do you find yourself going to the same places often?

Julie: There are four or five major destinations that we fly to more regularly than others. Yes, I've got to know some cities very well.

Sue: Oh, really? Which destinations are those?

Julie: Well, there's Paris, Frankfurt, Rome, Kennedy...

Sue: Kennedy Airport in...in Los Angeles?

Julie: New York...these are the most frequent destinations with British AirWorld.

Sue: So how do you deal with the changing time zones?

Julie: It's something you just have to get used to. Oh, everybody in the industry has a special tip to beat jet lag on longer flights. But me? I just make sure that I am regularly changing the time on my watch. I find that if I change the time little by little and fairly frequently, well, that seems to work well for me. You see, I have two watches: the one I'm constantly adjusting and the one with the original time at departure.

Sue: That sounds like a good idea.

Narrator: In the next part of the radio interview, complete the table with no more than three words for each answer. First, you have some time to look at the table and questions.

(10 second pause)

Now listen and answer Questions 26 to 30.

Sue: So, have you seen many changes in the type of services you offer?

Julie: Oh, yes. These days the competition is much tougher. I suppose the result is that the consumer, the traveller, has a much better deal. Well, the seats are bigger, more comfortable than they were 10 years ago – the in-flight entertainment, the films...now they are all recent release blockbusters. They weren't 10 years ago. But the two biggest improvements have been to do with the smoking restrictions and the upgrading of the meals.

Sue: Oh right, tell me about these two changes.

Julie: Yes, the restriction on smoking has had a two-fold benefit. Firstly, the atmosphere is much more pleasant, and, secondly, the fire risk is greatly reduced. You know, we used to have people dropping cigarettes, burning the seats. A dreadful fire risk. Can you imagine?

Sue: Terrible.

Julie: I, for one, never understood why anyone was ever allowed to smoke on aeroplanes in the first place.

Sue: Um...and the meals?

Julie: Ah, with so many carriers vying for passengers on the same route, you just have to offer more. Vegetarian meals, choice of two hot meals, interesting, exotic, gourmet food – all this is now commonplace in our economy class galleys. And for the business and first-class passengers, the food is as good as in any world-class restaurant – top chefs, great presentation, nutritious ingredients...really quite lovely.

Sue: And finally, what advice or words of warning would you give to school leavers considering a career in this industry?

Julie: That's a difficult question. I'd say think long and hard about why you want to do it. It's not all glamorous, and it can be very hard work.

Sue: Julie, it's been fascinating talking to you. Thank you for your time. And just before we go, next week we will be talking to...

Narrator: That is the end of Section 3. You now have 30 seconds to check your answers to Section 3.

(30 second pause)

Now turn to Section 4.

Section 4

Narrator: Section 4. You will hear part of an introductory seminar given at a Hotel Management School. First, you have some time to look at the questions.

(20 second pause)

Now listen to the lecture, and answer Questions 31 to 40.

Lecturer: Welcome to the first seminar of the International Hotel Hospitality and Management Course. My name's Garth Walters, and I'm one of the Career Advisors at the school, and, er...this afternoon, I intend to give you an overview of the four core subject options available to you in this course – one of which you will need to choose as your core or main subject by the end of the first week. Each core subject prepares students for work in one of four major career areas: front desk and reception work, drink and bar service, restaurant service, and lastly, guest relations. For each area that I have mentioned, we will explore the personal skills required, the professional qualifications needed, and the career opportunities available.

To start with, we are going to take a look at front desk and reception work. In some ways, the reception desk is both the...er...face and the nerve centre of a hotel. It's the first point of physical contact with the client, and a close and professional relationship should be immediately struck up. The psychology behind the need for creating a good first impression and maintaining it is fairly obvious, but how to do this effectively constitutes a major slice of the work that all students will be doing in the first few weeks of this course, regardless of the option that you choose.

Now, the type of person who is best suited for front desk and reception work is self-confident, caring and sensitive, intelligent, and also able to work calmly in the glare of the public eye, when it's as busy as it often gets, without appearing to panic. The ability to speak more than one language is, naturally, a great asset in this job, as is clear diction and familiarity with switchboard operating systems – a technical skill that is taught only in the front desk and reception core option.

Qualifications? Well, ideally, an Associate Diploma with at least one foreign language would be good, but this is not strictly necessary. You are encouraged, however, to take up another language. As for the career opportunities available, um...after a few years, competent front desk staff can begin working in reception management, that is, being responsible for the VIP guests, and coordinating and arranging conferences and meetings at the hotel.

We now move on to the second core subject option – drink and bar service. Usually, you need to have completed a recognised bar course to begin serving drinks in a top hotel, but you'll all be taught the basics, since a percentage of the work in each option is compulsory for all students.

Obviously, an outgoing and lively personality are prerequisites for this type of work, also, an ability to work late into the night. So, if you are a morning person, this type of work is definitely not for you! There is much more to skilled bar work than just serving drinks. It involves an intimate knowledge of most alcoholic beverages, mixers, wines, and beers, as well as mixing techniques, and the correct choice of drinks to accompany meals. An effective member of a drink and bar service team can eventually move into more specialised areas.

Two of the main avenues open are cellar management: dealing exclusively with wine and fortified wines...the, er...selection, purchase, storage, and general upkeep of the hotel cellar, and the other area is working in co-ordination with fine restaurants as a wine manager or consultant, with the emphasis placed more on the bonding of wine with food. Naturally, for both careers, a wide and thorough knowledge and appreciation of wine varieties and styles is essential.

The third core subject option is restaurant service. Well, a love of food and its presentation is a must for anyone considering this line of work. Also, life in a restaurant can be hectic, hot, and very busy. The hours are long, and the competition for certain positions within the industry is tough, but, by completing the International Hotel Hospitality and Management Catering core option, you will be able to enter restaurant service as an Assistant or Grade 3 chef. As a Grade 3 chef you will be responsible for the preparation of salads and desserts, stocking and cleaning the fridges, etc., and, as you learn, you can progress to Grade 2, and then, with time, Grade 1 or Chief chef. As you become more familiar with different styles of food and presentation, you may wish to specialise in a particular area, but, as I said, the competition, especially in the larger more reputable hotels, can be fierce. Right. Um...before I move on to the last option, guest relations, I want to say a few words about how you can best choose your core subject, but, er...are there any questions before I continue?

Narrator: That is the end of Section 4. You now have 30 seconds to check your answers to Section 4.

(30 second pause)

You now have 1 minute to check your answers for the entire test.

(60 second pause)

That is the end of the Listening Test. You are now given exactly 10 minutes to transfer your answers to the Listening Test Answer Sheet.

PRACTICE LISTENING TEST TWO

Narrator: Listening Test Two. This is a practice listening test which resembles the International English Language Testing System Listening Test. The test consists of four sections. Answer the questions as you listen to the recording. Note that the recording is played once only. Please turn to Section 1.

Section 1

Narrator: Section 1. Ewa is an overseas student who has just enrolled at the National Business College. Her friend, Jon, meets her on enrolment day. First, look at Questions 1 and 2.

(20 second pause)

You will see that there is an example already done for you. For this question only the conversation relating to the example will be played first.

Jon: Hi, Ewa. I see you've just enrolled.

Ewa: Oh. Hi, Jon. Yes, it didn't take long. What about you?

Jon: Oh, because I've re-enrolled for another year, I don't have to be here until this afternoon, but I thought I'd come along and help.

Ewa: Oh, that's very kind of you, Jon.

Jon says he does not have to be at the college until this afternoon, so the correct answer is C.

Now we shall begin. You should answer the questions as you listen because you will not hear the recording a second time.

Now listen carefully and answer Questions 1 and 2.

Jon: Hi, Ewa. I see you've just enrolled.

Ewa: Oh. Hi, Jon. Yes, it didn't take long. What about you?

Jon: Oh, because I've re-enrolled for another year, I don't have to be here until this afternoon, but I thought I'd come along and help.

Ewa: Oh, that's very kind of you, Jon. Maybe you could help me with this elective class timetable. It's for students who need more English practice, like me.

Jon: Yeah, it's a good idea.

Ewa: It's on Fridays, and I have to choose which timetable is best for me. There are four to choose from. Here, take a look.

Jon: Oh, I see. Well, what do you need?

Ewa: I need everything...but especially writing practice.

Jon: Well, do you want to go to the Writing Skills class in the morning or the afternoon?

Ewa: In the afternoon, I think.

Jon: OK. So, Grammar and Writing Skills in the afternoon.

Ewa: Grammar? Oh no. I don't want to study grammar.

Jon: Well, in that case, Reading and Writing in the morning, followed by Pronunciation...then Listening and Speaking in the afternoon.

Ewa: I don't think my pronunciation is too bad, do you?

Jon: No, no, you speak very clearly.

Ewa: Yes, but I do need more vocabulary.

Jon: If you study Vocabulary in the morning, you have to study Grammar in the afternoon. What about Listening?

Ewa: Oh, yes. I certainly need to practise more listening.

Jon: Then your best choice would be to study Listening and Vocabulary in the afternoon, and Writing, Reading, and Grammar in the morning.

Ewa: Do I have to take Grammar?

Jon: Well, if you want to improve your writing.

Ewa: Yes, I suppose you're right. And...um...Writing class first lesson in the morning?

Jon: I'm afraid so. How's your reading, Ewa?

Ewa: Oh, I'm a bit slow. Yes, I think I will study Writing, Reading, and Grammar in the morning...

Jon: ...and Listening and Vocabulary in the afternoon. Good choice. Now what do you have to do?

Ewa: Um...just give this form to my tutor tomorrow.

Jon: Do you have any classes today?

Ewa: There's a special introductory English class for foreign students later this morning.

Jon: What time's the class?

Ewa: We have to be at the Function Room at 11.00 a.m.

Jon: It's five past nine now...

Ewa: ...it's actually nine-thirty...

Jon: Oh, right. We've got time, so why don't I take you down to the Student Centre?

Ewa: OK.

Jon: Come on then...

Narrator: Jon and Ewa continue their conversation in the Student Centre. First, you have some time to look at the questions.

(20 second pause)

Now listen to the conversation, and answer Questions 3 to 5.

Ewa: Jon, how many years have you been studying at the College?

Jon: This is my second year. I started...er...well, one year ago. Tell me again. What is it that you're studying? Computing, isn't it? Basic Programming?

Ewa: Yes, I worked as a computer programmer after I graduated from university.

Jon: So why are you doing Basic Programming?

Ewa: No, no. Advanced Programming.

Jon: Right. Well, here we are at the Student Centre.

Ewa: Oh, it's huge!

Jon: Yeah, well, it has to be. There are 500 students on campus and 50 staff.

Ewa: Oh, look, there's some information about clubs.

Jon: I'm already a member of the Table Tennis Club *and* the Orienteering Club. Do you want to play table tennis?

Ewa: I'm not much good, I'm afraid. What else is there?

Jon: Fencing, tennis, hang-gliding...

Ewa: What about orienteering? How much is it to join?

Jon: For second year students it's cheaper. Only £10..., but for first year students it's £20, I think. Do you want to become a member? I joined last year.

Ewa: Why not?

Jon: OK. Let's go to the Student Information Office. Over here...

Narrator: At the Student Information Office Ewa wants to join the Orienteering Club. She has to give information about herself to the clerk. Listen to the conversation, and complete the information on the Club Registration form in the spaces numbered 6 to 10. First, you have some time to look at the form.

(20 second pause)

Now listen to the conversation, and answer Questions 6 to 10.

Jon: Hello. My friend Ewa is a new student, and she would like to join the Orienteering Club.

Clerk: No problem. All I have to do is fill in this registration form, and the cost is only £15 for first year students. To start with, I need your full name. Ewa, isn't it?

Ewa: Yes, E-W-A.

Clerk: Family name?

Ewa: Zaleska.

Clerk: Zaleska...how do you spell that?

Ewa: Z-A-L-E-S-K-A.

Clerk: Zal-eska. Very good. And you're from...?

Ewa:...Poland.

Clerk: Nationality: Polish. I went to Poland last year. Great place. OK, so what's your student number?

Jon:...Er...on your student card.

Ewa: Oh, right. Here it is: 3 4 9 6 8 – A P.

Clerk: 3 4 9 6 8 – A P. Got it. You must be doing the Advanced Programming course. Tell me about your orienteering experience. How long have you been doing it?

Ewa: Two years.

Jon: You're probably better than I am.

Clerk: Next thing is...do you know your blood type? Um...for safety reasons...

Ewa: Oh, right. Yes, it is A positive.

Clerk: When we climb we always nominate a partner; it's good for teamwork, and you both look out for each other.

Jon: OK. We'll be partners.

Clerk: Right. So, what's *your* name?

Jon: Jon. J-O-N.

Clerk: Family name?

Jon: Anderburg. A-N-D-E-R-B-U-R-G.

Clerk: Good. When would you like to climb?

Jon: Is Sunday morning good for you, Ewa?

Ewa: Not really, Jon. I go to church.

Clerk: We have sessions in the afternoon, too. Only on weekends though.

Ewa: Oh well, Saturday afternoon, is it OK for you?

Jon: Sure.

Clerk: Saturday PM. One more thing. I need a contact number if we need to ring you...change in the weather or something like that...er...what's your home telephone number?

Ewa: 0 1 2 2 2 – 5 6 5 2 4 8.

Clerk: 0 1 2 2 2 – 5 6 5 2 4 8. Now, all you have to do is pay the £15, and I'll fix you up with a Club Membership card. Here's an information sheet about the Club. See you later.

Jon: Bye. Hey, Ewa, we've still got plenty of time, let's watch some TV.

Ewa: All right.

Narrator: That is the end of Section 1. You now have 30 seconds to check your answers to Section 1.

(30 second pause)

Now turn to Section 2.

Section 2

Narrator: Section 2. When Ewa arrives at the Student Centre, she watches a television report on the European country of Estonia. Before you listen, look at Questions 11 to 15.

(10 second pause)

Now listen to the television report, and answer Questions 11 to 15.

Reporter: Good morning viewers. Today on "World in Focus" we take a look at the small but fascinating country of Estonia. Can you see it there to the right of your screen? Located on the eastern shores of the Baltic Sea – west of Russia, and to the north of Latvia – Estonia is a mere 45,227 square kilometres in size, which is, let's say, three-fifths the size of Scotland. The country is divided into 15 counties, 207 rural municipalities, and only 47 towns. The official population is 1,462,130, made up mostly of native Estonians (64.2%), followed by Russians (28.7%), Ukrainians (2.7%), and Belarussians, Finnish and others (4.4%). The capital, Tallinn, in the north-west, as you can see, quite a beautiful city, has a population of just 420,470.

We'll be back with a further look at this extraordinary nation. Stay tuned.

Narrator: Next, look at the summary of part two of the television report and Questions 16 to 20.

(10 second pause)

Now listen to the rest of the report, and answer Questions 16 to 20.

Reporter: Welcome back. Estonia is a rather flat country – the highest point is just 318 m above sea level. It has over 1,500 islands and more than 1,400 lakes. The chief industries are the manufacture of agricultural machinery and electric motors. Chief crops? Grain and vegetables. OK. Now, you're probably thinking – why don't we know more about Estonia? Well, it could be because the country only gained independence from Russia in 1991. Each year, it celebrates its Independence Day on February 24th. The constitution guarantees fundamental human rights, and Estonia, nowadays, is, in fact, a democratic parliamentary republic. The currency is the Estonian Kroon, worth one eighth of a German mark, or about 4.5 pence. The official language is Estonian, but, given that the nation shares a border with Russia, it's no surprise that a great many people speak Russian. And so, for the weather in Tallinn today. Estonians enjoy a mild climate in summer, and can expect partly cloudy skies and a top temperature of 61 degrees Fahrenheit, that is 16 degrees Celsius. Back to the news.

Presenter: Moscow. Talks today between the Russian Delegation and the Vice-President of the United States appear to have been successful...

Narrator: That is the end of Section 2. You now have 30 seconds to check your answers to Section 2.

(30 second pause)

Now turn to Section 3.

Section 3

Narrator: Section 3. Later that morning, Ewa attends a special class for students who are non-native speakers. The tutor is interviewing an ex-student of the College. First, you have some time to look at the questions.

(20 second pause)

Now listen to the interview, and answer Questions 21 to 30.

Tutor: Today I have with me Anna Cherney, who was a student at this College, er...how long ago?

Anna: I was here one and a half, no, two years ago now.

Tutor: Anna was a student in this English class when she was at the College, and she is here to tell us about the many problems facing a non-native speaker in a tertiary institution. What have you been doing since you graduated, Anna?

Anna: I...was quite lucky when I left the College because I got a job pretty quickly with the local council. I'm still with them.

Tutor: Tell the class what course you took here at the College?

Anna: Yes, I originally wanted to work in advertising, but I found it was too hard because of my English. And so I changed my direction, and, well, I'm glad I did because now I have a qualification in nutritional science, and that's how I managed to get a job with the council.

Tutor: What exactly do you do with the council?

Anna: I work with the Chief Dietician, making sure that the meals prepared for the elderly in the community are nutritionally balanced. The council provides food for those old people who can't get out of their flat or their house. It's a very demanding job, but I like it.

Tutor: You deliver the food?

Anna: No, no. I spend most of my day in a laboratory at the council, but sometimes I talk to older people to find out if the food is tasty enough, and,...er...that they like it. I spend a lot of time in the kitchens, too, making sure that the food is good quality.

Tutor: What exactly were the problems when you first arrived at the College?

Anna: I was very shy, you know. I couldn't communicate with the students in my class because most of them were native-speakers...my English was not very good. But I, I thought everything was OK, until I got the result of my first examination. The tutor was worried why I was so quiet in class. I told her it was because I was afraid to ask a question, and, anyway, she suggested that I talk to the school counsellor.

Tutor: What advice did the counsellor give?

Anna: Well, she was very kind and understanding, and I realised that I was doing the wrong course. You have to be an "extrovert"..., you know, outgoing. I think it's a personal thing with me. You had to give a lot of opinions, and I am shy. So, she suggested I ask more questions in class, so I made it a rule to ask at least one or two questions every lesson.

Tutor: So you swapped courses and began to talk more in class. Was there anything else that the counsellor suggested?

Anna: Yes, she said I shouldn't live with students from my own country. I should share a house with some English students, so I did, and my English improved much faster.

Tutor: Are there any problems that you currently have with English?

Anna: Oh, yes, I used to have problems with the technical vocabulary in my field, but you pick that up pretty quickly. Now, it's mostly...I have difficulty trying to understand the colloquial language of the English; the way they express themselves is sometimes very strange...

Tutor: I see. How do you increase your vocabulary, for instance?

Anna: I listen to the radio a lot. Interviews on radio, talk-back programmes, that sort of thing. I find that really helps me. It's better than just watching TV. And, actually, I keep a journal of the expressions I hear. Some people collect stamps, and I collect new words and English expressions.

Tutor: Let's talk some more about your course at the College. Do you remember any study projects that you were involved in?

Anna: Er, let me see...well, there was one study we made of the nutritional habits of English schoolchildren. We had to produce a questionnaire, for a group of 20 kids, and we discovered that, too many children either didn't have any breakfast at all, or else they ate foods for breakfast that were much too high in sugar. These are two major dietary problems.

Tutor: Why?

Anna: It's complicated, but breakfast is an important

meal because your metabolic rate – the rate at which the body burns up food – is faster the earlier you begin eating in the day. So, if you want to have lots of energy, eat a good, balanced breakfast; you need a higher metabolic rate, you see. Also, too much sugar in the diet can cause the blood sugar level to rise very quickly at first, and then drop too rapidly. For breakfast, this is bad because later you are more likely to feel sleepy and unable to concentrate. So, eat a good breakfast, you'll think better, concentrate better, and, yes, you'll probably score better in your exams!

Tutor: Um, one last question. What about your future? Have you any immediate plans?

Anna: Well, in the short-term I'll continue to work for the council and gain more experience there, I hope to get a position in a hospital, which would be much more challenging than my present job. After that, my long-term goal is...I have a dream to open my own business – an agency providing nutritional advice and giving consultations, or...I might have to go back to my own country instead and do what I can to improve the diet of my people at home.

Tutor: I see. Now, does anyone have any questions for Anna? Yes. In the first row...

Narrator: That is the end of Section 3. You now have 30 seconds to check your answers to Section 3.

(30 second pause)

Now turn to Section 4.

Section 4

Narrator: Section 4. You will hear part of the orientation in which Ewa is shown the College's computer laboratory. First, you have some time to look at the questions.

(20 second pause)

Now listen to the computer laboratory orientation, and answer Questions 31 to 40.

Donald: Well, as you can see, we have well over a hundred PC computers, as well as 20 Macintosh computers set up for those students who need to produce high quality graphic design work. Of course, maintenance of all these machines and the equipment that goes with them...printers, fax machines, modems, etc., takes up almost all of my time, so, we have a number of rules. All students are expected to follow the rules, or they will be unable to use the lab in the future – and just about everybody needs to use the lab at some stage.

First of all, log on procedure. All students have to log on, that is, enter their name and lab number before the program menu comes up on the screen. The reason is that, if anything goes wrong with the machine, we can find out from you what it was you were doing when the problem occurred, and this can save a great deal of time when trying to solve the problem. Which brings us to the second rule. If something goes wrong, you mustn't just walk away from the computer, or turn it off and pretend it hasn't happened. You must let me, or one of my assistants, know what has happened, and remember, we can always find out who was last using the machine! So, with these two simple rules, it becomes relatively easy to maintain so many machines. The third rule concerns the use of student disks. At no time are you allowed to bring your own disks into the laboratory. This lab is completely free of the need for student disks of any kind, because each computer is linked to a network, and there are four networks, each of which has its own file-serving machine. We don't want you to bring along your own disks for two very good reasons. The first reason is because of copyright laws. It's illegal to copy programs bought by the college. The second reason has to do with those nasty little programs called viruses, which can do a tremendous amount of damage. So, no student disks in the lab. We, therefore, insist that you leave your bags outside, too, which is rule number four.

Now, a network simply means a number of computers are linked together, in other words, can share information. There are three networks for the PC computers, and one network for the 20 Macintosh machines. That brings me to the fifth rule: students must only access the network that is set up for their use. One of the three PC networks is only for first year students to use – over here, another is only for second year students – over there along the back wall, and the third network – on the far right, is reserved for third year student use. The Macintosh computer network is reserved for second and third year students only, unless you are a first year student of the Graphic Design course. Rule five: you can only access the network that is set up for your level.

All networks have printout capability, and there is a charge per page on the laser printers. The dot-matrix printers, which, of course, do not give such good quality printouts as the laser printers, are suitable mainly for giving a rough copy of your work...er...um...they are free for student use during class hours. After hours a charge applies. Now, class hours, as you probably already know, are from nine in the morning until three-thirty in the afternoon, Monday to Thursday, and until midday on Fridays. The computer lab, however, is open an hour before class begins each day, and until six o'clock every afternoon, except for Fridays, when the lab closes at five.

Now, if you need any assistance with the software program you're working on, you can either look in the manuals located on the shelves below each machine, or, if you're still having problems, you can ask one of the lab assistants to help out. In addition, there is always help at hand on screen, in most cases simply by pressing function key number one at the top left of each keyboard. Well, that's about it. Uh. Oh, I forgot to mention the computer lab card which contains your log on number. By producing your card, you can borrow computer books and manuals from the computer lab library. Um...OK. That's all I need to tell you at this stage.

Narrator: That is the end of Section 4. You now have 30 seconds to check your answers to Section 4.

(30 second pause)

You now have one minute to check your answers for the entire test.

(60 second pause)

That is the end of the Listening Test. You are now given exactly 10 minutes to transfer your answers to the Listening Test Answer Sheet.

GLOSSARY

Check the meaning and spelling of the following words in a good English dictionary:

*(* indicates the word is included in the practice tests in this book.)*

A

abbreviation
ability*
abroad*
abuse*
access*
accessories*
accommodation*
accounting*
accurate*
acknowledge
acquire*
adapt*
additionally*
adequate*
adhere to*
adjust*
advantage*
advertise*
affordable*
agent*
aisle*
alternative*
ambition*
analogy*
analysis*
annually
anticipate*
appeal*
appendix*
appliance*
appointment*
appreciate*
approach*
appropriate*
approve
approximate*
arcade*
argument*
array*
article*
artificial*
aspect*
assemble*
assess*
asset*
assignment*
associate*
assume
assured*
atmosphere*
auditorium*
audio-visual*
auxiliary*
average*
avid*
avoid*

B

babysit*
balanced*
ban*
bargains*
basic*
basis
behaviour*
behind-the-scenes*
beverage*
bicentenary*
blockbuster*
bracelet*
brooch*
brainstorm
broadcast

C

cabin*
calculate
campus*
canoe*
cancel
canteen*
capable*
capacity*
capital*
catalogue
catastrophe
cater*
caution
celebration*
Celsius*
ceremony*
certification*
characteristic*
check-in*
circuit*
classify
click*
client*
climate*
co-ordinate*
code*
collapse*
colleague*
colloquial*
combine*
commission*
commit*
commonplace*
communicate*
commuter*
compare*
compatible*
compensation*
competent*
compile
complaint*
complex*
complicate*
comply*
compose*
comprehensive
comprise*
compulsory*
conceive
concentration*
concern*
conclude*
conduct*
confidence*
conscience*
conservation
constant*
constitute*
consultation*
consumer*
constitute*
context
contradict
contract*
contrast
controversial*
convict*
copyright*
core*
corporation*
correspond
cosmopolitan*
counsellor*
course*
craft*
creature*
credit
critical*
criticise*
cultural*
curriculum
cyclic*

D

damage*
database
deadline
debate
decade
declaration*
decline
degree*
demerit
demonstration*
density
department*
descending*
describe*
desirable*
desperate*
despite*
destroy*
detail*
deter*
determine*
development*
diction*
diploma*
directory*
disaster*
disclosure*
discourage*
discussion*
distinguish*
diversity
dividend*
divisive*
documentary*
domestic
doodle*
dot-matrix*
double-click*
downturn*
dramatic*
drawback
drought*

E

ecology
economic*
editor*
effective*
efficient*
elderly*
elective*
electronic*
eligible*
elongated*
emphasis*
enable*
encourage*
endangered*
endearing*
enormous*
enrolment*
ensure*
enthusiast*
entitle*

GLOSSARY continued

environment*
equipment*
eradicate*
ergonomic*
essential*
establish*
ethnic*
evaluation
eventual*
evidence
example*
exceptional*
exclusive*
exhibit*
expiry*
expose*
extensive*
extent*
extract*
extracurricular
extrovert*

F

facility*
factor*
familiar*
fascinate*
fatal
faulty*
feature*
feedback
field*
fieldwork
file-server
financial*
finite
first-hand
flowchart
flourish*
focus
folder*
forbid*
forecast*
foremost
former
formulate
fortify*
forum
foundation
fragile
function*
fundamental
funds*

G

gender*
generalise
generation*
global*
gourmet*
graduate*
graphic*
grievance*
guidebook*
guidelines*

H

habitat*
hail*
hardware*
harm*
harassment*
hazard*
heading*
heed*
hectare*
hectic*
hemisphere
hinder*
homestay*
hospitality*
hotline*

I

icon*
identification*
illustrated*
illegal*
immediate*
immense
impact
impression*
improvement*
inaccurate*
inadequate*
incidentally*
income
inconvenience*
increase*
independent
indicate*
inevitable*
influence*
inform*
ingredient*
in-house*
injustice*
innovative*
instance*
intake
instructor*
intensive*
interpret*
intersection*
intimate*
introvert
invalid*
inversely*
investigation*
involve*
irrelevant
issue*

J

jealousy*
jet-lag*
journal*
judgement
junction*
justification*

K

keynote*
kilometre*
kinesiology*
knowledge*

L

label*
laboratory*
laboured*
lack*
landlocked*
laser*
latter
lean*
lecture*
legible
leisure*
lesser*
licence*
limited*
linguistics*
location
long-term*
lush*
luxury*

M

magnificent*
maintain*
major*
majority*
mammal*
manage*
mandatory*
manual*
manufacture*
manslaughter*
marketing
marvellous*
materialise*
materials*
maternity*
maximum*
maximise
minimise
minimum*
media*
medium*
micro
minor
migrate*
minus
mock*
model*
modem*
modified*
monorail*
monitor*
multicultural*

N

national*
native*
natural*
negative
necessary*
necessity*
nervous*
northbound*
notify
numerous*
nutrition*

O

obligation*
obtain*
observant*
obstacle*
offend*
official*
offshore*
opinion*
opponent
opportunity*
optimism
optimum
option*
organise*
orientation*
original*
outgoing*
outline
outnumber*
overall*
overlook*
overtime*
overview*
overwhelm*

P

panic*
particular*
passage*
password*
pastime*
pastoral*
patron*
pattern*
pause*
per*

percentage*
period*
permanent*
personal*
persuade
peruse*
petition*
pie chart
placement
plus
pinpoint*
policy*
politics*
poll
positive*
possession*
possible*
post-mortem*
postgraduate*
postpone
potential*
practical*
precisely*
predator*
predict*
preferable*
preliminary*
premises*
pressure*
prevailing*
previous*
principal*
printout*
priority*
procedure*
process*
procrastinate*
profile*
programme*
progress*
project*
proposal
prosperity*
prospective*
protest*
psychological*
purchase*

Q

qualification*
quality*
query*
questionnaire*
queue

R

radiation
radius*
random*
range*
ranking
rapid*
ratio
react
realistic
reality*
receipt*
reception*
recession*
reconstruction*
recovery*
recreation*
redress*
reduce*
reference*
reflect*
refute*
regardless*
regards*
region*
register*
registration*
regular*
relatively*
relevant
reliable*
remote*
repetitive*
represent*
reputable*
request
require*
research*
resemble*
resent*
reserved*
resolution*
resource*
respondent*
response*
responsible*
resurrect*
restriction*
result*
résumé*
retrenchment*
review*
revise*
rigours*
robbery*
roster*
route*

S

sacked*
safety*
sample
scales*
scan
schedule*
scope*
score*
scruffy*
sculptor*
section*
security
selection*
self-confident*
seminar*
sensitive*
separate
sequence
series*
service*
session*
sharemate*
shift*
short-term*
shrink*
significant*
similarity*
situation
skill*
skim
software*
source*
specialised*
specific*
staff*
standard*
state*
statement*
stationary
statistics
steep*
stickers*
stress*
strict*
style*
substantial*
succeed*
suggestion*
sue*
suitable*
summary*
superannuation*
supreme*
survey*
syllabus
symbol*
synergy*
synonymous*
synthetic*
system*

T

target*
technical*
technique*
technology*
tend*
terraced*
tertiary*
timetable*
topic*
tradition*
transfer*
transgress*
trend*
trial*
tutor*

U

undergo*
undergraduate
unique*
update*
upgrade*
upkeep*
uppermost*
urgent*
utilise*

V

value*
varied*
variety
various*
vast*
vegetarian*
venue*
vehicle
viable
viewpoint*
villain*
virus*
vital
vocabulary*
voluntary*
vying*

W

well-equipped*
whitegoods*
widespread*
withstand*
worldwide
workforce
workshop

X Y Z

x-axis
y-axis
yield
zone*

INDEX TO 101 HELPFUL HINTS

IELTS TEST – BASIC HINTS

LISTENING TEST HINTS

READING TEST HINTS

101 Helpful Hints for IELTS is actually two books – one for each IELTS Module – Academic or General Training. Both include two practice Listening and Speaking Tests, four Reading and Writing Tests, and an extensive Help Section, covering all four sub-tests of the IELTS examination. The unique format of the books enables students to complete the first practice test and review their performance before attempting the next test. This is achieved by linking each hint to the appropriate pages of each test, so that students can identify problem areas and understand why they may have made errors. The tests increase in difficulty as students progress through the book. ***101 Helpful Hints for IELTS*** are comprehensive course books for use in the classroom or self-study.

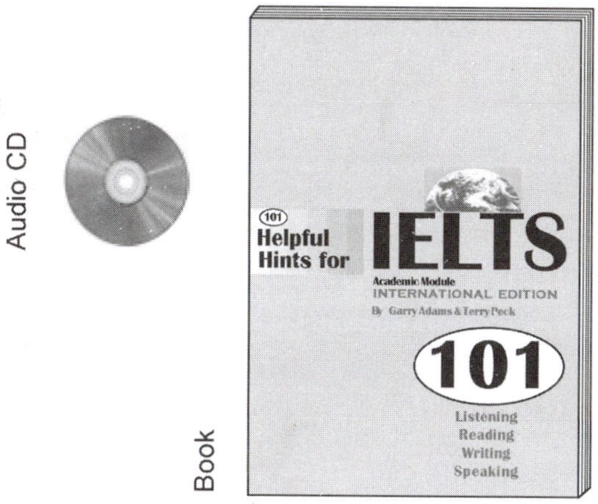

101 Helpful Hints for IELTS
Academic Module International Edition (Indian)
Book & Audio CD/DVD: ISBN 89-957634-1-8

101 Helpful Hints for IELTS
General Training Module International Edition (Indian)
Book & Audio CD/DVD: ISBN 89-957634-0-X

202 Useful Exercises for IELTS is our IELTS practice workbook, designed to give students of English extensive and guided IELTS examination practice. It is also a very effective learning aid for migrants and students taking EFL Secondary School Preparation Courses.

The book is divided into 5 sections, each focussing on a topic relevant to the examination, and contains:

- *27 listening exercises* – 8 news items, 5 academic lectures and 3 dictations, (all with complete tapescripts)
- 5 *reading passages* – with gapfill exercises, short-answer questions, sentence completion tasks, multiple choice, True/False style questions and matching tasks
- *10 writing tasks* – with complete Model Answers.

The 202 exercises complement the advice given in ***101 Helpful Hints for IELTS***. Also included are punctuation, spelling, grammar and vocabulary exercises. A complete Answer Key for all exercises and a comprehensive index are provided for reference.

202 Useful Exercises for IELTS
Academic/General International Edition (Indian)
Book & Audio CDs (2)/DVD: ISBN 89-957634-2-6

202 Useful Exercises for IELTS
Academic/General Australasian Edition
Book & Audio CDs (2): ISBN 978-0-9578980-5-9

404 Essential Tests for IELTS – General Training Module includes four complete practice tests for the General Training version of the IELTS examination. It has been written to give candidates extensive practice with instructions, question types and content used in the actual IELTS tests and includes detailed descriptions of the four test sections.

404 Essential Tests for IELTS
Academic Module International Edition (Indian)
Book & Audio CDs (2)/DVD: ISBN 89-957634-4-2

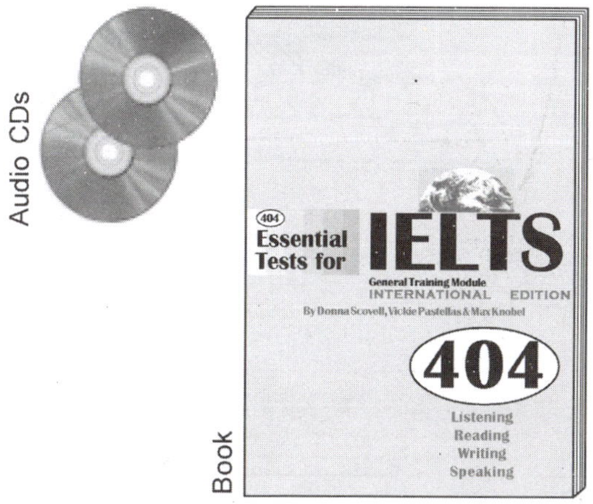